The Essential Department Chair

The Essential Department Chair
A Practical Guide to College Administration

Jeffrey L. Buller
Mary Baldwin College

ANKER PUBLISHING COMPANY, INC.
Bolton, Massachusetts

The Essential Department Chair
A Practical Guide to College Administration

ISBN 1-882982-99-1

Composition by Jessica Holland
Cover design by Jen Arbaiza Graphic Design

Anker Publishing Company, Inc.
563 Main Street
P.O. Box 249
Bolton, MA 01740-0249 USA

www.ankerpub.com

Library of Congress Cataloging-in-Publication Data

Buller, Jeffrey L.
  The essential department chair : a practical guide to college administration / Jeffrey L. Buller.
      p. cm.
  Includes bibliographical references.
  ISBN 1-882982-99-1
  1. Departmental chairmen (Universities) 2. Universities and colleges--Administration. I. Title.

  LB2341.B744 2006
  378.1'11--dc22

                                        2005035424

Table of Contents

About the Author

Jeffrey L. Buller is vice president for academic affairs and dean of the college at Mary Baldwin College. He began his administrative career as honors director and chair of the Department of Classical Studies at Loras College in Dubuque, Iowa before going on to assume a series of administrative appointments at Georgia Southern University. Dr. Buller has published widely on Greek and Latin literature, Wagnerian music drama, and higher education administration, including a large number of articles that have appeared in *The Department Chair*. Serving from 2003–2005 as the principal English-language lecturer at the International Wagner Festival in Bayreuth, Germany, he is widely known as an entertaining and popular speaker on such topics as literature, opera, and academic administration.

Introduction

Once upon a time, there was a wonderful and creative college—a college located not far from where you are reading these words right now—that had just one vexing problem: people could never agree on what they should call those administrators who were in charge of individual disciplines. Some people at the college believed that the appropriate term was "department heads" because, at this wonderful college at least, these were the people who made recommendations and personnel decisions about everyone else in the department. Others argued, however, that a better term to use would be "department chairs" because that would be a title reflecting the essentially democratic and collegial nature of the spirit at the wonderful college. During one particularly long faculty discussion of this issue, it happened that a well-respected senior professor remarked, "You know, I think I have the answer. We shouldn't call them 'heads' because I've got an uncle who served many years in the navy, and I learned from him that the expression 'going to the head' has a pretty unpleasant connotation to sailors." There was a moment of silence, and the faculty members began nodding in agreement with the wisdom of the insight offered by this particularly well-respected professor. But then a rather timid new instructor was overheard saying near the back of the room, "And yet, I'm not altogether sure that I'd feel comfortable working for a 'chair.' You see, *my* uncle served many years in the state prison and, to a convict, the expression 'going to the chair' has an even *more* unpleasant connotation."

Whether you are a department head, department chair, or some other administrator who works closely with the faculty and students of particular disciplines, welcome to the sometimes baffling world of college administration. The story I've retold above is probably apocryphal (at the very least, I've heard suspiciously similar versions of it at a number of different colleges and universities), but the basic situation that it presents is real enough. College administration is a place where, despite our best efforts, connotations are all too often unpleasant, the disagreements over terminology are neverending, and just when you think an issue is solved, that one voice from the back of the room makes you reconsider everything. Even with all of these drawbacks, however, if you are passionate about making a difference in the world, you have chosen your career path wisely. There are probably few opportunities you could have had in which you can affect, as significantly and as immediately, the way in which students are taught, scholarship is performed, and your discipline is served as you can at the departmental level. Unlike most of your institution's senior administration, you are likely to have meaningful and ongoing contact with students, faculty members, and other department chairs. You will know them by name, be familiar with their personal and professional histories, and be asked to make decisions that will affect their livelihoods and their lives. If you were looking for challenging but important work, in other words, you're in exactly the right profession.

This book contains strategies for how you can make a difference in people's lives on a daily basis. There are many guides for academic administrators that explore differing philosophies of administration, theoretical approaches to management and leadership, and exciting new trends in higher education administration. You probably have a shelf of such books in your office, and if you've read even a few of them, you know how useful they can be in getting you inspired to develop a major new vision for your discipline or perhaps for your entire institution. But in order to make that vision a reality, you've probably already realized that you've got to know, on a day-to-day basis, how to excel at the many administrative tasks constantly assigned to you. For instance, how do you cultivate a potential donor who can give you the resources you'll need to make your vision for your department a reality? How do you interview someone from outside your field if your dean assigns you to a committee searching for an administrator in a different academic area? How do you fire someone? How do you get the members of your department to work together more harmoniously? How do you keep the people who report to you motivated and capable of seeing "the big picture?"

This book is about the "how" of academic administration.

The chapters that follow are, for the most part, the result of a series of workshops in faculty and administrative development that I have given over the past 20 years at Georgia Southern University and Mary Baldwin College. What I have tried to do for each topic is to take the very essence of what administrators need to know and condense it to an easily read five- to ten-page summary that focuses just on the most important information you will want to have at your fingertips when you are facing a particular challenge or opportunity. Many of the chapters in this book first appeared as articles in the quarterly periodical *The Department Chair* (one of my own favorite resources when *I* was a department chair), and they have now been adapted and updated for this format. They have been grouped together, not as they appeared chronologically, but according to various themes and questions that you may have.

So, with that as an introduction, let me proceed immediately to the very first "how?" question you may have: How should you use this book so that it will be most beneficial to you and your ongoing administrative needs?

My suggestion is that you will probably not gain the absolute most from this book by reading it straight through from cover to cover in a single sitting. (Of course, you are more than welcome to do so if you wish, and you will earn my eternal admiration and gratitude just for wanting to make the effort.) No, most people will benefit by using this book as a desk reference or an occasional guide to help solve particular problems. It is intended to be what medieval authors sometimes called a vade mecum, a "go with me," the sort of ready reference that you pick up and put down as you need it. You may find, for instance, that you have a certain need or desire—you want to set up an innovative faculty development program in your discipline, the institutional advancement office calls you and tells you that they want you to meet with a prospective contributor, you find yourself exasperated by a faculty member who's using up all of your time with increasingly petty complaints—and you may find yourself turning to this work to discover (and my hope is that you will usually discover it in ten minutes or less) precisely what you need to know about how to address whatever your particular issue may be.

My guiding principle throughout has been to emphasize proven solutions over untested theories and to stress *what you need to know now* at the expense of how to develop a deep and abiding philosophy of higher education administration. (You already own all the books you will ever need on how to do *that*.) As an administrator, you have come to understand that your ultimate goal is to stop putting out fires and to begin making a difference. With that in mind, think of this book as your administrative sprinkler system. Scan the table of contents to find an issue that you're dealing with right now, and see if it can help you to turn a problem into an opportunity to make that administrative dream of yours come true.

In the meantime, good firefighting!

How to Write Job Descriptions and Position Announcements

Whenever administrators explore the topic of "decisions that seemed right at the time but that are now driving me crazy," department chairs are likely to think immediately of "the search that went wrong." Advertising, recruiting, hiring, and mentoring new faculty members—taken all together—form one of the department chair's most important responsibilities. Fulfilling these responsibilities effectively can lead to a department that is harmonious, productive, and dedicated to the success of its students. Doing even part of this entire process wrong can lead to departmental turmoil, the loss of the very faculty members whom you would most like to keep, and an overall decline in a department's reputation, either within the institution itself or throughout your academic discipline nationally. Hiring the right faculty members does not *seem* as though it would be particularly difficult, and yet it is all too often a far greater challenge than we imagine. How can you keep from making a misstep in faculty hiring and increase the odds that you will hire the best possible candidate for your department?

One of the best places to begin answering this question is to consider how your department writes its job descriptions and position announcements. All too often, the problem with an unsatisfactory hire starts at this point in the employment process, long before the first candidate has even been interviewed on campus, in fact, before the first candidate has even *applied*. The errors that most departments make in writing job descriptions include

- Not describing the type of employee you really need

- Not including the right type of information about the position or your expectations

- Not requesting the type of supporting materials that can help you make the best decision

Each of these errors results in its own sequence of problems for the department and stems from a misunderstanding of the department chair's role in setting up a search. For this reason, it is important to consider each of these three common errors individually.

Not Describing the Type of Employee You Really Need

All too frequently application deadlines pass and search committees find themselves confronted with a set of applications that, in their view, does not adequately represent the amount of gender or ethnic diversity that exists in their field. At other times, the problems appear only after an individual has already been hired. Perhaps the department becomes concerned when it discovers that a candidate who looked so wonderful on paper is an extremely poor teacher. Perhaps the very person who seemed so impressive throughout the interview process turns out to be highly uncollegial in his or her dealings with others. Perhaps the candidate who was the top choice of every member of the search committee now suddenly seems resistant to the idea of assuming an equitable role in committee work or advisement. In a surprising number of cases where these traits were among the most important factors in the success or failure of a new faculty member, they were *not even mentioned as desirable qualifications in the position announcement.*

The cause of this problem is clear. As academics, we have a natural tendency to focus on *credentials* and *areas of specialty* when we create position announcements, even though it is the *interpersonal and professional qualities* that tend to matter most in our day-to-day relationships with our colleagues. As a department chair, therefore, it is your responsibility to counterbalance a search committee's natural desire to build a position announcement around the precise subspecialty, type of academic credential, and amount of experience your faculty may initially be drawn toward and guide the position advertisement toward describing the sort of person you really need.

For instance, in diversifying your pool of candidates, it is not enough to include a cold and generic statement that "Women and minorities are invited (or even 'encouraged') to apply," particularly if the rest of your advertisement appears to emphasize precisely those qualifications and areas of specializations in which women and members of minorities are least likely to be represented. Be sure to ask repeatedly as your committee is developing its position description: "What is really most important here? Finding a candidate with experience in this precise area or achieving our department's goals in the area of diversity?" After all, if diversity is truly a goal, then perhaps it is worth broadening the disciplinary focus of the job description to include those areas where diverse candidates are most likely to be found.

It may expand your pool of acceptable candidates to modify statements like "Ph.D. in hand required at time of application" so that they are more inclusive, such as "doctorate required by time of appointment." The latter phrasing allows candidates pursuing Ed.D.s, Psy.D.s, and other types of doctorates to apply as well as individuals who are *close* to completing their degrees but who have not yet defended their dissertations. An even broader phrasing would be "ABD required for rank of instructor; doctorate required for rank of assistant professor." This phrasing allows you to consider a superior candidate who has not yet completed his or her degree, but it also emphasizes the priority your institution places on employing faculty members with terminal degrees. Furthermore, you will be likely to improve your recruitment of minority candidates if you replace unwelcoming phrases like "Women and minorities are encouraged to apply" with more inviting formulae, such as, "Our institution actively encourages applications from women, minorities, and individuals of every sexual orientation in keeping with its policy of promoting diversity throughout the institution." You may also wish to encourage your committee to give an expressed priority to applicants who have worked in a multicultural environment, had experience with diversity issues, or engaged in scholarship on how to teach your discipline to students from a broad range of cultural backgrounds. Statements of this sort send the message that your department is giving more than lip service to the importance of a highly diverse faculty. These and other suggestions on how to write position descriptions that will attract larger numbers of minority candidates may be found in two excellent books from the Association of American Colleges and Universities, *Diversifying the Faculty: a Guidebook for Search Committees* (Turner, 2002) and *Achieving Faculty Diversity: Debunking the Myths* (Smith, Wolf, & Busenberg, 1996).

If such matters as collegiality, excellence in teaching, and willingness to advise or perform academic service are important matters for your department, be sure to feature them prominently in your position announcement. Writing an advertisement in this way is simply the most sensible way to protect your department's interest: if you ever have to let this faculty member go, you will be on much stronger ground if you can demonstrate that the person you hired failed to demonstrate the qualities indicated as essential in your advertisement. (Conversely, imagine how weak your case would be in a lawsuit if it appeared that you were dismissing someone for not having qualifications that appeared to be secret or at least undisclosed.) Advertising for what you *really* need—as opposed to what certain members of your department may *think* you need—is the easiest possible way to attract individuals who actually possess those qualities.

For example, if developing collegiality is a goal in your department, require that candidates define and address collegiality in their letters of application; focus on collegiality in the reference calls and letters made on behalf of the candidate; include expressions like "team player," "strong departmental citizenship," and "cooperative attitude" in your description of the person you are seeking; where space permits, discuss *why* collegiality is essential to the mission of teaching, scholarship, and service of your department. If excellence in teaching is a major concern at your institution, have all applicants submit a statement outlining their philosophy of teaching; make it clear that a significant part of the interview process will be evaluating the candidate's quality of instruction in different pedagogical settings; suggest that development of a substantive teaching portfolio will be an absolute requirement during the successful candidate's probationary period. In cases where service or advisement is important, note this priority in the advertisement itself; while such statements may dissuade a few individuals from applying for your position, in the long run they are unlikely to be the sort of individuals who will succeed in your environment anyway. In sum, your basic rule as you charge your search committee should be: we may not always get the type of person we advertise for, but we are certain not to hire that type of person if we fail to mention the most important qualifications in our position announcement.

Not Including the Right Type of Information About the Position or Your Expectations

Unless a candidate already knows a great deal about your institution and department, he or she is unlikely to have a very clear idea of precisely what it would be like to hold the position that you are advertising. Is this primarily a teaching position, primarily a research position, or some mixture of the two? If it is primarily a teaching position, what is the course load? How many courses taught by the faculty member are likely to be at the introductory level? How many are likely to be at an advanced or graduate level? Will there be any opportunity for the individual to develop new courses? Will there be opportunities for or expectations of interdisciplinary work? If the position is primarily in the area of research, what are the expectations for research? Will startup funds be available? Will it be expected that the individual will need to secure external funding (and, if so, will there be the support of an office of research and sponsored programs)? If the position requires a mixture of instruction and scholarship, in what proportions are the two activities likely to occur? Will there be an expectation that the person hired involves students in his or her research, or are one's duties in the areas of teaching and scholarship usually unrelated?

Your department's position descriptions will be extremely ineffective if you are not clear about your expectations in any of these areas. For instance, if the advertisement states that you are seeking an assistant professor, how can an applicant tell if you also accept (or are *permitted* to accept) applications from individuals whose rank is already higher than this? If you state, "Minimum of one year experience preferred," is it clear to the search committee how they should use this preference in selecting candidates? What sort of experience will you consider? Does this experience have to be in a faculty position at a college or university? And what precisely do you mean when you say that you *prefer* this type of experience? Does this phrase imply that any experienced candidate will have an automatic advantage over any inexperienced candidate or that you are simply *reserving the right* to give precedence to experienced candidates, all other factors being equal?

In the long run, it is better for the search committee to develop a compelling reason from the very beginning of their discussions about the type of qualifications and experience that they regard as absolutely essential for this position. A guideline such as "Minimum of three years teaching experience at an accredited four-year college or university" may be clear, but it also means that you will not be able to consider any candidate who does not meet that criterion, no matter how desirable the candidate may be in other ways. Finally, assist your search committee in avoiding meaningless phrases like "Some teaching experience preferred"; this description actually tells an applicant nothing and gives the search committee no guidance whatsoever in selecting candidates to interview. The problem is that this pseudo-criterion is overly general. Even if a candidate has taught a first-grade Sunday School class for less than ten minutes, he or she has technically met the criterion. It is far better to have hard and fast requirements for the qualifications that you *really* need and to forego taking up advertisement space with statements that only *appear* to express preferences.

Not Requesting the Type of Supporting Materials That Can Really Help You Make the Best Decision

The final mistake that search committees tend to make in developing position announcements is to request all kinds of materials that don't give them any real help in selecting the best candidate. And, they may fail to ask for those materials that could really be important. You see this problem in job advertisements all the time: "In addition to letter of application and current curriculum vitae, submit three letters of reference, official transcripts of all college work, and samples of publications." What's wrong with such a request?

Letters of Reference

Letters of reference almost always tell you a good deal less than you are likely to learn by simply asking for a list of names, mailing addresses, telephone numbers, and email addresses of three to five references. To begin with, anyone can locate three individuals who are willing to write reasonably positive, upbeat letters on his or her behalf. What you really want is the opportunity to ask follow-up questions, to describe your precise position and inquire whether the candidate is a good "fit," and to ask the one question that you really need to know (and that you will almost never learn from reference letters): "Do you know anything about this candidate that, if I were aware of it, might make me hesitant to extend a job offer?" Furthermore, some—possibly very desirable—candidates will not apply for your position simply because you have asked for letters of reference up front. No one likes bothering their references to prepare letters for positions until they know that there is a very good chance that they will be seriously considered as a candidate. Moreover, some candidates will not want current employers and colleagues to know that they are considering new positions; these candidates are likely to rule out applying for any position that requires letters of recommendation at the very start of a search.

Official Transcripts

There are almost no searches in which a department needs to request *official* transcripts as part of an application. To be sure, accrediting agencies do require institutions to obtain official transcripts—defined as transcripts marked with an official seal and mailed directly from the registrar of the issuing institution to the institution requesting them, without ever being in the possession of the candidate—*once an individual is hired.* For this reason, the submission of official transcripts is often a requirement that is expressed in an initial contract of employment. But there is almost never a reason for a search committee to compel a candidate to undergo the burden and expense of requiring official transcripts at the time of application. Some candidates will choose not to apply for your position rather than supply you with the transcripts. If your faculty members believe that it is absolutely necessary to review an applicant's coursework and grades in order for them to prepare a "short list" of semi-finalists, be sure to request "*unofficial* transcripts" or "*photocopies* of transcripts." This phrasing will provide you with the information that you need without creating an obstacle for the candidates you would like to have in your pool.

Samples of Publications

Evaluating the scholarship of applicants is certainly an important part of every academic search process. But ask yourself whether it is truly necessary to review the publications of every single person who applies for your position or whether it would not be better to request these materials from a select group of applicants only after an initial screening has been completed. Mailing books and offprints is an expensive proposition for candidates. Returning these items at the end of a search, should a candidate request them (and the vast majority of candidates will) is an expensive and time-consuming process for your department. Furthermore, depending on the position you are advertising, you are likely to receive between 60 and 200 applications. Is it going to be worth the time it takes your committee to examine all of the scholarly products submitted (in fact, are they really going to examine them with any care?) and is it going to be worth the space to store these items, even temporarily? In most cases, the answer to these questions will be "no." Screen applicants on the basis of the information that they provide in their cover letters and résumés; request actual samples of publications only later in the search or to be brought to the interview.

If many departments ask for items that they do not really need in a search, they also fail to request submission of those items that could really help them: statements of a candidate's philosophy of teaching, administration, scholarship, or service; a sample syllabus or final examination; a brief description of the best student project ever submitted to that candidate; suggestions about the "one book every student (or faculty member) in our discipline should read"; or a brief faculty development plan for teaching, scholarship, and creative activity over the next five years.

Of course, certain decisions about position descriptions can only be made in the context of individual institutions and particular positions. For instance, do you ever refer to salary level in a job advertisement and, if so, do you provide a range or merely say something general along the lines of "Salary commensurate with experience?" In making this decision, there can be no hard and fast rule. (Your institution may, however, have very definite guidelines on this issue.) If you provide a salary range, you run the risk of losing certain candidates who believe that the range offered is inadequate for their current needs. You may decide that such a situation is preferable to incurring the expense of bringing a candidate to campus only to discover that the individual is out of your price range anyway. On the other hand, your institution may offer certain intangible benefits—a beautiful location, extensive cultural opportunities, or a safe and congenial community—that candidates will need to experience in order to appreciate. One general guideline is to avoid stating that a salary range is "commensurate with experience" if the remuneration for this position is already largely fixed. Your statement would be inaccurate in such a case and likely to cause hard feelings or worse later on in the search. In a similar way, many institutions consistently make the mistake of terming their salaries as "highly competitive" and their benefits packages as "excellent," when neither of these is actually the case.

Other aspects of the position description should *always* appear, regardless of the type of job you are advertising or the nature of your institution. These inflexible guidelines include:

- Always clearly indicate whether the position is tenure-track, temporary, or for a set term.

- Always indicate whether any required qualification applies at the time of application or at the starting date for the position.

- Always provide the starting date for the position.

- Always list the documents required for the application to be complete.

- Always provide the full name and contact information of the search chair.

- Always specify whether applications are acceptable in hard copy, electronically, or both. If the search committee or institution has a preference for how the application should be submitted, state it.

- Always clarify whether dates are postmark deadlines or deadlines for receipt of material. (It is a wise idea to make sure that this date is not a Saturday, Sunday, or postal holiday.)

As a starting point, therefore, you might adapt the following position description to meet the needs of your department. The entire sample advertisement is almost certainly too long for many publications, but it does provide a template that may be adapted to your department's individual needs.

DISINGENUITY STUDIES. Tenure-track position (instructor through associate professor, depending on qualifications and college-level teaching experience). ABD required by the starting date of the position, August 1, [YEAR]; doctorate preferred. Preference *may* be given to applicants with coursework or previous experience in teaching the methods of disingenuity or the Theory and Practice of Dilettantism. Duties will include teaching the introductory-level course "Disingenuity Studies for Non-Majors," as well as other undergraduate and graduate courses in a large, interdisciplinary program. Initial screening of selected applicants will occur at the AADSP conference in San Francisco on February 3–6, [YEAR]. Send letter of application, curriculum vitae, statement of teaching philosophy, sample syllabus for "Disingenuity Studies for Non-Majors," and the names, addresses, email addresses, and telephone numbers of five references to Professor Lionel O'Cueshon, Chair, Search Committee #999666, Department of Disingenuity Studies, PO Box 8555, East Central Southern University, Northfield, West Dakota, [ZIP]. (Electronic applications not accepted.) **Postmark deadline: January 15, [YEAR]**. East Central Southern University actively encourages applications from women, minorities, and individuals of every sexual orientation in keeping with its policy of promoting diversity throughout the institution. Persons who require accommodation(s) in the application process under the Americans with Disabilities Act should notify the search chair.

References

Smith, D. G., with Wolf, L. E., & Busenberg, B. E. (1996). *Achieving faculty diversity: Debunking the myths.* Washington, DC: Association of American Colleges and Universities.

Turner, C. S. V. (2002). *Diversifying the faculty: A guidebook for search committees.* Washington, DC: Association of American Colleges and Universities.

2

The Department Chair's Role in Successful Faculty Searches

The *defined* role that department chairs play in faculty searches can vary considerably from institution to institution. For instance, at some schools, the chair is a member of every single search committee that happens to fall within his or her discipline; at times, the chair may even be appointed to head every search that takes place within the department. At other institutions, the chair may participate in searches only where there is a direct and obvious connection between his or her field of specialty and the area in which the new hire will be made. At still other institutions, the search committee operates independently of the chair, preparing a list of acceptable candidates that must then be screened by the chair, the dean, and the provost who ultimately select the finalists or the individual who will be offered the contract. Despite this wide variety in institutional practice, however, there tends to be extremely little difference in the *undefined* role that the chair should play in faculty searches. After all, one of the central duties of the chair when it comes to faculty searches is to serve as an advocate for the discipline as a whole, to make sure—either by direct involvement with the screening committee or indirectly through mentoring and moral suasion—that institutional search procedures are being followed, and to provide guidance so that the search committee will take all the appropriate steps necessary to locate and solicit applications from the best possible pool of candidates for the department and the discipline.

However different chairs may choose to perform these various duties, there will always be three major aspects to the chair's role in every successful faculty search.

Focus

The chair will need to ensure that the search committee's attention is consistently directed toward those particular traits and criteria that will most effectively assist the department in fulfilling its central missions of instruction, scholarship, and service. Accomplishing this task is not always as easy as it sounds. Frequently, once a search gets well under way, a committee will become distracted by certain types of qualifications that do not advance—and may even end up being detrimental to—the overall success of the search. For instance, when reviewing the applicants' submitted materials, a committee may notice a particularly interesting achievement cited in the materials submitted by one candidate and then begin to screen out other candidates (sometimes consciously, sometimes unconsciously) because those applicants do not have a parallel achievement—*even though that criterion was never stated in the search advertisement, never discussed as desirable during the department's original planning sessions for this position, and never before regarded as relevant to the strategic plan of the institution, division, or department.*

Similarly, a search committee may, at times, become preoccupied with a particular type of supporting document that one candidate has submitted—the document might be a statement of research philosophy, a letter of support from a nationally prominent individual, or a particularly unusual set of instructional materials—and then begin to give significantly less attention to other candidates who may be equally qualified or even superior in terms of what the department really needs, all because those candidates did not submit a part of the application that *the search committee had never requested in the first place.*

Finally, it is not at all uncommon for search committees to misunderstand their proper roles and try to make decisions for the candidate. It may come to your attention that the search committee is saying such things as, "Oh, we could never really interest this candidate. We wouldn't even be close to the salary that the person is making right now." Or, "We couldn't offer the rank this candidate currently has, and I'm sure this person would not accept an offer at a lower rank." Or even, "Well, I can't imagine why these applicants would leave their current institutions to come *here.*" In all of these instances, search committees have been distracted from their primary responsibility of applying the search announcement's stated criteria in order to identify a pool of highly desirable finalists who can provide what the institution and the department need.

In such situations, the department chair can serve as an effective advocate for reminding the search committee what they really are looking for and what its overriding responsibility must be. If the chair is a formal member of the search committee, this goal can be accomplished very directly at screening meetings. The chair can say, "Well, let's not forget what we set out to do when we planned this position. We said that what we really needed was X, not Y. And it's not fair to the other applicants (or possibly even legal) to go applying a different set of standards. If that's what we want to do—and I'm not really convinced that it is—then what we really ought to do is to cancel this search, re-advertise the position, and *state* that this is what we want."

In other situations, the chair could say, "I'm just not comfortable making that decision for this candidate. Now, the individual applied for our position, and I believe we need to take this application seriously. Maybe the candidate has family in the area or is interested in working in a different sort of environment, and right now *that* seems more important than salary (or rank or whatever other extraneous factor seems to be distracting the committee). I suggest that we screen for the criteria we agreed on and then, if we end up making an offer, we let the candidate decide whether or not to accept it."

In situations in which the chair is not officially a member of the search committee, guidance of this type may have to be offered in a more indirect manner. Depending on the situation, it may be appropriate for the chair to ask to meet with the committee in order to ask for an update while the search is still in progress. Or, the chair may need to consult with a trusted member of the committee to ask about the criteria that are being used in selecting finalists.

Regardless of the situation, be on the alert for the following indications that the focus of a search committee has shifted from its original purpose.

- In searches where the successful applicant's primary responsibilities are going to be in, for instance, instruction, watch out for a *disproportionate* amount of attention being paid to research, offices held in scholarly associations, and other matters not particularly relevant to the department's instructional mission. In these cases, it can be extremely useful to say things like, "Well, all of that's great, but remember the single most important thing we said we need right now is a superb teacher."

- In searches where the department is making a genuine and significant effort to diversify the faculty, be on the alert for a disproportionate amount of attention being paid to specialties unlikely to attract women or minorities or to qualifications that, while certainly desirable, are in the long run less important to the institution than a faculty that best reflects the gender and ethnicity of the student body.

- In any search, look out for the use of a set of screening criteria and weights that is significantly different from that stated in the search announcement. "Secret criteria," like hidden agendas, are never desirable in a department that wishes to avoid lawsuits and earn a reputation for candor and transparency.

Clarify

When candidates are invited for on-campus interviews, the department chair can play a valuable role by helping the search committee to clarify what specifically it is attempting to accomplish by the end of the interview process. Search committees may need to be reminded that interviews are expensive and time-consuming activities. For this reason and for the sake of increasing the likelihood that the best possible candidate will be found, it is extremely important that the resources devoted to the on-campus interview should be used wisely. Interviews should never be seen as opportunities "just to take a closer look at" a candidate and determine whether that person is qualified; qualifications and general suitability to the position can be checked through examination of written materials, reference calls, and telephone or video interviews with the candidate off site.

On-campus interviews should focus on those activities that can *only* be done or at least *best* be done on site and in person. How does the candidate relate to the sort of students with which he or she will be dealing in this particular position? As the candidate observes the facilities and opportunities for research, scholarship, or creative activity, is there a good fit between what the institution can offer and what the individual brings in terms of experience, interest, and talent? Is there a reasonable amount of rapport between the candidate and coworkers? Does the individual understand and support the mission of your institution and department?

The department chair can also clarify that on-campus interviews are never times for "courtesy interviews" of candidates whom you would never actually hire. At times, individuals having some contact with the department—internal candidates, adjunct faculty members, alumni, friends of current faculty members—are given consideration by a search committee that extends far beyond their suitability for the current position. People often ask, "What harm would it do just to interview them? They're here anyway. It wouldn't cost that much. And it would make them feel good." These attempts to spare someone's feelings by including that person in an interview process without a significant chance to obtain the position frequently lead to disaster. Rather than making the person feel better, they end up making that person feel far worse by giving a false impression that he or she has a very good chance of obtaining the position. Situations such as this also produce a great deal of litigation as both the "insider" and other candidates who were not interviewed because they were not insiders may feel that the search process was not legitimate.

To avoid these problems, the department chair should always help a search committee clarify its purpose in conducting on-campus interviews: *to examine one or more individuals who are already considered to be extremely highly qualified for the position and likely to be good additions to the department in order to determine whether any one candidate is the best possible "fit."*

When search committees are not clear about their purpose in conducting on-campus interviews, they are far more likely to conduct interviews poorly, possibly even alienating the very candidate whom you would most want to impress. The following are some of the most common errors made by search committees in scheduling interviews, because they have not sufficiently thought through their overall purpose.

Over-Scheduling

When search committees lack a well-defined idea of what it is that they are trying to accomplish in an interview, they tend to lapse into either planning too many activities, thus running a candidate ragged, or planning too few, leaving the impression that no one was taking the candidate seriously. Over-scheduling may occur when a search committee assumes that they will develop a better understanding of the candidate by planning as many individual appointments as possible; alternatively, they may actually be trying to help candidates by exposing them to everything they can about what is occurring in the department and institution. The schedule then becomes one of taking the candidate to breakfast, shuttling the candidate around to appointment after appointment throughout the morning, taking the candidate to lunch, filling the entire afternoon with another series of meetings, and then ending the day with taking the candidate to dinner, possibly followed by a social event or other campus activities.

When questioned as to why the search committee has not allowed the candidates any time to explore campus on their own, rest their voices between appointments, or even collect their thoughts, the answer frequently given is, "Well, we want them to see as much as possible, and we want to see as much of them as possible. Besides, it gives a good impression of how busy things can be around here." As a department chair, you are in an excellent position to warn against this dangerous thinking. Over-scheduling interviews gives your best candidates an extremely poor impression of your department and campus. It makes you come across as individuals who do not respect one another's time, have difficulty planning even a fairly simple schedule like an interview, and have so little respect for visitors that you grill them with questions mercilessly even while they are trying to eat. Encourage your search committee to plan an interview with at least a little bit of "down time." Do not let them plan so many different events and appointments that, instead of impressing your candidate, you end up making applicants feel harried and exhausted.

Under-Scheduling

In an effort to avoid over-scheduling, some search committees will go to the opposite extreme and under-schedule an interview. While not planning at least some free time exhausts candidates and does not allow them to perform at their best, too much free time can also give the impression that you have not planned the visit well or even that the faculty members, administrators, and students do not care enough about this position to share their days with the candidate. The key goal should be planning and deciding what the interview process can reveal that can *best* be learned only in person. One possibility, if you feel that an interview schedule is seriously under-planned, is to offer the candidate different options: take a walk, tour the library, chat with some students, go over a map of the campus, make use of a room to go over his or her presentation or just to regroup, get a cup of coffee, visit the art gallery, or see neighborhoods in town with a realtor. These options allow you to respond with sensitivity to a candidate's needs and interests without resorting to activities that are tiring for the candidate and uninformative for you.

Mis-Scheduling

As we have seen, the most effective way of being certain that the interview schedule is not too full or too empty is to develop a clear notion of what it is that you most want to discover in the interview and how best to discover it. If teaching is the most important aspect of this position, schedule sessions where you get to observe candidates teaching the sort of students who actually enroll at your institution and interacting with them in settings similar to those of day-to-day activities on your campus. Don't expose the candidate only to honor students or your best majors; find out how well they relate to the full variety of students in your program. If research is the primary focus of the position, have the candidate present recent research findings, critique your current facilities and library holdings, and discuss with you an anticipated research agenda for the foreseeable future. Most important of all, schedule these events *instead of* other activities that may initially sound important but that, in the end, give you very little information that will help you in making a decision.

"Courtesy visits"—opportunities to meet the president, provost, dean, and other campus officials—should be either relatively brief or even omitted, unless the person whom the candidate visits will be playing an active role in selecting the candidate. The basic question you should always ask your search committee about each planned activity is: "What will we gain from this appointment or event that we are not gaining from any other activity that has already occurred?" If you cannot come up with a compelling, significant answer to that question, then skip that event and allow your candidate more free time to pursue the various optional activities that you have offered.

Caution

Search committees, particularly when they are composed of faculty members inexperienced in conducting faculty searches, will probably need some guidance in the types of questions they either should or should not pose to the candidates. It is all too easy, during casual conversation with an applicant, to ask questions that may accidentally lead you into unacceptable areas. For this reason, you may wish to caution your search committee and the other members of your department to take special care against asking even seemingly innocent questions that could later result in a complaint against your department or the failure of a search. A few examples of these "seemingly innocent" questions include those dealing with:

- *Marital status.* How shall I address you? As Miss or Mrs.? Do you have a family? Will your wife be accompanying you when you visit? What are the ages of your children?

- *Clubs, organizations, and religion.* We have quite a number of wonderful civic and religious groups here in town. Would you be interested in hearing about any of them?

- *National origin.* What a fascinating name! What nationality is that? It *is*, however, permissible to ask: Are you legally authorized to work in this country? In fact, before hiring a candidate, your institution will be *required* to ascertain the answer to that question.

- *Age.* These are very impressive credentials for someone your age! How old were you when you started teaching? Why would you want to move so far away from home when you'll be retiring in a couple of years?

You should remind your faculty that it does not matter whether these questions are asked at social occasions or during formal interviews. The essential thing is to ensure that all questions—regardless of where they are asked—deal solely with qualifications, experiences, and attitudes that are directly relevant to the professional position itself. A good general rule should always be to treat applicants with the same courtesy and fairness that we ourselves would wish to receive.

Interview Questions That *Should* Be Asked

If your faculty members find it difficult to formulate appropriate questions for candidates in light of these restrictions, the following is a list of questions that should be asked of each candidate for an academic position:

- Why are you interested in this job?

- How would you describe your teaching philosophy?

- Do you have any experience in teaching students of non-traditional age? Teaching students from a diversity of social or ethnic backgrounds? Teaching graduate students?

- How would you go about promoting active learning and a high level of engagement among your students?

- What is the most interesting book you've read in the last six months?

- Have you done anything that provides evidence of support for inter-disciplinary studies or for academic disciplines outside of your own field?

- If there were one book that all freshmen in college were required to read, what should it be?

- What makes you unique as an individual?

- What part of academic life gives you the most pleasure?

- What part of academic life annoys you the most, exasperates you, or is a pet peeve?

- What do you regard as the biggest challenge facing college and university professors today?

- What is your most significant accomplishment in your present position?

- What would you regard as the proper balance between scholarship and teaching for a faculty member?

- What is your greatest strength as a faculty member?

- If I were to speak to those who know you best, what would they describe as your greatest weakness?

- What achievement would you like to look back on after your first year as a faculty member here?

- Describe a mistake that you made in your professional life.

- Describe a problem that you have solved in your professional life.

- How would you describe yourself? How would those who know you best describe you?

- What do people who don't like you say about you?

- What are some examples of your creativity and innovation as a teacher?

- What is your favorite word in the English language? Why?

- If you could converse with any particular leader or historical figure, who would it be? Why?

- What three sources do you use most to gain information about recent trends in your field?

- (Give each candidate a list of the essential job-related functions of the position.) Let's go through this list, and I'd like you to tell me how you would accomplish each of these tasks.

- If you could develop your knowledge or skills in any one area, what would it be?

- What do you regard to be the single most important asset for a faculty member in higher education today?

With a few well-chosen questions and a carefully planned interview schedule, candidates will give you the information and impressions your search committee will need in order to make the best possible recommendation. Your candidates will be impressed by the department's professionalism, courtesy, and consideration.

3

How to Interview Candidates for Administrative Positions

Department chairs are frequently asked to serve on search committees for other administrators at their institutions. Sometimes this opportunity arises because there are a number of discrete programs in the chair's own department and a search must be conducted for a new program director or, at least, for an assistant chair to help with the workload. At other times, the chair may be asked to serve as an external representative on another department's search for its own chair. And quite often chairs are invited to serve on search committees for deans, academic vice presidents, or other senior administrators.

These opportunities, while usually welcome, do at times pose a problem. After all, most department chairs are relatively experienced at interviewing candidates for faculty positions; we know what questions to ask and how to gain, relatively quickly, the information that we need the most. But this is not always the case when interviewing candidates for administrative positions. It is not always immediately apparent which sort of question will reveal to you what you really want to know and will do so in a way that allows the candidate to demonstrate something of his or her personality, creativity, or individual style. As a result, we rely all too frequently on trite or uninteresting questions such as, "What is your management style?" "Tell me about one of your faults," or "What first attracted you to this position?"

Rather than reverting to overused questions, which most candidates have been asked dozens of times anyway, it is better for the chair to plan for an administrative interview by considering what it is that he or she needs to know about the candidate in each of the following five areas: experience, knowledge, point of view, approach, and fit with the particular position and with your institution as a whole.

Once you determine what it is that you need to know in each of these areas, it will be relatively easy for you to come up with a question that allows that precise information to emerge, that probes a bit more deeply beneath the surface, and that allows the candidate to draw upon his or her own experience and relate it to the new responsibilities of the particular position.

Frequently, it is best to ask more general or open-ended questions, then follow up more precisely if needed. Just as you would probably not ask a candidate for a faculty position "Would you be willing to teach a course in X?" (since even the most inexperienced candidate knows that the only correct answer to this question is, "Yes, of course"), it is equally unproductive to ask an administrative candidate a question like "Are you interested in helping us do Y?" A far more productive question to the prospective faculty member is, "As you examine our current curriculum, what are some of the areas where you would have the greatest enthusiasm about teaching? What areas not currently in our curriculum would you be most interested in developing?" In the same way, it is more revealing to ask administrative candidates questions that do not offer them simple yes-or-no choices, but instead allow them to elaborate and draw upon their own perspectives.

Here are a few possible questions in each of the five areas outlined above. While all of these questions have been thoroughly field tested in actual interviews, it is probably more useful for you not to ask them in their current form, but to consider them as a way of stimulating your own thinking. How can you come up with questions somewhat similar to these, but more appropriate to your institution, your department, and the specific position that you are searching for?

Questions About Experience

- What would you regard as your most significant accomplishment in your present position?

- If you were to leave your current position, what quality or aspect of your work would others at your institution miss the most?

- Describe the biggest professional mistake you ever made and how you fixed it.

- What was the toughest decision that you ever had to make in your career? How did you go about making that decision? What made it so difficult?

- What was the most unpopular decision that you ever had to make in your career? How did you go about making that decision? What made it so unpopular?

- Give me a specific example of a problem that you have solved. What resources did you use in solving that problem?

- What is the most creative or innovative thing you have ever done?

- What have you learned about managing growth in an academic setting? What have you learned about managing retrenchment or cutbacks?

- If I had to select between you and a candidate who happened to have more experience in this area, what are some of the reasons why I should still choose you?

Questions About Knowledge

- What three sources do you use most often to gain information about recent trends in higher education?

- How do you think Boyer's (1990) four functions of scholarship might apply to faculty development and evaluation in our program? (This is really a two-pronged question. First, you're exploring the candidate's familiarity with one of the classics of higher education administration. Second, you are providing an opportunity for the candidate to demonstrate creativity in applying the central argument of this work to a given situation.)

- What principles would you use in allocating scarce resources among compelling critical needs?

- Which recent work about issues in higher education do you believe every member of our department might profit from reading?

- In which professional organizations should administrators in our area maintain active memberships? Which professional organizations do you believe have the most productive and informative meetings?

Questions About Point Of View

- What is the most interesting book you have read in the last six months?

- If you had an opportunity to have a conversation with anyone—either a contemporary or some historical figure—who would it be? Why?

- What is your favorite word in the English language? Why?

- What do you do to relax?

- What makes you unique as an individual? What would you add to our area that we would be unlikely to get from another candidate?

- What would you describe as your own personal core values? What, in other words, are the values or principles that you regard as simply non-negotiable?

- Where do you see yourself in five years? In ten years? Why is that particular plan, goal, or trajectory important to you?

- What tends to give you the greatest satisfaction in your work? What tends to frustrate you the most?

Questions About Approach

- If you could choose just one book that all of our students would read, what would that book be?

- What is a current trend in higher education that you believe is really a wrong direction or, at least, a fad that will not last very long?

- What is the biggest challenge facing higher education today?

- What specific problem or challenge would you want to address first if you were to receive this position?

- If you were to be offered this position, how would you spend your time preparing for it in the interim before you actually started?

Questions About Fit

- What do you like least about your current position?

- What tends to annoy you? Describe for me a number of specific situations that, when they occur, cause you to feel that there is a real problem that needs to be solved.

- How will I know when you are angry? Serious? Kidding?

- What do people who don't like you say about you?

- Over the course of your entire career, which three students are still the most memorable to you? What made them particularly memorable?

- If I were to speak to the people who report to you in your current position, how would they describe you? (It is useful to compare the candidate's answer to this question to what those individuals actually say. That correlation, or lack thereof, can tell you a great deal about the candidate's self-awareness and candor.)

RESOURCES

In addition to the questions listed in this chapter, there are a number of useful resources that can guide you further in formulating your interview questions and steer you away from areas that may be inappropriate or legally questionable. Some of the resources that you may wish to consult include:

DeLuca, M. J. (1997). *Best answers to the 201 most frequently asked interview questions.* New York, NY: McGraw-Hill. (Although not really intended for the academic market, this book can provide an additional source of useful interview questions, as well as some indication of what a well-thought-out answer might sound like.)

Falcone, P. (1997). *96 great interview questions to ask before you hire.* New York, NY: AMACOM. (Another book that, while focused more on the business market than the academic world, can help guide you to phrasing more informative and appropriate interview questions.)

McCabe, L. L., & McCabe, E. R. B. (2000). *How to succeed in academics.* San Diego, CA: Academic Press. (This book contains a section on searching in the academic setting and on conducting interviews [albeit from the candidate's perspective] on pages 23–29. It deals primarily with the natural sciences, particularly the health sciences.)

REFERENCE

Boyer, E. L. (1990). *Scholarship reconsidered: Priorities of the professoriate.* Princeton, NJ: The Carnegie Foundation for the Advancement of Teaching.

4

How to Let Someone Go

There is a common image of academic administrators as individuals who relish lavish displays of their own power, enjoy the authority that comes with their positions, and take great delight in refusing even the simplest request. Certainly despotic administrators exist in academia, just as they do in every other profession. The vast majority of college administrators regard giving employees bad news as the absolutely worst part of their jobs. And the hardest thing that any administrator ever has to do is to fire somebody. Letting an employee go has a severe, and sometimes lasting, effect on that person's income, career, and self-esteem. There are relatively few situations in which one can claim that a termination is "nothing personal." To the individual who will now be out of work, it is a very personal matter indeed. Probably more than any other part of their positions, firing someone is what keeps department chairs awake at night. They worry about potential lawsuits, about coping with the employee's hostility (or possibly even violence), and about the look in an employee's eyes just after receiving the news that his or her career at the institution has ended.

Nothing can be done to make this distressful task palatable. Nevertheless, there are a number of actions that you can consider in order to protect yourself, your institution, and even the person whom you are terminating. The following are among the most important steps you can take when letting someone go.

Get Advice and Support

There is never any reason to "go it alone" when you're terminating someone. Before you take any action whatsoever, contact the appropriate person on your institution's human resources staff. In most cases, you will also want to touch base with the legal affairs office or your campus attorney; we live in a litigious society and terminations can be extremely litigious matters. Your human resources staff and legal counsel will advise you on which institutional policies must be followed, when and in what form notification needs to be given, whether witnesses must or should be present (see next section), how much of a "paper trail" is adequate for this dismissal, and even whether you ought to be taking this action in the first place. At the very least, consulting capable, discreet individuals who have probably dealt with significantly more terminations than you have will provide you with an "external scan" to make sure that you have asked the right questions, followed the right procedures, and prepared yourself to be asked some potentially difficult questions.

Act Sooner Rather Than Later

Many times department chairs delay letting someone go because the task of dismissal is unpleasant, and there is always a chance that the situation may improve. Doing so is almost always a mistake. While there are undoubtedly a few cases somewhere of a chair who later regrets letting someone get away, nearly every seasoned chair can tell you stories about people who should have been dismissed but who were allowed to remain on at an institution until it was far too late. The faculty member who goes up for tenure, with full anticipation of being approved, only to be denied should be the rare exception in academe. If your institution does not have a systematic, formal pre-tenure review in a faculty member's second, third, or fourth year of service, start one in your own department. In fact, it is probably desirable to conduct some sort of formal review of tenure-track faculty members *each* year. Some of these reviews can be formative; these sessions can be collegial and supportive meetings with the chair and a few members of the senior faculty in which constructive advice is given and a plan for the future is developed. Some of these meetings should, however, be summative; the faculty member should be told clearly whether adequate progress is being made toward tenure and promotion, where improvements are required, and whether the individual's performance to date has met the expectations of the department and institution. While you will want to conduct some of these sessions yourself, it is inadvisable for the chair to be the *only* individual who reviews tenure-track faculty members annually. Tenure decisions are, after all, usually based on committee recommendations and tend to require ratification at higher administrative levels. Whenever possible, see if your own evaluation matches that of your departmental personnel review committee, the dean, and the provost. It is better to find out sooner rather than later that different levels draw different conclusions about the adequacy of an individual's progress in instruction, scholarship, and service.

In any case, it is always better to non-renew a contract just as soon as there is a clear consensus that the faculty member is not a good match for the institution or the duties assigned. It may seem merciful to keep giving an unsuccessful teacher or researcher numerous additional chances, but it is actually not. The longer individuals remain at an institution, the more difficult it is for them to explain their involuntary departure to future employers. People may also feel that sheer length of service is itself an endorsement of their performance, sending a false or mixed message that you will certainly wish to avoid.

For tenured faculty members, the difficulty of your task increases tremendously. But you should remember that, despite the manner in which tenure is viewed at some institutions, it does not guarantee continued employment to faculty members who fail to perform the duties of their position, violate either the law or institutional policy, or behave in a manner that is seriously detrimental to your program or your college. What tenure provides for an individual is the right to: 1) be given a reason for the dismissal and 2) respond to that reason through some form of due process appropriate to your institution. There will certainly be very specific and detailed procedures for the steps you must take in dismissing a tenured faculty member. You will *always* want to have legal counsel in these situations both before you take any formal action and at each step along the way. But you should never rule out dismissing a seriously underperforming faculty member or one who has flagrantly violated a major institutional policy simply because that person is tenured. Always ask yourself, "What does more harm for our students and for the institution as a whole: letting this person remain or letting the faculty member go?"

In cases involving staff members, your institution will almost certainly have established policies and procedures outlining what sort of notice you need to provide and on what timetable. If you work in a unionized environment, these guidelines are likely to be quite specific. If your institution happens to be located in an "At Will" state, you may not be required to give the staff member whom you're terminating any explanation for your action; you may, however, be required to pay unemployment compensation to any employee you dismiss without providing a reason.

Have a Witness Present, If at All Possible

Even at institutions where witnesses are not required, it is always advisable to have a third party present when you are dismissing someone. The third party's presence can be extremely useful if there is ever a question at a later date about specifically what was said, promised, and done. Particularly in cases where the chair and the employee are of different genders or sexual orientations or where there has been a history of tension and animosity, a witness can verify that the proper policies were followed and that nothing inappropriate occurred behind closed doors. When selecting a witness, you may wish to have present someone from your institution's human resources or legal affairs office who has dealt with other terminations and can offer you guidance about what to say. Meet privately with the witness before joining the employee you will dismiss in order to plan your strategy, go over precisely who will say what, whether a written dismissal will be given to the employee, and remind one another of the importance of discretion and courtesy in matters of this sort.

Read and Follow Your Institution's Internal Procedures Scrupulously

In cases of dismissals, more problems—including legal vulnerabilities—occur because of failure to follow internal, institutional guidelines and procedures than from any other cause. You have come to this difficult decision after much anxiety and soul-searching; you don't want it all to collapse as the result of a technicality. Be sure that all timetables for various types of notifications have occurred. If your institution requires a series of oral and written warnings before you can proceed to a dismissal, be certain that you have taken these steps. Notify all the individuals that your institution requires you to notify. Prepare a checklist of all the steps your institution requires you to take, and be certain that all these steps have been taken.

Maintain Good Documentation

You are on the safest ground if you have maintained a clear "paper trail" that leads up to this dismissal. In most cases, you will want a series of performance appraisals that indicated the employee was informed of improvements that needed to occur, a timetable by which to take these actions, and indications that the required action has not been taken. Even in situations where the documentation is not this clear, however, it is extremely useful to have documentation of conversations held in which you spoke to the employee about concerns with his or her performance, email messages illustrating the problems for which the employee is being dismissed, timecards or attendance records suggesting the employee's failure to perform the full functions of the position, or other clear, written evidence that will suggest, to a reasonable observer, that you were justified in terminating the employee.

Don't Reveal More Than You Need

When it comes to letting someone go, less is definitely more in terms of what you say. The more you tell the employee being dismissed, the more you run the risk of legal challenges, misinterpretations, and multiple appeals. For staff members, if you are living in an "At Will" state and your institution is willing to pay the required weeks of unemployment benefits, you are better off providing no reason for your action at all. Similarly, in the case of untenured faculty members, unless you are specifically required by your institution, it is far preferable to give no reason for a non-renewal. Some department chairs don't realize that you are never required by law to provide a reason for dismissing a untenured faculty member at the end of a contract. In fact, some institutions and state systems *forbid* stating reasons for dismissing an untenured faculty member. The reason is that, unlike tenured faculty members, untenured faculty members are on annual employment contracts and have no legal right to expect their extension during their pre-tenure, probationary period. The difference is roughly akin to that between contracting someone to paint your house and contracting someone to deliver your daily newspaper. The house painter works for the duration of the contract and, when that period is over, has no right to expect future employment from you *unless you specifically offer a new contract.* The newspaper service, on the other hand, will keep delivering a daily paper to you *unless you specifically instruct them to stop.* Though the comparison is certainly not perfect, the untenured faculty member is like the house painter: after the expiration of each contract, you can part ways for no reason whatsoever. The tenured faculty member is more like the person who delivers your newspaper: there is an expectation that the relationship will continue unless you specifically give instructions to the contrary.

Even in cases where a tenured faculty member is being terminated, it is better to say less rather than more. In these situations, there is rarely only one reason or one occurrence of an action that has led to the dismissal. In cases where there is only one reason, the violation of policy will have been so egregious that the result is likely to seem fairly clear cut. The tendency of many department chairs, when dismissing a tenured faculty member, is to want to "throw the book at 'em" and cite every single reason in an effort to justify the termination. In many cases, this approach is a mistake. Certain reasons are likely to be stronger and more compelling than others. By including a large number of weaker reasons in an effort at justification, department chairs can actually undermine their own cases. They can open more opportunities to appeal and make even their strongest reasons seem trivial in the context of so many weak explanations. The result, therefore, is that it is far better in situations where there are multiple reasons for dismissing a tenured faculty member to place your emphasis on the *one indisputable* reason than to attempt an approach that sacrifices the quality of your argument for the quantity of explanations you can introduce.

Be Humane, But Honest

No matter how your relationship has been with the employee whom you are terminating, it is important to realize that the situation will be stressful for that person, possibly devastating to his or her career and self-esteem. You will want to extend all the courtesy, respect, and professionalism you can possibly bring to the situation. As you review in your mind how you will approach the situation, ask yourself how you would wish to be treated—or how you would wish your child to be treated—if you were in a similar position. At the same time, our tendency to want to make a painful situation more bearable can lead us to say things that we don't really mean. Because of a terminated employee's tears or look of hurt, we may start to praise aspects of the person's performance that, in other situations, we might not regard as of particularly high quality. It is important not to send mixed messages about the individual's performance that can end up complicating your task later. Be clear and direct in stating what you had planned to say, but do not be unnecessarily heartless in either your phrasing or demeanor.

Understand That the Employee Will Require More Than One Conversation on This Topic

When employees hear that they have been terminated, it is rather like hearing a death sentence. Their reaction is one of shock and, for a significant time afterwards, they may not really be processing everything that you are telling them. After they digest the news that you have given them and discussed it with their family and friends, they will inevitably have additional questions, concerns, and possibly even anger. You should expect that the employee *will* engage you in further conversations, or that at least the person will *try* to do so. The difficulty with this development is that, while you have fit the initial conversation into your schedule and prepared carefully for it, you may not know when the next conversation will occur. The employee may make an appointment a day or so after the original encounter; the conversation may also occur impromptu when you are blindsided in the hallway, washroom, or off campus. Be prepared for these follow-up conversations.

Know in advance precisely what you will say and where you will draw the line in saying anything more. In truly difficult situations, you may need to say, "I've told you everything I have to say about this matter. From this point further, you'll need to direct those questions to the Office of Human Resources (or to the college attorney)."

If you have decided not to provide reasons for the non-continuation, don't allow the unexpected nature of these encounters to make you deviate from this plan. You may be tempted, for instance, in a less formal encounter with the employee to provide additional information about what he or she could have done better as a means of helping that person in the future. This type of mentoring may seem valuable but it is fraught with perils. The "informal guidance" you give the employee may be construed as supplying the reason for the dismissal. So, be kind, be as supportive as you can, but don't provide any information in a later conversation that you intentionally omitted from your initial meeting.

RESOURCES

Consult the resources that you need: There is no need to reinvent the wheel when terminating someone. This is an area of administration in which there are numerous excellent sources. Among the best are:

Covey, A. (2000). *The workplace law advisor: From harassment and discrimination policies to hiring and firing guidelines—what every manager and employee needs to know.* New York, NY: Perseus.

Falcone, P. (2002). *The hiring and firing: Question and answer book.* New York, NY: American Management Association

Fleischer, C. H. (2004). *The complete hiring and firing handbook: Every manager's guide to working with employees—legally.* Naperville, IL: Sphinx.

Horowitz, A. S. (1999). *The unofficial guide to hiring and firing people.* New York, NY: Macmillan.

Levin, R., & Rosse, J. (2001). T*alent flow: A strategic approach to keeping good employees, helping them grow, and letting them go.* San Francisco, CA: Jossey-Bass.

Repa, B. K. (2000). *Firing without fear: A legal guide for conscientious employers.* Berkeley, CA: Nolo.

Weiss, D. H. (1999). *Fair, square, and legal: Safe hiring, managing & firing practices to keep you & your company out of court* (3rd ed.). New York, NY: American Management Association.

5

How to Write Outstanding Letters of Recommendation

There is one fact of life that all department chairs must sooner or later learn to accept: if you don't like writing letters of recommendation, you're going to have a very tough tenure. Every department chair ends up with an almost unbelievable number of requests for letters of recommendation. Students need them for employment or for admission to graduate school. Faculty members need them when they are submitting grant applications, applying for promotion, and even when they are seeking positions at other institutions. But your obligations in this area do not end even with the boundaries of your department itself. Your chair colleagues in other departments may ask for letters of recommendation when they undergo performance evaluations or seek new opportunities in college administration. Since writing letters of recommendation will be such an important aspect of your position, is there any way in which you can make this task easier? And, at the same time that you are making the task easier, is there any way in which the letters that you produce can be more informative to the person who is reading them and truly outstanding from all the other letters that may receive little more than a cursory glance?

The letters of recommendation that you write will be more effective and less of a burden for you to produce, if you systematically ask yourself each of the following questions before you begin to draft the letter:

- How strong of a recommendation do I wish to write?

- On what basis am I making this recommendation?

- Which three central points do I therefore wish to make?

- What examples can I provide for each of these three points?

- What insights can I provide that the reader can gain nowhere else?

Spending just two or three minutes reviewing these five questions will instantly give you insight into what you need to say, how to organize your letter, and how to keep it focused enough for it to be effective. Let's examine each of these in turn.

How Strong of a Recommendation Do I Wish to Write?

The first thing that you should do when beginning a letter of recommendation is decide in advance what overall impression you wish to create. Where, in other words, along the overall spectrum of "recommendability" would you place this candidate? Do you wish to leave the reader with the impression that the person about whom you are writing is one of the very best individuals with whom you have ever worked? Is this a candidate about whom you have no reservations whatsoever, someone on whom you would stake your reputation? We all have students and colleagues we might place in that category and, when these select individuals are requesting a letter, you will need not hold back the superlatives in your praise. But usually a person who is asking for a letter of recommendation is not a denizen of these exalted regions, but rather a person not unlike the vast majority of us: good, perhaps even extremely good, at certain things, less capable at others. In these cases, try to develop a clear picture of precisely how you would rank the person. Is he or she in the top 2% of all the people you might recommend for this position? No? Perhaps in the top 5%? The upper quarter? The best third? The top half? Or, is this an individual who, for whatever reason, you do not feel you can give a particularly strong recommendation, at least for *this* opportunity?

It is important at the start to have a clear impression of the degree of support you wish to convey: If you are not certain yourself, there is no way in which your reader will be certain after seeing your letter. Deciding in advance on the strength of your recommendation involves far more than simply determining how emphatic your adjectives will be; it involves knowing what one thing you want the reader to know most of all. Try to state that one, overall impression to yourself in twenty words or less. If you are unable to frame your basic message that concisely, your reader will not be able to interpret your message—no matter how carefully you craft your prose or select the anecdotes that you will relate.

On What Basis Am I Making This Recommendation?

Once you have decided the overall strength and tone that your recommendation will take, your next question will be to decide the basis on which you are writing this letter. This question is a little more complicated than simply knowing that you are creating the letter as the person's colleague, mentor, or advisor. It is a matter of developing a clear image in your mind of the reason why you feel that you can serve as a reference for this particular can-

advised, transformed, etc.) rather than abstractions, too many adverbs, and weaker, less action-oriented verbs (e.g., supported, approved, served, etc.). In each paragraph, be sure that you have stated, not merely *that* the person is good, but *why* the person is good and what specific *behavior* or *accomplishment* has led you to this observation.

What Insights Can I Provide That the Reader Can Gain Nowhere Else?

Finally, ask yourself if you have provided the reader with insights or observations that could not be gained (or, at least, not *easily* gained) from another source. One of the mistakes that many writers of reference letters make is simply to repeat information that the recipient already knows from a transcript, curriculum vitae, or the applicant's own letter. In a letter written on behalf of a student, for instance, it makes very little sense simply to state the individual's cumulative GPA. At best, this statement will merely repeat information that the reader already knows from other sources and will make it look as though you are "padding" your letter because you don't have anything else positive to say. At worst, either your information or the transcript mailed by the student may be out of date, and the recipient will end up giving undue attention to why the student's cumulative GPA is listed as 3.83 in one place and 3.77 in another. Rather, if you believe that the student's grade point average could be particularly important to the reader of your letter, place that information in a context that only you can provide. Say something like, "While this student's cumulative GPA was an impressive 3.43 at the end of fall semester [YEAR], it should be noted that in advanced practica and seminars—where students are competing against the most accomplished of their peers in the most rigorous of conditions—the student's average reached a perfect 4.0, the only such example I have known in my 22 years of teaching."

In all cases, try to select specific examples of achievement that are unlikely to be documented in standard sources such as résumés and transcripts. Since the individual selected you to be a reference, what opportunities have you had to experience this person's work that are unlikely to be shared by other observers? Which examples provide the most informative picture of the candidate as a person, even if the reader of your letter has not yet met the person about whom you are writing? The more you can tie your examples to things you have directly experienced, and the more you can bring the person about whom you are writing to life for your readers, the more effective your letter will be.

didate's suitability to this particular opportunity. In most cases, your letter will be based on at least one of the following:

Experience

A letter based on experience argues that the candidate has already had prior success in programs or positions similar to the one about which you are currently writing and, therefore, would be an excellent choice for the position at hand. Because the candidate is likely to have amassed experience in situations relevant to the current opportunity, your letter will be filled with more examples of obstacles overcome and opportunities seized than is usually the case in other types of letters. The best cases that you can cite are those that help clarify for the reader how the person approached the challenges that arose, made effective decisions, and grew in responsibility over the time that you had direct observation of the individual. Try to cite situations in which you directly observed the candidate's strengths or information that goes beyond what is probably contained in the person's letter of application and curriculum vitae.

Potential

A letter based on the candidate's potential or promise would be appropriate when that person is seeking an opportunity that goes significantly beyond or is substantially different from his or her past experience. For instance, examples of individuals for whom you may decide to write a letter based on their potential include an undergraduate who is applying to graduate school or for a first job, a teaching colleague who is seeking a first deanship, and a graduate student who is trying to find an initial appointment on the full-time faculty of another institution. Although they may not have held a position identical to the one for which they are currently applying, you might cite examples of somewhat similar activities that the person has successfully accomplished. Have they been a teaching assistant, demonstrated leadership on a committee, or excelled at coursework at all similar to what will be involved in this new opportunity? In a letter based on promise, you should build your case around experiences that are similar, though obviously not identical to, the proposed position and extrapolate the candidate's likely success from these other situations.

Intelligence

A letter based on the candidate's innate intelligence is most suitable when you are asked to write a recommendation for someone who is applying for a position far outside of his or her prior experience. Since you may not even know of appropriate *comparable* achievements, you might talk about how quickly this individual learns to succeed in unfamiliar situations, masters challenges, and demonstrates unusual insight into the root causes of various problems. Your central point should be that, although the person has not yet had the opportunity to demonstrate success in this area or in similar areas, he or she is bright enough to adapt to any sort of challenge that may come along. You are arguing that the person is a "quick study" (providing, of course, a number of specific examples to back up your claim), even if that talent has not yet been applied in an area similar to the current opportunity.

Character

Letters of reference based primarily on a person's strength of character should be used only in certain situations, and then only advisedly. While it is always appropriate in any letter of recommendation to describe the candidate as principled, having a strong sense of values, and trustworthy (providing that you believe such claims to be true), most letters that over-emphasize an applicant's personal qualities strike reviewers as rather weak. They appear to be saying that the applicant is unqualified for this opportunity, that you recognize this lack of qualifications, and that you are intentionally avoiding making reference to the central criteria on which this decision will be made. In most cases, you should focus your letter on the applicant's character only if that is the type of letter that is specifically requested by the institution (as may be the case, for instance, with an applicant to law school or seminary) or if that is the primary capacity in which you know the individual (if, for instance, you are writing a letter, not primarily as the applicant's chair but as his or her spiritual advisor or colleague in a religious education course).

Which Three Central Points Do I Wish to Make?

Having now decided on the strength of your recommendation and the basis on which you will be framing your letter, your next task is to decide how to be as helpful as possible to the person or committee who will be receiving your letter. You will want to be concise. Long letters of recommendation simply are not read. Although you may feel that your pages of eloquence are serving the candidate's best interests, your efforts may actually be counter-

productive. A five- or six-page letter will be set aside and ignored, along with all of your arguments on behalf of this candidate. Other, potentially less qualified candidates may end up getting more attention because the letters of recommendation written on their behalf were concise and easily digested.

For the most part, therefore, you will want letters of recommendation to fit on one side of a single sheet of paper. In certain rare instances (for example, that truly rare advisee who will undoubtedly go on to a distinguished career in your discipline), you may allow yourself to extend onto a second page for perhaps a paragraph. But under no circumstances should you ever write a letter of recommendation that is longer than two pages. The task facing you is thus to make your point as clearly, crisply, and directly as possible. Don't allow valuable information to become lost in excess verbiage.

The best way to do this is to ask: what three things are most important for the reader to know about this candidate's potential (or experience or intelligence or character)? Make each of those three points the topic sentence of a brief paragraph, and your letter will largely structure itself. For instance, when writing a letter on behalf of a student who is applying to graduate school, you may decide that the most important information the reader can receive is: The student was highly original in selecting research topics, the student is a good "self-starter" and independent worker, and the student recovers easily from unexpected set-backs in his or her academic work. For a faculty member applying for promotion, you might decide that your three observations will be: The faculty member has introduced classroom techniques that greatly enhanced the engagement of his or her students, the faculty member's research is highly respected in the discipline, and the faculty member's college-wide service commitments, while few in number, have made a tremendous impact on the good of the community. For a colleague who is applying for a senior administrative position, you might note that this individual takes a highly collegial approach to problem solving, sees the central issue of a problem very quickly, and strives to ensure that every side of an issue is examined.

What Examples Can I Provide for Each of These Three Points?

Once it is clear to you which three observations will provide the central structure of your letter, you will want to support each point with one or two clear, specific examples. Try to focus on a substantive instance in which the individual has demonstrated the positive quality that you are describing. Use concrete "action words" (e.g., developed, recruited, founded, increased

Additional Guidelines

There are two other principles to keep in mind while writing letters of recommendation.

Make Your Task as Easy as Possible for the Reader

Recipients of letters of recommendation are frequently dealing with dozens of letters at once. Keep their needs and interest in mind. The first time that you mention the subject's name, place it in **bold face type**. Open your letter, for instance, with language similar to the following: "**Jennifer G. Student** has asked me to write you in support of her application to the [PROGRAM]. I am delighted to do so because . . . " Use of this type of font and structure keeps the reader from having to sift through the entire letter trying to discover about whom you are writing. (It also makes it easier for the person sorting the mail to know how your letter should be filed.) When addressing a letter to someone outside of your department or institution, try to consider what they will know and what you will need to explain to them. Will it be clear to your reader that the "APA" you feature prominently in your letter is the American Philological Association and not the American Psychological Association, the American Psychiatric Association, the American Payroll Association, the Audio Publishers Association, the Allied Pilots Association, or the American Planning Association? (All of these are real organizations, and they are all widely known as "APA" among certain groups of academics.) Will your reader know whether the "ENG 101" that you mention is a literature course or a composition course? Will it be obvious that GR 300 is a German rather than a Greek course and that IN 411 is an Independent Study course rather than an International Studies course? (As a general rule of thumb, always use course names rather than course numbers. They tend to be more easily understood.) Proofread your letter to be sure that every reference—including references to people who may be known locally in your department but not in wider academic circles—is either obvious or explained.

Be Judicious About Writing Negative Letters

There are very few instances when you should write a letter of reference that is not, on balance, far more positive than negative. If you are asked for a letter by the individual himself or herself and do not feel that you can write a positive letter, the kindest suggestion that you can make is for the person to seek someone else to serve as reference. In most cases, merely making this suggestion is all that you will have to do. Certain people will press you, however, in order to learn the reasons why you are reluctant to write a letter on their behalf. In these cases, it is far preferable to provide one or two concrete reasons face-to-face, as uncomfortable as that may be, than to give the false impression that you are submitting a positive letter.

In all letters of recommendation, you should only state what you are 100% certain and can document. This rule is even more important in the case of less than completely positive letters of reference. Even letters for which the subjects waive their rights to see cannot be guaranteed to remain confidential. The subject may see your letter at some point in the future, which could result in a legal challenge that should have been avoided. As a general rule, write nothing in a letter of recommendation that you would not want the subject to read and to be quoted in a large circulation newspaper. In a worst case scenario, both of those contingencies could occur.

RESOURCES

There are a number of useful sources to consult in developing additional insights about writing outstanding letters or recommendation. These sources include:

Bell, A. H. (2004). *Writing effective letters, memos, and e-mails,* (3rd ed.). Hauppauge, NY: Barron's Educational Series.

Fawcett, S. (2004). *Instant recommendation letter kit: How to write winning letters of recommendation.* Montréal, Québec: Final Draft! Consulting and Communications.

Mamchak, P. S., & Mamchak, S. R. (1999). *Educator's lifetime encyclopedia of letters.* San Francisco, CA: Jossey-Bass.

Whalley, S. (2000). *How to write powerful letters of recommendation.* Minneapolis, MN: Educational Media Corporation. (Even though this book is intended for people who are writing on behalf of high school students who are applying to college, it contains good ideas for any kind of reference letter. Best of all, the book includes 52 sample letters that you can adapt and expand upon in developing your own letters.)

6

Sharpening Focus

One of the most perplexing challenges for department chairs is how to mentor those faculty members who, while excellent in many ways, do not focus their energy or attention to achieve all that they are capable of accomplishing. The unfocused faculty member may exhibit the following characteristics:

- He or she is always flustered, complaining about how much there is to be done and rushing off to do it, but rarely producing any substantive results from all of this frenzied activity. While most of your faculty members may tolerate—or possibly even thrive in—all the demands that academic life places on their time, the unfocused faculty member too frequently seems overwhelmed even by minor challenges.

- He or she gives you critical information, such as self-evaluations, annual budget requests, and textbook orders, either after the deadline or at the moment they are due. If on more than one occasion you find the same person's report slipped under your door late in the evening on the day you needed it or emailed to you only when you are printing your own summary report to the dean, this is a faculty member who could desperately use your mentoring skills.

- He or she receives student evaluations that routinely say the professor's courses did not remain "on track" or "lacked structure." Unfocused faculty members frequently carry a lack of organization from their departmental behavior into their courses. When students repeatedly comment about "a general lack of organization" in someone's courses, you may find that this criticism corresponds rather well with the concerns you are sensing in other areas of this faculty member's performance.

Although it can be a difficult mentoring challenge to help habitually disorganized people achieve a greater degree of focus in their work, this is not an impossible task. The advice needed by the faculty member will vary, of course, according to individual work habit and personal style, but there are some general guidelines that you should use in either a formal performance review or an informal conversation. In all cases, the faculty member may be more receptive to advice if you mention that you have personally found these suggestions helpful in organizing your time.

Set Goals and Deadlines in a Timely Manner

Unfocused faculty members frequently feel compelled to work on whichever problem has just caught their attention. You can provide useful advice about how to set priorities according to the overall importance of a task and its due date.

Devote a Certain Amount of Time Each Day to Critical, Ongoing Work

Guide the faculty member in setting aside a specific amount of time, perhaps an hour a day, for consistent work on his or her most important tasks. These tasks will not necessarily be fires that need to be put out right away. Rather, they are likely to be the jobs that have the greatest significance for the discipline or for that faculty member's professional development. Encourage the faculty member to find a time that can be devoted to work each day without interruption. The period he or she sets aside should not be during regular office hours, and the faculty member should not even attempt to answer the phone during that period unless it is likely to be an emergency.

Don't Over- or Underestimate the Amount of Time That Commitments Will Require

A frequent challenge for unfocused faculty members is taking on too many different obligations or assuming that they can complete a task in far less time than it ultimately requires. Encourage the faculty member to say no to low-priority tasks and to develop the habit of budgeting worst case time scenarios rather than being overly optimistic. Have the faculty member limit the number of meetings and appointments to a realistic number on any given day. Always leave room in the person's schedule for emergencies and sudden changes that cannot be anticipated.

Track Use of Time

Ask the faculty member to keep a time log that records how his or her time is being spent each day, and then group these blocks of time into various categories. Work together with the faculty member to explore ways in which certain tasks can be done more efficiently or discarded entirely in favor of more productive activities. If the faculty member's appointments and meetings tend to go overtime, ask the faculty member to consider why this occurs: Does the person who is conducting the meeting focus on its primary purpose immediately, or does it take some time to get to the main topic? Do people tend to linger and talk long after the main purpose for the meeting has been completed? If you observe that the faculty member frequently seems rushed when trying to keep appointments, help the faculty member analyze his or her use of time; encourage the faculty member to time how long each appointment actually runs. Go over these results with the faculty member and, by working together, try to develop a more realistic estimate for how much time should be blocked off for these appointments in the future.

Set Time Limits for Certain Tasks

Unfocused faculty members can sometimes become perfectionists when completing tasks that simply do not require perfection. Explain to the faculty member the difference between a major report to an accrediting body that should be as flawless as possible and ordinary email messages that do not need to be proofread until they are free of every typographical error. Explain to the faculty member that not every email message may be worth answering and that the vast majority of these messages can be answered in a sentence or two at most. Also, be sure to explain that it is perfectly acceptable to work on minor tasks for a set amount of time and then, when that time is up, to move on to something else.

Leverage Time

Assist the faculty member in pursuing opportunities that have multiple benefits. Are there scholarly projects that can also result in curricular innovations for your department or involve students in research? Are there creative service opportunities at your institution that could be developed into conference presentations? This type of two-for-one assignment can teach the faculty member to focus by clustering his or her time into a more manageable group of projects.

Take Advantage of To-Do Lists, But Don't Become Overly Dependent on Them

Establishing a clear list of items that need to be completed can be useful for setting priorities. All too often, however, people become enslaved to their to-do lists because the lists merely serve as unwelcome reminders of all the things they will never get done. The following guidelines can help make to-do lists truly productive.

Never Record Any Item too Large to Be Accomplished in a Single Session

Any item that is too large to be finished in one day should be broken down into multiple tasks that can be accomplished in one day each. Checking off these items as they are completed will provide a greater sense of accomplishment and will keep the faculty member from being overwhelmed by the size of the tasks on the list.

If an Item Has Remained on the To-Do List for More Than a Few Weeks, It Should Be Removed From the List

Any item that gets carried over from list to list for several weeks is unlikely to be completed anyway. Rather than being tyrannized by this item, you should encourage the faculty member to refocus his or her priorities on tasks that can and will be accomplished.

At the End of Each Day Spend No More Than 10 Minutes Reorganizing the List for the Next Day's Priorities

A small amount of time spent on setting priorities can become a useful exercise in focusing one's energy. Too much time spent on this task, however, simply becomes one more unnecessary distraction.

Fake It Until You Make It

Faculty members may be surprised how much more productive they can be simply by changing their attitude and approach. Encourage them, the next time they are tempted to complain about how much they still have to do, to speak instead about whatever it is they have just completed. After doing this a number of times, the faculty member will begin to feel that they are getting a lot done. Before they know it, they will actually have many more of their formerly overwhelming responsibilities well in hand.

In an initial conversation, it is frequently best to tell the faculty member that you are offering these suggestions only in a spirit of being helpful. If, in making these suggestions, you appear to be too intimidating at first, your advice may come across as "simply one more thing to do" rather than an approach that will ease the faculty member's workload. Be sure to address one or two aspects of the faculty member's performance that seem meritorious. By doing so, you will be perceived as a true mentor who is trying to make good work even better, rather than as a mere supervisor who is offering criticism for its own sake.

7

Increasing Productivity

The vast majority of faculty members work hard, devoting long hours to educating students to the full extent of their abilities, conducting research in their chosen disciplines, and serving on a wide variety of committees. Occasionally, however, a department chair will encounter a faculty member who is either unwilling or unable to match the productivity of his or her colleagues. This faculty member might be relatively new to the department and appear distracted from the central mission of the discipline by personal matters or outside interests. Or he or she might be a more senior member of the department who is marking time until retirement and no longer interested in providing instruction, scholarship, and service at what might once have been a very high level. These cases of what is sometimes disparagingly called deadwood can pose serious problems to the department's productivity and image. Department chairs can mentor these individuals to help increase their job satisfaction and the productivity of the department.

Determine the Causes

The chair must first ascertain the reasons for the faculty member's lack of productivity. It is rarely due to laziness. Even when individuals lack the work ethic of their peers, it is not usually because the faculty member does not care how he or she is perceived or takes no pride in the quality of the work being performed. A supportive but candid conversation, behind closed doors and in an encouraging, nonthreatening environment, can provide useful information about the origins of the behavior that concerns you. Sometimes even your expression of concern—coupled with the fact that you and others have noticed a decline in satisfactory productivity—is enough to bring about a noticeable change of behavior. Even if this does not happen, you might gain insights into problems that you can solve or reasons that you can address to begin changing the faculty member's behavior.

Look for Possible Sources of Pride and Motivation

Try to determine what still motivates the faculty member. What attracted this individual to the discipline in the first place? Is that still an aspect of academic life that inspires interest or enthusiasm for the faculty member? If so, what might be some of the ways in which this person can be reconnected with these vital interests? If not, are there other aspects of academic life that might still be stimulating for this person? As you explore these possibilities with the faculty member, try to determine what he or she still gets excited about. That source of motivation may be an opportunity that lies outside of your department, even outside of the academic affairs division of your institution. In these cases, you may wish to discuss the matter with your dean (or, if appropriate, your president) and explore together the ways in which the faculty member may be reconnected with the institution. Although few of us are able to design the specific job that we want, you might be able to work out a modification in the faculty member's assignment—perhaps coupled with some development opportunities or retraining—that leads to more of the challenges that the person still enjoys.

Be Clear About Responsibilities and Priorities

Occasionally a faculty member's productivity has suffered because we have been unclear about our expectations. If, for example, you feel that someone has not assumed their fair share of advisees, consider the extent to which your expectations have been outlined in plain and unmistakable language. As a department, you might want to establish guidelines about such matters as the number of office hours per week that are expected in your discipline (perhaps even mentioning that these must be on multiple days of the week), the amount of internal and college-wide committee service your department members should undertake, and your recommended practice about advising another faculty member's students in the absence of the students' own advisor. In private conversations with the faculty member whom you are mentoring, you might provide specific observations about where these departmental expectations have not been met. If necessary, you can look for ways to restructure the faculty member's assignment so that there are more opportunities to address the issues that you consider to be of higher priority.

Assign a Peer Mentor

As a department chair it is your responsibility to mentor faculty members in your area, but there are times when it is more effective for one of the faculty member's colleagues to act as a mentor. This is particularly true of junior faculty who might see you more as an authority figure than as a colleague and find it difficult to be completely candid with you. In these cases, assign the faculty member a mentor whom he or she trusts and with whom there is already an established rapport. Discuss with the mentor the issues that need to be addressed before his or her work with the faculty member begins. Establish a plan of action, and then give both the faculty member and the mentor the freedom to make this plan work. You can easily undermine your own efforts if you hover too closely over this process or if the faculty member comes to regard the mentor simply as a conduit of privileged information to you. Nevertheless, you should expect definite results, and you should measure and assess the level of progress while still providing sufficient space for those results to emerge.

Remove Any Obstacles That You Can

Every college or university has its own amount of bureaucracy and red tape. Some faculty members are more immobilized by these obstacles than others. Thus, if a faculty member is routinely late in submitting necessary documents—such as book orders, self-evaluations, or budget requests—see if you can determine whether the process itself is proving an impediment for this faculty member. Are there mechanisms you can provide that will simplify the process? With a little bit of ingenuity and some computing skill, many cumbersome tasks of gathering and organizing data can be made almost automatic. For instance, databases of textbooks can automatically create individualized book orders for faculty members each semester based on past textbook assignments and current enrollment patterns. As new textbooks are adopted, a secretary or administrative assistant can update this information in the system so that "pre-completed" textbook orders can be generated on time and as needed. In a similar way, departmental clearinghouses can be established to ease the process of preparing annual self-evaluations. Whenever publications are accepted or awards are received, these achievements can be entered into a database and then produced when annual reports are due so that the faculty member doesn't have to start a self-evaluation from scratch every year. Examining your departmental processes on a regular basis will allow you to determine where you are helping and where you are hindering the productivity of your own faculty members.

Provide Public Recognition

Some faculty members cease to be productive because they feel that their contributions are never recognized or rewarded. You can reduce this likelihood by making a habit of publicly recognizing the contributions of individual faculty members. Public praise is a powerful motivator. It encourages the individual being praised to try even harder and stimulates others to seek their own moment in the spotlight. In environments where budgets are tight—and for most academic institutions this is a perennial problem—significant public recognition can make the difference to someone who wants to go the extra mile and someone who is content with a minimal amount of effort. Also keep in mind that public recognition does not have to be given only in formal settings. Praising the extra achievement of one faculty member to another in a private conversation, if properly done, can boost the morale of everyone. An impromptu commendation in the midst of a casual conversation can be all the more gratifying because it was unexpected.

Keep a Paper Trail

If you have legitimate concerns about a faculty member's level of productivity, be sure to keep records documenting your efforts to fix the problem. Maintain a log of your conversations and the advice that you have given. When you are writing a formal evaluation, be candid and precise. State clearly what your expectations were, how they were not achieved, and what should be done about the situation in the future. Although much can be done to improve the productivity of your faculty members, not every problem is fixable. In the event of a negative personnel decision, you will want clear documentation outlining precisely when you first recognized the problem, how you brought it to the faculty member's attention, what steps you took to improve the situation, and why you remain dissatisfied with that individual's productivity.

8

Promoting Collegiality

Every department chair understands the importance of promoting collegiality within his or her department. Few factors can bring the productivity of a department to a standstill and destroy its reputation as quickly as can the presence of even a single uncollegial faculty member. Continued breaches of collegiality have been known to destroy departmental morale, alienate capable students, cost the department some of its most valued faculty members, and decrease a department's competitiveness when it applies for grants and other forms of external support.

Like many aspects of higher education law, the role that collegiality can and should play in personnel decisions is still not perfectly clear. Nevertheless, even as these legal issues continue to unfold, several precedents suggest that collegiality can indeed be a valid factor when faculty members are reviewed. In the landmark case of *Mayberry v. Dees*, for instance, the Fourth Circuit Court recognized collegiality as a criterion in tenure decisions alongside such widely accepted criteria as teaching, scholarship, and service. Moreover, in the case of the *University of Baltimore v. Iz*, the Maryland Appellate Court ruled that collegiality may be considered when personnel decisions are being made even if an institution's governance documents do not expressly cite collegiality as a distinct criterion. (On the case history of collegiality issues, see Connell, 2001; Connell & Savage, 2001; Fogg, 2002.) To be sure, since collegiality affects the quality of a faculty member's teaching, scholarship, and service, it may well be regarded as an appropriate *implicit* factor—much as showing up for work on time and not plagiarizing another scholar's research are frequently unstated implicit criteria—when personnel decisions are made.

Yet even though it is in both a faculty member's own interest and in the interests of the department as a whole for coworkers to treat one another in a collegial manner, department chairs are often at a loss as to how they should mentor a faculty member whose uncollegial behavior causes problems. What, they may ask, is the best way to promote departmental collegiality and foster mutually respectful interactions among peers?

Begin With a Department-Wide Dialogue on Collegiality

A surprising number of faculty members do not understand what is generally meant by "collegiality." They assume that it merely means "being polite," "getting along," or "saying hello" to their colleagues in the hallway and inviting them (or accepting their invitations) to an appropriate number of parties. What faculty members frequently do not understand is that *collegiality consists of all forms of appropriate professional activity that promote, to the greatest extent possible, the primary functions of the institution.* In other words, collegiality is not just "being nice" and it is certainly not the same thing as "never criticizing anyone." Rather, collegiality is a central ingredient in academic professionalism. It is one of our obligations as academic professionals to our disciplines, departments, and institutions. But it is not the same as "being nice;" it is perfectly possible for a "nice person" to lack collegiality because that person avoids a fair share of committee service, unnecessarily prolongs routine departmental processes, and squelches the free exchange of ideas during discussions. By contrast, other faculty members may offer criticism, even repeated criticism, in a perfectly collegial manner by voicing their opinions in a proper forum and by using a manner that is civil, conducive to the academic mission of the institution, and professionally respectful. The real test of collegiality, therefore, is this: Does the behavior in question *contribute to* or *make more difficult* the central mission of the institution with regards to teaching, scholarship, and service?

Develop a Departmental Code of Conduct

One way to work through the issues of collegiality is for a department to attempt to define a code of acceptable behavior. Departments can even increase their reputations on campus by serving as leaders in discussions of professional civility. As a chair, you can set the goal of developing a departmental code of civility or collegiality that you will share with other departments on campus. Such a code might look something like this:

> As members of the Department of X, we undertake to communicate with others, both orally and in writing, in a manner that is polite, respectful, and courteous. Whenever we disagree with someone, we restrict our differences to the issue itself while continuing to respect the individual with whom we disagree. All of our discussion and argumentation will be conducted in a polite, courteous, and dignified manner.

Once you have established such a departmental code, you will then have a vehicle with which to initiate conversations with faculty members when, in your professional judgment, serious breaches of that code have occurred. Those discussions can carry particular weight if the faculty member you are addressing is one of those who voted in favor of the code or if the code was reviewed with the faculty member when that person was hired as part of the interview or orientation process.

When Public Breaches of Collegiality Occur, Intervene Sooner Rather Than Later

If, for example, discussions at a department meeting are on the verge of dissolving into rancor, it is best to step in at once. Abruptly adjourn the meeting or call a temporary recess. Invite the principals into your office for a private conversation (where they can cool down or at least rephrase their concerns without "grandstanding" in front of other colleagues). Explain to them—calmly but firmly—the reasons why you could not allow the discussion to continue as it was. Similarly, if you encounter an uncollegial discussion or exchange of messages among members of your department, it is your duty as chair to intervene and to see if you can redirect the focus of the dispute. Intervention does not mean that you will become involved in every faculty disagreement; many disagreements are healthy and actually serve to keep the department vigorous in its consideration of new ideas. Nevertheless, if it is clear that a discussion is about to become personal rather than professional or to involve matters that are inappropriate and irrelevant to the topic at hand, it is important for you to become involved.

Whenever Possible, Address Breaches of Collegiality Privately Rather Than Publicly

In many instances, if you attempt to handle uncollegiality by openly "calling the guilty party on the carpet," you will end up making that person defensive and possibly even less cooperative in the future. Handling lapses in professional demeanor privately, including such phrases as "what I just heard was so unlike you" and assuring the individual that you have his or her best professional interests at heart will make your conversation more clearly a mentoring session than a disciplinary procedure. As you talk over the matter with the faculty member, try to determine the reasons for the breach of collegiality that you observed. Was the person unaware of the impact that his or her actions might have or was the person fully aware of what was occurring and simply indifferent to the result? Determining this will guide you in formulating your response. For if the faculty member was unaware that he or she was being uncollegial, it may be useful to have that person internalize the impact of the situation. Ask such questions as, "How would you feel if . . . ?" Or, "How do you imagine that Professor X is going to respond to you now that you . . . ?" On the other hand, if you suspect that the faculty member actually intended to cause discomfort and was simply bullying a colleague, then it is far more productive for you to keep your focus directly on the uncollegial faculty member and the inappropriateness of his or her action. Say such things as, "Let me tell you why what you did was unprofessional . . . " And, "Here's why your actions have done a disservice to our department . . . "

Confront Rumors and "Ancient History" Head-On

There are few things more poisonous to departmental collegiality than rumors, innuendo, and constant reference to long-past grievances. If you have reason to believe that a faculty member has been guilty of spreading rumors or malicious gossip, speak to that person about the damaging effect of these actions. Remind the faculty member that, in extreme cases, he or she might even become legally liable if someone's professional reputation or livelihood is threatened. Whenever necessary, debunk rumors publicly in department meetings. Then, if the rumors are mentioned again, adopt the "broken record" approach: Just keep repeating, "As I already said in an earlier meeting, the reason why that's not true is . . . " Be particularly careful to quash false rumors about members of the upper administration. Being associated with misinformation of this sort can jeopardize your department on any number of levels. Similarly, if a faculty member repeatedly brings up past grievances, make it clear that you are not interested in rehashing earlier problems. Say things like, "I think there ought to be a Statute of Limitations on how long we can complain about . . . " or, "We all already know about that. We can't change the past, and I'm not going to hold this department's progress hostage to something I can't do anything about. Let's move on."

Mentor Faculty Members in the Art of Constructive Criticism

Sometimes violations of collegiality occur because a faculty member does not have the proper "people skills" or experience to raise objections forcefully but constructively. When this occurs, you can provide a valuable service to that person by offering instruction in collegial disputation. Start by explaining the difference between criticizing an idea and appearing to criticize the person who is advancing that idea. Offer a few verbal tips on ways in which objections can be raised more positively, such as "I think that's a great idea, but we might be able to refine it a bit by . . . " or, "Well, I'm not sure I agree with you about that particular approach, but since we're both enthusiastic about achieving the same goal, maybe we could . . . " Note that it is perfectly acceptable to advocate strongly for one's own ideas, but there are both appropriate and inappropriate ways of critiquing the ideas of others. Encourage the faculty member to stick to the topic at hand, making a rational and unemotional argument about why one approach is superior to another, while remaining open to and supportive of the ideas that others may have. Point out unintended subtext conveyed through posture, facial expression, body language, and the level of one's voice.

Seek Common Ground

Sometimes faculty members are uncollegial in their treatment of others because there is a personality conflict between them or they just "got off on the wrong foot." In these situations, the chair has an opportunity to serve as a catalyst for improving professional relations by exploring areas where the faculty members share common outlooks, approaches, or aspirations. It often takes a third party to hear voices of commonality where the faculty members cannot hear any agreement for themselves. Point out any shared areas of interest. Say things like, "Isn't that just another way of saying this . . . And didn't I just hear you say that . . . " Decrease the intensity of the confrontation by using yourself as a buffer. Ask such questions as, "Maybe I'm not quite understanding this correctly, but haven't you both been saying essentially that . . . ?"

Maintain a Focus on the Real Benefits of Collegiality

Finally, what do you do in the case of that passive-aggressive faculty member who, while outwardly polite, is hindering the work of the discipline by avoiding a fair share of departmental service or by unduly prolonging meetings with excessive questions, comments, and requests for further clarification? Be candid with this individual about the detrimental effects that his or her actions are having on the department. In a private conversation, state clearly why it is essential for everyone to take a turn in accepting a few more advisees, recording the minutes at a meeting, or drafting a report for a committee. Point out how everyone else has needed to take on these responsibilities, and, while you understand the sacrifice that will be required, you find it necessary that he or she take on a fair share as well. Describe the time constraints that require a decision to be made without further delays caused by a discussion that, while perhaps valuable and extremely interesting, is not bringing the issue to resolution. Suggest other ways for certain questions to be asked—a departmental listserv, a bulletin board in a common area, a threaded discussion on a faculty web site—rather than devoting scarce meeting time to these discussions. Frequently, the lack of response to the faculty member's questions once they are posted publicly can be used to suggest tactfully to that individual that perhaps others were not as concerned about these issues as he or she may have thought.

REFERENCES

Connell, M. A. (2001). The role of collegiality in higher education tenure, promotion, and termination decisions. *Journal of College and University Law, 27*(4), 833–858.

Connell, M. A. & Savage, F. G. (2001). Does collegiality count? *Academe 87*(6), 37–41.

Fogg, P. (April 26, 2002). Nevada supreme court rules against professor who was denied tenure. *The Chronicle of Higher Education*, p. A14.

Mayberry v. Dees, 663F.2d 502 (4th Cir. Ct. 1981).

University of Baltimore v. Iz, 716A.2d 1107 (Md. Ct. App. 1998).

9

Dealing with Chronic Complainers

Constant complainers may be found throughout all professions and are not unique to academic life. If you examine nearly any manual devoted to personnel management, you will find chapters exploring the "whiner," "griper," or "chronic complainer" and the destruction that this type of person can do to the organization. One of the first highly successful books on challenging personalities in the workplace, Bramson's (1988) *Coping with Difficult People* contains a large section on complainers, and this practice has been followed by such works as Lloyd's (1999) *Jerks at Work*, Topchik's (2000) *Managing Workplace Negativity*, and Scott's (2004) *A Survival Guide for Working With Humans*. In fact, one recent internet article on personnel management, Kirk's (2003) "Don't Duck Chronic Complainers," is focused *exclusively* on this topic.

Perhaps inevitably, personnel guides for academic department chairs have also contained advice for coping with chronic complainers. For instance, McDaniel's (2002) "Dealing with Department Chair Detractors: Strategies That Succeed," includes the complainer as one of the chair's most persistent personnel challenges. Yet despite the pervasiveness of the chronic complainer in all walks of life, department chairs soon realize that there are several important ways in which the way this type of personality displays itself in academic life can be distinctly different from its counterparts in other professional environments. For instance, most business-oriented management guides report that chronic complainers tend to express dissatisfaction on a broad range of issues, never focusing on a single complaint for very long; the moment that you actually try to address one purported problem, these guides conclude, the complainer will invariably be off in pursuit of some other alleged grievance. This pattern of behavior rarely applies to academic complainers. They are rarely fickle in their objections, raising a single complaint over the course of many months or even many years, sometimes even drawing some perverse sort of satisfaction from the fact that none of their colleagues is "enlightened" enough to champion this particular cause—at least with the proper amount of vehemence and persistence.

Academic complainers are less likely to be drawn to an unrelated range of issues and more likely to be drawn to one particular "hobby horse" (such as faculty salaries, workload, or support for scholarship) that they are willing to discuss at length even when no one else in the department seems particularly interested, even when you may think that, as chair, you have already addressed and solved the complainers' "problems." Similarly, business-oriented management guides will frequently talk about chronic complainers as employees who can only identify problems, never pausing long enough to develop a plan of action that would actually deal with the problem. Academic complainers, on the other hand, regularly develop plans of action—even quite detailed plans of action—which may be wholly impractical, excessively self-serving, or completely oblivious to the larger needs of the institution, but they are plans.

Books on personnel management usually assume that chronic complainers cause most of their difficulties for coworkers, not in official meetings or in formal planning sessions, but in casual conversation, around water coolers and during coffee breaks, or in spontaneous lunchtime "gripe sessions." The academic complainer is attracted to no particular venue when wishing to voice a concern; the complainer will speak openly in faculty meetings, behind closed doors in committees, to your face and behind your back, anywhere that a captive audience may be found for discussing a well-nursed grievance.

Perhaps it is because we, as academics, tend to focus on problems and problem-solving for a living that the challenge of dealing with our own breed of chronic complainer seems particularly severe. Nearly every department either has or has had at some time or another at least one individual who has long ago ceased being merely a loveable curmudgeon and has threatened to ruin morale, bring departmental business to a standstill, and encouraged other members of the faculty to seek employment elsewhere, all because of the complainer's incessant carping.

As department chairs, we have both an opportunity and an obligation to mentor these individuals who both harm our departments and render themselves miserable in the process. Unfortunately, not every chronic complainer wants to or can be helped—and certainly not every mentoring strategy helps in every case—but the following are some proven techniques that may help you assist the chronic complainer in the academic setting.

Model the Behavior That You Want the Faculty Member to Emulate

Sometimes complainers feel that it is acceptable to become fixated on their objections because they observe others doing so. One of the ways in which to break this cycle is to be a mentor to members of your department by modeling constructive behaviors and approaches to problem-solving. Monitor your own behavior to make sure that you never resort to morale-diminishing complaining, even when you are faced with the frustrations of dealing with chronic complainers. Try to maintain as positive an attitude as possible about the challenges confronting your department. Attempt to suggest several possible solutions each time you are forced to address a problem. Seek to find something good to say in even the most trying of circumstances. In a surprising number of instances, this behavior will begin to wear off on your faculty members, and they will start being more constructive and upbeat in their own approaches to you and their departmental business.

Try to Determine the Reason for the Individual's Negative Attitude

Not all complaining is alike. Some chronic complainers are seeking attention, even if it can only be negative attention, because they do not believe that they are being taken seriously. Some are unhappy about other aspects of their life that may have little or nothing to do with their function in your department. Some complainers may even be clinically depressed and in need of professional help. Some may simply need some guidance into more constructive ways of making suggestions for improvement. According to Israel (2003) in "Managing Difficult People: Turning 'Negatives' Into 'Positives:'"

> Dr. Mike Weber, superintendent of the Port Washington–Saukville (Wisconsin) School District, has classified three types of "complainers."
>
> - The "helpful complainer" has a specific gripe about an issue, but offers constructive feedback that could resolve the problem.
>
> - A "therapeutic complainer" is experiencing a temporary setback and draws out a confidante to vent frustrations, rather than liberally spreading doom and gloom.
>
> - The "malcontent complainer" is the one to watch out for, warned Weber. "They have ongoing, persistent problems with many issues, but offer no constructive suggestions. They are energy drainers," he stressed. (Knowing the Difference section)

Since, as Israel and Weber point out, not all chronic complainers are motivated by the same need, you will need to determine why an individual has such a need to focus on problems in order to help that person overcome his or her own problem. You will not be able to diagnose the root cause of chronic complaining, however, unless you make a concerted effort to understand the individual who is causing the problem (as difficult as that may be in many cases) and what benefit they perceive themselves as deriving from an activity that is so distressing to others.

Confront the Destructive Behavior Head-On

While it is far from always the case, there are situations in which chronic complainers have no idea whatsoever how their repeated criticisms are perceived by their peers. They may even be shocked when the reaction of others is pointed out to them. Start a conversation—always behind closed doors—by asking, "Why is it that almost every time you speak in a meeting, you voice a complaint?" And then listen very carefully to the person's answer. When taking this approach, it is important always to keep attention throughout your discussion focused on *what* the individual is doing that is harmful to departmental progress or morale, not on the merit or contributions of the individual who has voiced the complaint. Appearing to attack chronic complainers themselves frequently makes them defensive, a situation that can backfire on you and provide them with still one more thing about which they can complain.

As a mentor of the faculty members in your department, therefore, it is far more useful for you to guide the chronic complainer into more productive *behaviors*. Are there ways in which you can guide the faculty member into raising the points that he or she feels necessary to address, but in a more positive, morale-building manner? Are there more appropriate venues for raising these concerns than under the conditions that are currently causing the problem? Is it possible to explain to the individual how his or her behavior comes across to individuals who have frequently heard these issues many times before and feel that there are simply other matters meriting their concern? You may be able to point out to your faculty member that raising the complaints in the manner that he or she has done is really counter-productive. "It's not that your issue is unimportant," you might say, "but rather that people have stopped listening to you because you bring this up so frequently. The result is that your issue is just getting lost by the way in which you discuss it."

Give the Complainer an Opportunity to Tackle "The Problem"

Channeling the complainer's energies into action rather then mere grumbling may also be effective in certain cases. It sets the tone that you, as chair, value doing something about problems rather than simply whining about them. At times you can direct the complainer's energy towards the very issue that is the subject of the complaint. Ask that the details of the complaint be put in writing. Specify that concrete solutions must be recommended and that, if these proposed solutions have any budgetary implications, you will also need recommendations about where this funding can be reallocated from current expenditures. Sometimes, complainers might then say, "That's your job, not mine. I'm supposed to identify the problems; you're supposed to fix them and figure out how to pay for them." This will give you an opportunity to explain that this is not how the department is going to work under your administration. You could say, for instance, that you see all of your colleagues as a team; for this reason, you and your faculty are *jointly* responsible for doing the business of the discipline. "Now, this was an issue that you brought to my attention," you might say. "If we're going to make any progress on it, I'll need your help and the help of every other member of the department." The complainer then has two choices: either to let this topic drop or to write up a recommendation. In situations in which you receive a written recommendation, you can introduce it at a department meeting—again modeling a more positive approach to problem solving than simply griping about problems—and let the author see in person how much, or how little, support there is for the changes that have been recommended. In situations where the topic is dropped, don't relax too much: It is likely to emerge again later in a slightly different form; all that you have won is a reprieve.

Provide Opportunities to Make More Constructive Changes in Your Department

In certain situations, it may not be possible to put the chronic complainer in charge of fixing the very problem that was the subject of the complaint. At times like this, it may be useful to direct the individual's energies to some *other* matter of importance to the department. This can be a particularly effective solution in those cases where you believe that the individual is complaining because he or she feels marginalized or no longer taken seriously by the other members of the department. Offering the person an opportunity to develop an important new grant opportunity, revise (or even develop for the first time) a handbook of departmental procedures, improve the advising system in the department, or take on some other administrative matter that actually needs to be done can help renew the complainer's sense of purpose in the department. Meet with the individual several times as the project is under way in order to provide mentorship in those skills needed to make this project effective. How can this proposal be presented to others in the department in the most positive way? How can the faculty member demonstrate the benefit that others will receive from this project? How will this undertaking strengthen the discipline or the institution as a whole? Demonstrate that this task is important, not just busy work intended to divert energy from the "real problem."

Enlist the Help of Other Members of the Department to Ensure That the Disruptive Behavior Is Not Being Reinforced

Complainers frequently continue voicing their objections either because the attention that they receive in department meetings makes them feel that they are raising valid issues or because they interpret the silence that follows their remarks as tacit consent. When this happens, you may need support from other members of your department in order to make solving this problem a group effort. If even one or two other people say such things as, "No, I really don't think that is our most important issue right now," or, "We keep hearing about this but, frankly, I think we've got other more urgent matters to address; let's just move on," you may have an opportunity to say something similar to the following: "I'm hearing several of you saying that you really don't want to take up any more of our meeting time on this issue. How many of the others of you feel that way? Maybe we should just table this topic and leave it, since we do have other items that need our concern."

Declare a Moratorium on Bringing Up Alleged Past Grievances

One topic to which complainers will frequently devote a great deal of attention is how a previous policy or decision created an inequity which is still harming the department today. Frequently, these alleged past injustices resulted from actions taken from previous chairs or even previous administrations at the institution. In these cases, it may be necessary to impose a Departmental Statute of Limitations on complaints. It may be effective to say such things as, "I understand your concerns. I really do. But I can't change the past, and my whole attention has to be devoted to where this department needs to go in the future. So, understand that, rather than dealing with that,

I'm going to be focused on moving us forward." At such times, it will probably be necessary to enunciate such a policy as your administrative perspective and then to keep reiterating it as the issue comes up: "As I've said before, that issue goes way beyond my Statute of Limitations. Now, instead of going back once again to that issue, let me tell you what we're going to be addressing today . . . "

Provide Positive Mentoring in More Constructive Ways of Voicing Disagreements and Solving Problems

Some chronic complaining is simply the result of poor social skills. If you discuss with a faculty member more constructive ways of getting a point across or raising objections, you may end up both making the faculty member a more effective member of your academic community and avoiding a great deal of grief in your department. Some chronic complainers, when you attempt to coach them out of their disruptive behavior, may accuse you of attempting to silence them or of interfering with their academic freedom. Always make it clear that your goal is not to deprive the faculty member of the right to express an opinion—even if it is an opinion with which you do not agree—but rather to make them more effective in their vital role as a citizen of your academic community. Remind the complainer that, just as you would have a duty to assist a faculty member whom you observed being ineffective in an approach to instruction, so now you have an obligation to assist this particular faculty member with a behavior that is ineffective and, in fact, becoming increasingly counter-productive. Develop a strategy with the faculty member for how the complaint will be raised, in what type of forum, and (for the greatest effectiveness) with what sort of frequency. Remind the complainer that we all cease to hear voices that are heard too often, and that now might be an appropriate time to adopt a different strategy in addressing this particular problem.

Establish Clear Boundaries for When Complaining Is Acceptable

Everyone needs to vent every now and then. The difficulty is that the chronic complainer vents so frequently and repetitively that it is causing difficulties for the other members of the department. At times, the only effective way to deal with this problem is to create "griping time" that only occurs every now and then. Establish in advance a clear amount of time—usually no more than half an hour—in which complaining at a department meeting will not only be tolerated, it will be encouraged. Use this periodic opportunity, built into the schedule perhaps once or twice a semester, for airing the frustrations in the department. Then, if the chronic complainer reverts to typical behavior at other meetings of the department, in private conversations, or when you are meeting for some other task, you can step in and insist that these complaints have to be saved for the next official "griping time." The advantage of this approach is that you will have an opportunity to mentor your faculty member that there is a time for venting frustration and a time for action, and that the latter should be a more common occurrence than the former. One other advantage is that, by opening up "griping time" to the whole department, you may learn about some issues that are affecting some of your more silent and long-suffering faculty members. Finally, your chronic complainer may even learn through this process how frustrating it is to listen to the complaints of others.

Declare Your Department a "Complaint Free Zone"

Work with your faculty members to develop a more positive philosophy of solving problems. Create a departmental code of conduct that includes a statement along the lines of:

> As members of the Department of X, we seek to work together positively for the solution of problems and the resolution of conflicts. Rather than complaining, we are interested in solutions. We attempt to determine a plan of action that we ourselves can take to improve a situation, and then we put that plan into effect. Rather than assuming the worst of others, we take it for granted that every member of the department and of the institution as a whole is working toward the good of our students. Rather than becoming preoccupied with the faults of others, we prefer to focus on their strengths, providing positive and constructive mentoring to the best of our abilities.

A departmental code of this sort can become an important ingredient of your new faculty orientation, and it will give you a way to address the issue of excessive complaining openly and directly when it occurs.

As with many personnel challenges, mentoring the chronic complainer requires patience and is not always successful. In those situations where you *are* able to make a difference, however, you will find that, not only will the atmosphere in your department reflect a distinct improvement, but the former complainer will also have improved relationships with colleagues and be a more effective member of the academic community.

REFERENCES

Bramson, R. M. (1988). *Coping with difficult people.* New York, NY: Dell.

Israel. (2003). *Managing difficult people: Turning 'negatives' into 'positives.'* Retrieved December 1, 2005, from http://www.educationworld.com/a_admin/admin/admin313.shtml

Kirk, J. F. (2003). *Don't duck chronic complainers.* Retrieved August 18, 2005, from http://www.workopolis.com/servlet/Content/tprinter/20030808/duck

Lloyd, K. (1999). *Jerks at work: How to deal with people problems and problem people.* Franklin Lakes, NJ: Career Press.

McDaniel, T. R. (2002) Dealing with Department Chair Detractors: Strategies That Succeed. *The Department Chair, 12*(4), 13–15.

Scott, G. G. (2004). *A survival guide for working with humans: Dealing with whiners, back-stabbers, know-it-alls, and other difficult people.* New York, NY: AMACOM.

Topchik, G. S. (2000). *Managing workplace negativity.* New York, NY: American Management Association.

10

Helping to Resolve Personality Conflicts

In the best of all possible worlds, department chairs would never need to worry about personality conflicts. Every member of the department would get along amicably with every other member. The departmental faculty would all respect one another's individual contributions, value their opinions even when they disagree with them, and work harmoniously for the overall good of the department, its students, and its reputation.

Unfortunately, relatively few departments function this perfectly in the real world. At least, they rarely function this perfectly at all times. Periodically, a personality conflict will arise among two or more faculty members, creating tension and affecting the department's effectiveness, either for a brief period or, in the worst situations, over an extended period of time. At times, too, the relationship between two faculty members will become so fractious for so long that the department chair will begin to wonder whether the individuals involved are not somehow deriving a type of satisfaction from prolonging their conflict. Otherwise, it would hardly seem worth all of the time, energy, and sacrifice that the individuals regularly invest in keeping their dispute going.

Resolving personality disputes is rarely as easy as determining that one of the participants is clearly at fault, while the other is a purely innocent bystander. Situations are almost never as simple—or simplistic—as those who are involved in them tend to allege. At times, neither side in the dispute are "right," and the department chair is placed in the awkward position of making both sides equally unhappy. (In certain situations, the result can be an ironic sort of rapprochement between the two feuding faculty members who now find in the chair a shared focal point for their discontent.) Even more commonly, each of the disputants have some justice on their side while at the same time being responsible for a share of the rancor, lack of collegiality, and poor judgment that has led to the impasse. As La Rochefoucauld said, "Disputes would not last long if the fault were on one side only" (Les querelles ne dureraient pas longtemps, si le tort n'était que d'un côté. Maxim #496). Solving the problem (or at least improving it to the point where the functioning of the department is not unduly hampered) requires diplomacy on the part of the department chair, a special amount of sensitivity to the foibles of human behavior, and a great deal of that very precious commodity: *time.*

In most cases, the following action plan will provide you with at least a start toward dealing with the most serious cases of personality dispute.

Begin by Gathering as Much Specific Information as Possible

It is almost always counterproductive to intervene in a faculty personality conflict by saying things like, "You two just need to get along better." Advice of this sort is so general that it will prove to be unhelpful in the extreme. Besides, most parties in a conflict already know that they cannot get along; what they do not know is how to improve the situation. Another inappropriate response is making a generalized announcement in a faculty meeting along the lines of "We've been having some personality disputes in our department, and I want those who are responsible to stop it." The individuals to whom you are referring in such a statement may not even realize that you are talking about them. Even if they do understand you, they are still being given no help whatsoever in what to do to *solve* the problem.

Rather than attempting to address the problem as a general matter of intra-departmental relations, therefore, what you need to do is learn all that you can so that you may identify the difficulty with great specificity. Determine as precisely as possible *who* is having conflicts with *whom*, *which* behaviors tend to be causing serious problems for your department, and *what* the problematic results of these behaviors have been. In other words, reflect on what it is that has led you and others in your department to be aware that there is an issue needing to be addressed, the conditions under which the problem tends to arise, and what the negative consequences for your department have been. As you gather your information in preparing to solve the problem, focus as much as possible on *detrimental behaviors*, not on *perceived character flaws*. In other words, the specific behaviors that you might observe could include: directing public criticism at a person rather than at a policy or an idea; continually bringing up "ancient history" that most faculty members in the department would prefer to leave behind; uncollegial slights and omissions, such as failure to recognize the contributions of others to a project or to apprise others of important developments in a timely manner; or blindsiding other faculty members in meetings with information or objections that could easily have been shared with colleagues in advance. The conditions under which these behaviors might be demonstrated could include formal department meetings and other large gatherings of faculty members ("grandstanding"), private confrontations with the other individual in an office or some other location where witnesses were not present ("bullying"), catching the other person off-guard in the hallway or during conversations with students ("humiliating"), or by means of excessively harsh and unprofessional communications, such as memos or emails ("flaming"). The negative consequences of the individual's action might include: preventing important departmental business from being conducted in an efficient manner; loss of potential students or majors in your program who are alienated by this unprofessional behavior; a poor reputation for the department at your institution or at national meetings of your discipline; or decreasing faculty morale that could even lead, in extreme cases, to high faculty turnover. By giving close consideration to these issues, you will know more clearly the message that you want to provide to the faculty members involved in the personality conflict. You will be able to say specifically, "Here's what each of you is doing that is causing problems for yourselves and others. Here are the situations that seem to provoke these actions. And here's the difficulty that it's causing for us. Now, let's discuss what we're going to do to *fix* this situation."

Pick Your Battles Carefully

Resolving personality conflicts will almost inevitably involve difficult, prolonged effort on your part. You can easily make a difficult task all but impossible by failing to distinguish pet peeves (annoying habits that don't really cause any lasting damage to the department) from the truly severe personality issues that can end up destroying a program. As you examine each behavior that seems to be causing difficulty, ask yourself the following four questions:

- What's the best that I could hope for if I intervene to change this behavior?

- What's the best that I could hope for if I simply do nothing?

- What's the worst-case scenario that could occur if things backfire when I intervene to change this behavior?

- What's the worst-case scenario if I simply do nothing?

Only in those situations where the benefits clearly outweigh the disadvantages is direct action by the department chair likely to be desirable. Like all administrators, you need to develop a fairly thick skin against those frequent, but ultimately petty annoyances that occur in every management situation. Your voice will become less effective if you begin being seen as a micromanager of idiosyncrasies instead of what you want most to be: your institution's leading advocate for your discipline.

Prepare a Clear Action Plan for Your Intervention

In most cases, it will be best if you meet privately with each of the individuals involved in the personality conflict. Scheduling these preliminary conversations will take some sensitivity since, no matter which faculty member you speak with first, he or she may be *perceived* as the real culprit, while the second person is perceived as the innocent victim; it may be desirable, therefore, to offer a number of times and dates to each party, allowing each to select the one that seems most suitable. In these initial conversations, explain what it is you are trying to solve, why finding a solution is important, and what an acceptable outcome will be. Avoid giving the impression that you are "taking sides" in the dispute: your goal must always be to fix the problem, not to fix the blame. Concentrate on what your future expectations will be and state, politely but firmly, what consequences will occur if those expectations are not met. Throughout this conversation, continually direct both your attention and that of the faculty member toward what *will* occur, not toward past grievances. Each faculty member may need to vent; a little bit of griping and self-pity is acceptable, but only to a point. If the faculty member appears unwilling after a reasonable amount of time to let go of the past, you may need to say something like, "I understand that's how you feel. But you have to understand that it's my job to make certain that the work of this department gets done. And right now one of the things that's preventing that is all of this past history. We need a new start, and as of right now that's what we're going to have." If the individual begins offering excuses or justification for his or her treatment of the other person, simply refuse to accept them. Remind your faculty member that there can be no excuse or justification for any behavior that harms the education of your students, the scholarship or creative activity for which your department is responsible, and the other essential business that needs to be performed by your department.

Do not end this initial meeting with each faculty member until you have outlined the clear course of action that you have determined in advance, underscored the seriousness of the issue, and summarized the next steps that all of you will be taking. Then follow up this meeting with a brief memo of understanding that summarizes and reiterates what your expectations are. In the majority of cases, your next step should be to meet with both faculty members together to reinforce the new working arrangement that will be in place from this point forward, to demonstrate your continued emphasis on resolving this issue, and (it is hoped) to provide an opportunity for the faculty members to begin to build a new sense of rapport. If one or both of the faculty members begins returning to old, destructive patterns of behavior during the course of this joint meeting, acknowledge what has occurred immediately, describe the negative impact of these actions, and reiterate—politely but very firmly—the consequences that will occur from repetitions of this activity.

Make Your Purpose as Precise and Clear as Possible

When attempting to resolve personality conflicts, chairs may be accused of trying to mandate that the members of their departments "like one another," that they socialize with and invite one another to lunch or parties, and that they must expand their working relationships into a deep and abiding friendship. These assumptions are far from the case. You should make it clear that, as academic professionals in a free country, we are all entitled as individuals to choose our own friends and to like or dislike whomever we wish. Personal preferences are not the issue here; *the effectiveness of the department* is the issue. Whenever someone's behavior interferes with the ability of the department to attract and retain students, secure its necessary resources, provide the quality of education to which it aspires, or produce the level of scholarship that is expected by your college or university, then your department has a problem that must be addressed. You are not seeking to control anyone's attitudes, rights, or feelings. What you *are* trying to do is to promote behavior that allows your department to succeed at its mission. Just as a faculty member would not wish to be *pedagogically* ineffective because of his or her attitudes toward a particular student, that faculty member should not wish the discipline as a whole to be ineffective at your institution because of a relationship with a colleague. It is, then, your purpose in speaking to faculty members about this issue to ensure the proper operation of your department at all of its various tasks. You have absolutely no desire (and no right) to control any individual's personal likes and dislikes.

Scheduling Follow-Up Sessions as Appropriate

If a personality conflict is severe enough to require your intervention, it is unlikely to be resolved with a single meeting. You will need to schedule a certain number of follow-up sessions both with the faculty members as individuals and together as a group in order to monitor progress, reward steps forward, and address reversions to earlier destructive behaviors. Do not expect the path toward resolution of the personality conflict to be one of smooth and steady improvement. There will be backsliding, particularly at those times of the academic year when stresses are high and tempers are short. These lapses should be dealt with swiftly, firmly, and (whenever possible) in private. Nevertheless, the trend of the relationship between the two faculty members should be one of overall improvement in collegiality and professionalism. If that is not occurring, you will need to begin again by considering what specific behaviors tend to be causing a problem for the department, under which conditions these behaviors tend to occur, and what undesirable results are occurring due to those behaviors. Make it clear to both individuals that their actions are still a long way from where they need to be and, as a result of your previous statements about the consequences for failure to improve, you will now need to take certain actions. If, however, real progress is finally made, be generous with your praise and recognition, understand the difficulty of the task undertaken by the faculty members, and congratulate them on their excellent spirit of collegiality toward one another and other members of the department.

While taking these actions will help improve (though perhaps not necessarily eliminate) a large number of personality conflicts in the academic setting, there are still two types of situations that require special consideration and separate attention.

What Should I Do If *More* Than Two Faculty Members in My Department Seem to Be Participants in a Personality Conflict?

The more parties there are to a departmental personality conflict, the greater the challenges will be in overcoming it and the longer your time commitment as chair will be to solving this problem. Somewhat less obvious, however, is how the challenges in these situations can increase *exponentially* with each additional faculty member involved. To begin with, it is rarely the case that a personality dispute involves three or more faculty members, each having *equivalent* grievances about all of the others. Far more common in these complex disputes is the development of factions, blocs, or cabals in which several faculty members will join forces against another, at times creating a shifting pattern of alliances and counter-alliances. Second, the sheer number of issues that needs to be worked through in these more complex personality conflicts is likely to be greater than in cases in which you are dealing with only two individuals. In such instances, while your basic method of approaching the problem (individual meetings with the various faculty members, followed by a group meeting of all those involved in the dispute) probably remains the same, you may wish to supplement this tactic with one or more of the following, depending on the particular details of the situation and the severity of the departmental rift.

Mediation

Someone from outside the department who has training and experience in mediating workplace conflicts can bring a fresh perspective to a situation that members of your department (including yourself) may only be able to see as insiders. External mediators can free you from appearing to take a partisan interest in the conflict, work behind the scenes in ways that you cannot, and draw the participants' attention to the genuine seriousness of their problem.

Training

While general training in "workplace relations" or collegiality is likely to be of only limited value in complex personality conflicts, a more focused departmental retreat on techniques that will help your faculty move beyond departmental tension, foster teamwork, and achieve greater professionalism in their relationships with colleagues can be one useful step in particularly large departmental conflicts. Constructing a half-day workshop around one of the following works can help provide an ongoing context for resolving personality disputes in your department.

- *The Complete Guide to Conflict Resolution in the Workplace* (Masters & Albright, 2002)

- *Work and Peace in Academe* (Coffman, 2005)

- *Listening to Conflict* (Van Slyke, 1999)

- *Is It Always Right To Be Right?* (Schmidt et al., 2001)

- *The Eight Essential Steps to Conflict Resolution* (Weeks, 1994)

- *Wired for Conflict* (Vansant, 2003)

Receivership

In the most extreme cases of personality conflict, you may wish to consider the desirability of some form of receivership. Is there some shared project, facility, or enterprise that appears to be provoking repeated outbreaks of the conflict? If so, then assigning that responsibility to a neutral party—with a clear understanding of *what changes in behavior* will be required for reconsideration of this assignment at some future date—may be necessary to underscore the severity of the problem. Receivership is not always a possible or desirable option, but in certain cases where no other solution seems possible, it may be the chair's last hope when other attempted solutions have failed.

What Should I Do if *I* Am One of the Parties Involved in the Personality Conflict?

Your awareness that one of the challenges facing your department is a personality conflict involving you and at least one of your faculty members means that you either have a remarkable degree of self-understanding or an unusually candid colleague who has confided in you. In either case, congratulations! We rarely see disputes involving ourselves as personality conflicts, preferring to characterize them as simply the other person's fault. If, however, you have good reason to believe that you are a contributing party to a personality conflict that is affecting your department's function, you should consider taking at least one of the following steps.

Clear the Air

Sit down and talk to the other person with whom you seem to be in conflict, openly admitting that your differences are hampering your department's work and stating your dissatisfaction with this result. Try to formulate a working arrangement that will minimize differences and avoid those situations that tend to aggravate your conflict.

Consult a Neutral Party

Just as you may sometimes have a better view of the causes of conflict between faculty members than the faculty members themselves may have, an impartial third party (another department chair, a trusted senior faculty member, or an unbiased party from elsewhere in the institution) may be able to provide you with insight that you cannot gain from other sources. If your institution employs trained mediators, these individuals may be able to assist you with reducing departmental tensions in an objective manner that is simply not possible within the department itself. In all such cases, it will be important for the neutral party to be fully aware of the confidentiality that will be required in this situation; while trained mediators will already be fully aware of the need for confidentiality and discretion, more informal mentors may need some guidance—or at least a polite reminder—in this area.

Delegate Appropriate Responsibilities

If there are certain departmental decisions that seem to be exacerbating the conflict you have with another faculty member, try to seek processes that remove as much personal tension as possible from the situation. A committee that reviews departmental travel requests, an assistant chair who must also sign off on departmental course rotations, or a process that bases certain decisions on seniority or other non-subjective factors can help reduce the number of situations that lead to tense encounters and perceptions that decisions are based on personal likes and dislikes.

In every case involving a personality conflict between yourself and another faculty member, remember that there may be at least a perception of a power differential. Whether you see it or not, the other faculty member may view you as "the boss" and, particularly in cases of junior faculty members for whom promotion and tenure decisions are in the future, that person's perceptions may not be that the issue is merely a dispute among equals. Always go out of your way to be sensitive to how you may be perceived by faculty members simply because of your title, position, and authority. Issues that may not even occur to you as being stumbling blocks in your relationship with another faculty member may be the very reasons why your personality conflict appears so difficult to resolve.

REFERENCES

Coffman, J. R. (2005). *Work and peace in academe: Leveraging time, money, and intellectual energy through managing conflict.* Bolton, MA: Anker.

Masters, M. F., & Albright, R. R. (2002). *The complete guide to conflict resolution in the workplace.* New York, NY: American Management Association.

Schmidt, W. H., & et al. (2001). *Is it always right to be right?: A tale of transforming workplace conflict into creativity and collaboration.* New York, NY: AMACOM.

Vansant, S. S. (2003). *Wired for conflict: The role of personality in resolving differences.* Gainesville, FL: Center for Applications of Psychological Type.

Van Slyke, E. J. (1999). *Listening to conflict: Finding constructive solutions to workplace disputes.* New York, NY: American Management Association.

Weeks, D. (1994). *The eight essential steps to conflict resolution: Preserving relationships at work, at home, and in the community.* New York, NY: Jeremy P. Tarcher/Putnam.

11

Coping with the Passive-Aggressive Faculty Member

A particularly difficult mentoring challenge for the department chair is the faculty member who, while possessing a number of otherwise admirable qualities, simultaneously undermines the chair, his or her own colleagues, and possibly the department as a whole through repeated passive-aggressive behaviors. The passive-aggressive faculty member who will be addressed in the pages that follow is not, it should be noted, the sort of pathological individual who can be clinically diagnosed as passive-aggressive. If you believe that an employee who reports to you may possibly be passive-aggressive in this more severe, clinical sense, you should consult your dean or Office of Human Resources about whether your institution allows you the possibility of referring this individual for professional evaluation; there is probably very little that you yourself can do for such a faculty member unless you are a trained clinical psychologist. (And under such circumstances, it would be unethical and inappropriate, not to mention unwise, to confuse your clinical role with your position as department chair.) Severe passive-aggressive behavior stems, after all, from a personality disorder; those afflicted with it are often intractable and may not respond well even to therapy. In these cases, you are better off allowing the problem to be handled by professionals and turning your attention to other matters where you are more likely to make a real difference.

On the positive side, it is not at all common to encounter a faculty member who demonstrates these extremely severe tendencies. On the negative side, what you *are* more likely to encounter is the type of individual who:

- Has a history of agreeing to change behaviors that are destructive—and frequently may even express gratitude to the chair for pointing out these destructive behaviors and helping with them—but later fails to act upon any of strategies that he or she had eagerly declared to be appropriate

- Blames others for problems and claims to be "as confused as you are" as to why he or she always seems to attract so many complaints and objections

- When assigned responsibilities that he or she does not want to do or had resisted when they were initially proposed, performs the task very slowly or in an unsatisfactory manner, thus "proving" that the idea or assignment was a poor concept from the beginning

- Has a highly inflated opinion of his or her contributions to the department and institution, frequently claiming to be unappreciated, even though you may find the person's performance to be weak or substandard

- Impedes departmental work simply by failing to answer routine requests, memos, or emails in a timely manner

- When challenged about poor performance or uncollegial behavior, routinely projects the worst of his or her own character traits onto others

Unlike other kinds of behavior problems, mild passive-aggressive tendencies often seem to give little if any distress to the faculty members demonstrating them. By contrast, chronic complainers may well be aware that they make themselves as miserable as they make others. Outright hostile faculty members frequently realize that their aggressive tendencies alienate those around them, even though they may be powerless to control those tendencies. Passive-aggressive faculty members, on the other hand, are often so convinced that they *are* trying to improve, that the problems still occurring are the fault of others, and that the animosity others may show them is simply the result of jealousy or their own problems that they remain blithely unaware that they have a problem.

The behaviors demonstrated by even mildly passive-aggressive individuals are probably deeply ingrained. For this reason, you are unlikely to create dramatically improved behavior in such a faculty member, even if you make a consistent attempt to do so. There are, however, three strategies you may wish to attempt in order to cope with someone's passive-aggressive tendencies and to reduce the difficulties that are occurring in your department.

Establish With the Faculty Member, Not Mere Goals for Performance, But Specific Timetables for Their Implementation

As we have seen, it is often not at all difficult to get passive-aggressive faculty members to agree that an existing problem needs to be changed. The real challenge comes in prompting significant improvement in behavior without addressing the underlying causes of the difficulties. If you wish to see real changes, you will need to establish a clear and reasonable timetable with the faculty member, monitor that timetable effectively, and adopt rewards or sanctions based on whether the goals you have set are actually met.

At a performance appraisal meeting with the faculty member, set a specific goal that you would like the individual to achieve and impose a clear deadline. This first task you assign should, in most cases, be relatively easy and the deadline should be relatively soon: 48 hours to one week. What you are asking the faculty member to do might involve completing a long overdue memo or annual report (provided, of course, that this task can reasonably be accomplished in the time that you have allowed), contacting a committee in order to set the date of its next meeting, or returning a graded course assignment that should have been handed back some time ago. Get progress reports, if you feel it is necessary, even before the deadline arrives. Let the faculty member resent the pressure you are applying if he or she must, but take the steps that you feel are necessary to get the assignment done. In truth, the resentment may or may not subside once the task is complete, but remember that your ultimate goal is increasing your department's overall productivity and service to your students, not generating the contentment of this particular faculty member.

When the task is complete, review it with the faculty member, being generous with your approval where it is warranted, but not accepting shoddy, inferior, or slovenly work. If improvements are necessary, be very clear about what you would like changed and why that is important. Set a new deadline (perhaps breaking the task into even smaller parts, each of which must be approved in turn) and begin the process again. If the assignment was successfully completed, praise it appropriately and begin setting new deadlines for new tasks. Start by planning various assignments perhaps six weeks out or until the end of the current semester. Establish a sufficient number of concrete steps along the way so that you will always know whether the faculty member is making progress in a timely manner. Then provide the faculty member with frequent, candid, and constructive feedback regarding the rate of progress being made.

Allow the Faculty Member Some Flexibility and Choice in Work Assignments Where This Is Possible, With Standards of Performance in These Areas Set Proportionately High

One of the justifications frequently made by passive-aggressive faculty members for their unsatisfactory performance is that they are asked to take on too many responsibilities, not assigned tasks that are truly worthy of their talent, or called upon to work in areas where they have relatively little training, experience, and interest. One way to respond to this ploy is to allow some flexibility in the faculty member's work assignment where this is possible and desirable. If the faculty member is given a chance to play an active role in selecting the assignment that he or she will take and in setting the deadline (within limits), then there can be no such excuse as "this was something I really didn't want to do in the first place." It can be useful to have the faculty member provide you with a list in writing of those committee assignments, tasks, or reports that he or she is really most interested in. Then, if deadlines go by unmet or a pattern of excuses begins to emerge, you will have this written document to go over with the faculty member, saying "But I'm confused as to why this isn't getting done. Back on such-and-such a date, you sent me a memo telling me that you really wanted to do this."

When allowing the faculty member some leeway in selecting responsibilities and deadlines, it is appropriate to combine this flexibility with correspondingly higher standards of achievement. Since you are dealing with a task that the faculty member has personally selected, poor performance or missed deadlines should not be an option. Remind the faculty member that with increased freedom comes increased responsibility, and that your expectations rise proportionally with the added self-determination you are offering in this task.

Require More Frequent Updates and Progress Reports From This Faculty Member Than You Might Expect From Most Employees

While your goal is ultimately to wean the faculty member from the constant supervision and frequent deadlines that you will use at the beginning of your mentoring process, you should realize that faculty members with mild passive-aggressive tendencies will always require a higher level of guidance and supervision than other faculty members. When you see that genuine progress is being made, reduce the number of mentoring sessions to once a month, and eventually to once or twice a semester. At those sessions, you can review progress towards goals, set new objectives, celebrate targets that have been reached, and speak candidly about any lapses or backsliding. Keep the meeting as task-oriented as possible: don't reinforce the faculty member's tendencies to complain or to shift blame to others by acknowledging this behavior. You should not expect progress to be either smooth or rapid. Remember that, unlike other mentoring challenges, you are far less likely to "fix" the difficulties arising from the passive-aggressive faculty member than simply to manage and reduce them.

Your institution's Counseling Center or Human Resources Office may be able to assist you with further techniques that could be effective in your individual situation. You may also wish to consult Lieberman's (2005) *How to Change Anybody* and Topchik's (2001) *Managing Workplace Negativity* for the specific advice they give on dealing with passive-aggressive temperaments.

Whatever strategy you take, avoid the temptation of trying to solve the faculty member's problem by addressing his or her underlying issues of self-image, problems with authority figures, or past trauma. As an effective mentor for the members of your department, your role is to help them grow as *professionals* through your guidance and example. Being a good mentor does not mean becoming an employee's spiritual counselor, therapist, or confidante. Whatever other role you may play in other situations, you are still the faculty member's *boss*, and you are entitled to expect a certain amount of professionalism regardless of the problems that faculty member has had or is having.

For this reason, keep your focus on the behavior you want the faculty member to demonstrate, not on the person's underlying reasons or justifications for past actions. For instance, are there aspects of this faculty member's performance that you can legitimately praise and cite as examples of the type of accomplishments that he or she should continue to pursue? Is the faculty member a good organizer of plans (though perhaps not as successful at carrying out those plans)? Does the faculty member tend to work effectively one-on-one with students (though perhaps less effectively in committees)? Is the faculty member a polished writer (even if it takes a very long time for his or her written works to be completed)?

As you would with all your faculty, conduct your mentoring of the faculty member by focusing on these areas of demonstrated strength, perhaps even changing a few of his or her assignments (where appropriate) as a means of playing to that person's strengths. Having established a baseline of understanding about "This is what you do well . . . ," you then can turn to the areas of performance that really are causing problems for the department. Start with general observations about the individual's poor performance ("On the other hand, you have a tendency to miss deadlines and to request extensions repeatedly that causes a number of problems for us.") Give a few specific examples, but don't pile on so many instances of poor performance that the faculty member reverts to self-defense. If you do happen to notice a tendency towards defensiveness, simply ignore it. Don't let your focus deviate from the faculty member's *actions* and don't give in to comforting the faculty member or discussing any justifications that he or she may give you for poor performance.

Similarly, if the faculty member keeps blaming others for his or her poor performance, routinely ignore these statements. (Either say nothing at all or rapidly return to your primary subject: "Well, that's not the issue. What we're talking about is how *you* can be even more effective.") The important impression that you wish to establish with the employee is that: 1) there *are* good things that he or she does, and these contributions are both recognized and appreciated by the department; but 2) there are also some areas in which the faculty member can improve, and these are areas for which the individual needs to take personal responsibility, not assign blame to colleagues.

Coping with the passive-aggressive faculty member is likely to require a great deal of patience and, even then, the situation may well cause you repeated frustration and irritation. In the most difficult of times, it may be useful to remember that the individual's behavior is not caused by anything that you, your department, or your institution has done. Ultimately, it is the individual's own problem and, while you can take steps to cope with the departmental challenges resulting from it, it neither is nor should be your responsibility to solve it. Only the individual faculty member can do that.

REFERENCES

Lieberman, D. J. (2005). *How to change anybody: Proven techniques to reshape anyone's attitude, behavior, feelings, or beliefs.* New York, NY: St. Martin's Press.

Topchik. G. S. (2001). *Managing workplace negativity.* New York, NY: American Management Association.

12

Tips for Conducting Effective Faculty Evaluation Sessions

At most colleges and universities, department chairs are expected to conduct annual, face-to-face evaluation sessions with faculty members. Despite the great significance of this duty, many department chairs are not trained in the basic techniques of how to conduct performance appraisals and, as a result, feel uncomfortable whenever evaluation sessions occur. Some institutions may have specific requirements for conducting evaluation sessions. Nevertheless, the following tips do provide good, general guidance for department chairs, particularly for those who are relatively new to the process of conducting evaluation sessions.

Keep Good and Timely Records

The day to start planning a faculty evaluation session is not the day of the session; it's the day *after* the session. That's when you begin planning the faculty member's evaluation for *next* year. Keep something to which you can add notes concerning every faculty member under your supervision. You may wish to keep these records in a word processing file, a spreadsheet, a database, or on a legal pad. Whichever method you choose, be sure to prepare a backup copy and keep both the original and the backup in safe, confidential locations. Organize your notes into whatever sections you will need for the evaluation itself: teaching, scholarship, service, overall, or the specific categories used by your institution. Throughout the year, whenever the faculty member does something significant—whether good or bad—make a clear, dated record in your notes. Be specific. If the faculty member did something that you regard as worthy of criticism, what exactly was the problem and what was the result of the faculty member's action? What could the faculty member have done differently? If you wish to offer praise, why was the faculty member's action so successful? How did it benefit the department, the students, and the academic community? How can the faculty member have similar successes in the future? Be sure to record positive accomplishments as well as specific suggestions for improvement; you'll be glad that you have a list of commendations to make when you are preparing for your next evaluation session.

Prepare Carefully for the Evaluation Session Itself

You will prepare for your face-to-face meeting while you're creating the written evaluation that you will send to the faculty member and place in his or her personnel file. In addition to this, however, just before your meeting, give yourself at least 15 minutes to clarify in your mind precisely what message you want to convey. Decide in a single sentence what the message of the meeting will be. In most cases, that one sentence will be all that the faculty member will take away from the session. Because of this, be sure that this sentence—what I'll refer to as your "central message"—is clear in your mind beforehand. As a general rule, adhere to this principle: If you can't summarize a faculty member's evaluation to yourself in one sentence, then you haven't refined your thoughts clearly enough. Never permit yourself to go into an evaluation session cold. If you don't have enough time to prepare for the meeting, try to reschedule it. Evaluation sessions are far too important to be done carelessly or off the cuff.

Begin the Evaluation Session by Clearly Stating the Result

Don't keep the faculty member waiting as to what the outcome of the session might be. The following are some examples of what you might say to a faculty member, although you should rephrase each message in your own words.

Completely Positive Evaluation

"The one thing that I want you to take away from today's meeting is that this has been an absolutely first-rate year. What we're going to be doing is taking a look at a lot of successes, and I think you should be congratulated for that."

Positive Evaluation With Suggestions for Minor Improvement

"The most important thing I want you to remember about today's session is that this has been a very, very good year. I want you to be proud of what you've done; it's really been extremely good. Now, we're also going to talk about one or two areas where I think we can work to make some improvements. But I don't want any of that to overshadow the central message I'm going to try to convey: This has been a really wonderful year."

Negative Evaluation With Suggestions for Improvement

"What I'd like to focus on today are a number of areas where I think we've seen some problems during the past year. Basically, what I'm going to tell you is that I think you could've done better. And I want to help you do that."

Negative Evaluation With Specific Warning

"I don't want to sugar coat this. I think this has been a year where your performance just wasn't what it should have been. I'm going to give you some specific examples of that, and I'm going to try to explain how I think you could have done better. And the message that I want you to take away from this meeting is that we're going to have to see some changes and see them real soon. If I don't see the improvements I suggest by [DATE], then what's going to happen is this: [STATE LIKELY OUTCOME]."

Especially when you give extremely bad news, you've got to remember that, to the faculty member being evaluated, what you say will be like hearing a death sentence from his or her doctor. The faculty member is going to stop absorbing what you say for awhile. Don't expect all of the details to be remembered; you'll need to follow up with a thorough written report.

Take Your Time Conducting the Face-to-Face Meeting

A repeated criticism that is heard from faculty members is that evaluation sessions with their chairs tend to be perfunctory. The reason for this is that we, as supervisors, don't feel comfortable in conducting evaluation sessions. Giving both public praise and candid criticism tends to embarrass us. Nevertheless, remember that when you're being praised, you want to take some time to revel in it. If you're being critiqued, you want information about what you've done wrong and how you might improve. Faculty members feel precisely the same way. Don't just speed through your sessions with them. Plan on spending a half hour or more with each person you evaluate.

Don't Mix Meetings

One of the ways in which supervisors send mixed messages is by holding multipurpose meetings. Talking about a curriculum proposal for the future makes the faculty member assume that he or she will be part of that future. Discussion of departmental successes implies that the faculty member has contributed to those successes. If you feel you must cover several different agenda items in a single session with a faculty member, then schedule a separate time for the formal evaluation session itself. Make it clear that this is a special meeting conducted simply for the purposes of evaluation. Don't allow a general conversation just to segue into a performance appraisal.

Give Specific Examples

Telling a faculty member "you did a great job" is really not helpful; it gives the faculty member absolutely nothing to go on in order to repeat the success. In much the same way, saying "next year teach better" is of little use. What the department chair must do instead is offer specific advice. If quality of instruction is an issue during an evaluation session, offer the faculty member suggestions on how to improve. Is there a Center for Excellence in Teaching on your campus? Are there faculty development workshops that deal with pedagogy? Can faculty development funding be used for off-campus improvement of instruction? Is there a formal or informal mentoring program that you can suggest? Also, make it clear to the faculty member on what basis your criticism is being made. Was there a repeated concern raised in student ratings of instruction? Were there problems noted in peer evaluations? Have you received student complaints? Rather than issuing a general complaint or concern, try to deal with the specific behavior that you would like to see improved.

Set Specific Standards

If you are concerned that a faculty member's level of scholarship has not been sufficient, what would it have taken for you to feel that adequate progress has been made? What were you looking for in the faculty member's performance that you didn't see? If the faculty member provides that level of achievement next year, will you be satisfied or are standards increasing each year?

Repeat and Clarify Your Message

In what is essentially a positive evaluation, be sure to follow criticism with some specific praise. But take care not to do this when you want the overall message to be negative. Tempering bad news with praise in order to make the faculty member feel good may actually just send a confusing message. As uncomfortable as it may be, it is better to stay "on message" as much as possible throughout the session.

Be Aware of Subtext

As you conduct your session with the faculty member, be alert to any signals you may inadvertently be sending. What are your facial expressions? What is your body language? Are you undermining your words by nonverbal communication?

Record in Writing the Central Message of the Session

There should be a clear connection between the overall focus of the oral and written evaluations conducted for each faculty member. If possible, have your one-sentence summary of your central message stated verbatim in the overall section of each evaluation, oral and written.

Be Forward-Looking in Addition to Reviewing Past Performance

Set goals for the coming year with the faculty member. Discuss with the faculty member possibilities that might lead to a more positive evaluation next year.

End by Reiterating Your Central Message

In other words, evaluation sessions should "sandwich" the central message. In your notes, you may wish to outline your plan for the performance appraisal as follows:

- State central message.

- Provide specific details.

- Make other comments that the faculty member needs to hear.

- Allow the faculty member to ask questions and make observations.

- Restate your central message.

- Be certain that the faculty member understands your central message. If you need to do so, ask the faculty member to repeat the primary thrust of your meeting.

13

How to Write First-Rate Faculty Evaluations

At most colleges and universities, the department chair plays an important role—frequently *the* most important role—in preparing each faculty member's annual performance evaluation. Often the result of this evaluation directly affects the amount of an instructor's annual merit increase or salary adjustment. Sometimes, however, the chair submits an evaluation to a dean or other administrator who in turn is responsible for allocating an increase from a faculty salary pool. At times, too, evaluation systems have been devised that are completely separate from the process of setting salaries, either because the institution is unionized or because the evaluative process is considered to be formative and "mentoring" rather than summative and "judgmental."

Writing effective performance appraisals for faculty members is an activity that all chairs must and should take seriously no matter how central or peripheral a role the chair may play in conducting these evaluations. Few processes are subject to the sort of repeated and vigorous challenges that tend to be associated with annual faculty evaluations. Few processes are as daunting for department chairs, because so much of the professional development—even the very livelihood—of each faculty member depends on his or her chair's ability to exercise skill and judgment properly when preparing faculty evaluations. Some institutions have made the evaluation process much more consistent by adopting a standardized evaluation form (or at least a standardized evaluation format) that must be used in all performance reviews. At many institutions, however, the chair's evaluations are either "free form" or subject to a great degree of flexibility and personal discretion. If you are in the latter situation, you are probably quite eager to receive some guidance in how to write and structure the evaluations of the faculty members you supervise.

Surprisingly, even positive evaluations can be extremely difficult to write; we want to praise the people who report to us without being either tepid or excessive. Positive remarks often become repetitive through the excessive use of a few over-used superlatives, such as "excellent," "outstanding," and "exceptional." At the other extreme, it is a challenge to write an evaluation in which a faculty member is criticized, because these evaluations are likely to be the very documents that will be given the greatest scrutiny and might even be defended in grievance hearings or legal challenges. Good administrators always want to offer advice in a positive manner so that the criticism they feel obliged to make does not cause discouragement or reduce morale. They also understand the reason for providing a clear paper trail in case the improvement they are recommending does not occur in a timely manner.

The department chair's goal is to create a set of annual evaluations that are as useful as possible to the faculty members and to the department's growth, professionalism, and service to its students. The chair needs to record, candidly and fairly, all of the areas in which each faculty member is expected to improve. Weaknesses should be documented in an appropriate manner so that the individual can continue to work toward progress. Strengths should be celebrated enthusiastically so that these activities are more likely to be continued in the future. Most importantly, in order to write first-rate faculty evaluations, it is necessary for the chair to ask the right questions at every single stage of the process.

Questions That Should Be Asked Before Writing Any Evaluations

What Is My Purpose in Writing These Evaluations?

Formative faculty evaluation processes are concerned with mentoring or improving a faculty member's performance. *Summative* processes are concerned with reaching a conclusion—for instance, the amount of a salary increase, whether promotion should be granted, or the terms under which a contract should be renewed—based on the faculty member's past performance. More common, however, are those evaluation processes that seek to be formative and summative simultaneously. This type of evaluation is the most difficult to complete effectively since offering any type of advice about how a faculty member can improve in the future may be read by the recipient as implying that *there is going to be a future at the institution*. It is important, therefore, for chairs always to consider what purpose they are trying to achieve in the evaluation process itself. For instance, in a formative evaluation, you should use the individual's past performance as the basis for suggestions about future goals and needed changes. In a summative evaluation, you should include numerous evaluative remarks, specifically categorizing each aspect of the instructor's performance as "sufficient," "appropriate," "exceptional," "inadequate," "not up to our standards," or "meeting our departmental expectations." In an evaluation that must be both formative and summative, the chair will need to achieve a careful balance of both of these ingredients, citing areas where improvement is needed without causing the faculty member to lose morale—unless, of course, the situation is so dire that drastic improvement is urgently needed or the faculty member is likely to be terminated anyway.

What Are My Institution's Established Criteria for These Evaluations?

One of the problems that chairs inadvertently cause themselves in writing faculty evaluations is discussing matters that turn out to be irrelevant to the stated criteria of the institution for faculty evaluation. To avoid this problem, chairs may wish to structure their evaluations around the specifically stated criteria of their institutions. For instance, if a college states that annual evaluations are to be based 50% on teaching, 30% on scholarship, and 20% on service, it may be useful to create a template for each evaluation that contains three separate headings, clearly designating the three major criteria with <u>underlining</u> or **bold face**. It may be valuable to cite in the evaluation template itself where these criteria are defined or illustrated in the institution's evaluation procedures or in a faculty handbook. Then, as you are writing each faculty member's evaluation, ask yourself repeatedly, "Are these statements germane to the criteria I'm supposed to be using and to the specific definitions that have been established at my institution?"

What Resources Are Available to Me?

As with many administrative matters, there is no need to "reinvent the wheel" when doing faculty evaluations. There are numerous books, web sites, and software packages that deal with performance reviews or employee appraisals. Although the vast majority of these resources are designed for a business environment, their advice is easily tailored to an academic setting. Books that are particularly useful in this regard include:

- *Perfect phrases for performance reviews* (Max & Bacal, 2002)

- *The #1 guide to performance appraisals* (Neal, 2001)

- *How to do a superior performance appraisal* (Swan, 1991)

- *10 minute guide to performance appraisals* (Furtwengler, 2000)

Useful web sites to examine when preparing for annual faculty reviews are the Guidelines for Faculty Evaluations for the College of Arts and Sciences at Jacksonville State University (http://www.jsu.edu/depart/cas/guidelines.html), the Faculty Evaluation Center of Austin Community College (http://fe.austincc.edu/), and the Guidelines for the Evaluation of Faculty: Annual Evaluations, Promotion, and Tenure at the University of Nebraska–Lincoln (http://www.unl.edu/svcaa/hr/tenure/tenureguide.shtml). Software programs that can assist chairs with the evaluation process include Lominger Edition Software's EMPLOYEE APPRAISER™ (http://www.lominger.com/67_329.htm) and Knowledgepoint's Performance Now™ (http://www.notjustsurveys.com/HR/KPBIGPFS.htm). In addition, Falcone (1999) includes a disk in his book that has sample evaluation documents in Microsoft Word format that can be revised and adapted to your department's needs.

Questions That Should Be Asked Before Writing Each Evaluation

What Is the Overall Message That I Wish to Convey to This Particular Faculty Member?

The National Council for the Accreditation of Teacher Education (NCATE) requires that all of the teacher education programs it accredits must have a clear *conceptual framework* underlying the entire program. This conceptual framework serves as a unifying structure that gives a program both its meaning and its direction (NCATE, 1997–2004). Similarly, the chair's evaluation of each faculty member should be based on a clear conceptual framework of the message and advice that a particular faculty member most needs to receive from you as chair. If you are unable to summarize each evaluation you have written in a sentence of 20 words or less, then you have not made your overall message clear enough. It is useful to include that single sentence in **bold face** prominently somewhere in the evaluation itself.

The philosopher George Edward (G. E.) Moore was famous for challenging the statements made by others with the refrain "What exactly do you *mean?*" (Edmonds & Eidinow, 2001, p. 60). If you are not able to answer Moore's question easily about a given evaluation, then you have not yet refined your thoughts thoroughly enough to convey them to someone else.

How Can I Be Specific Enough in My Criticism, Citing Examples Where Appropriate?

The most frustrating type of criticism is that which is vague, since we can neither challenge it nor be improved by it. Whenever you make a criticism, be sure that you have based your remarks on something that you have observed or on data that have been reported to you. Do not keep these observations secret. Make it clear *why* you have concerns about certain aspects of the individual's performance. If you believe that a faculty member's teaching has not been up to departmental standards, state the specific reasons why you have developed this belief. Are student ratings of instruction for this individual consistently low? Are the faculty member's peers expressing concerns directly to you? Have students consistently reported their concerns to you? Are you basing this observation on something that you witnessed yourself? Are the materials for the instructor's courses outdated or the exams too dependent on multiple-choice questions? Similarly, if there have been problems with a faculty member's scholarship, be specific about what those problems are. Is the faculty member not submitting articles to the right sort of journals or not making presentations at the appropriate type of conferences? Is it a matter of productivity, and does the faculty member simply need to bring more projects to fruition? If so, how many projects, articles, reviews, or other publications would have been appropriate? Why? Is the faculty member's research agenda veering so far from the discipline that it is difficult for you to assess it effectively? By asking yourself such questions as these, you will be able to give clear, specific guidance to the faculty member rather than make vague statements, such as, "Your quality of instruction has not been sufficient," or, "We need to see further growth in scholarship."

How Can I Be Positive and Constructive in My Criticism, Even When I Have to Point Out Some Genuine Weaknesses?

Particularly in evaluations that contain both a formative and a summative component, it is important to give criticism that preserves a faculty member's morale and supports his or her willingness to take whatever steps are necessary in order to make improvements. In most cases, achieving this goal is merely a matter of adopting a tone that conveys recommendations for improvement in a manner that is overtly helpful and positive. Read over each sentence that you write and ask yourself, "How would I feel if a superior wrote this to me? If I had to be given this advice, how would I want it to be phrased?" In many cases, you can include some phrase that makes the appropriate point without causing an unnecessary blow to the person's ego or implying that the individual has failed in some irremediable manner. For instance, a constructive tone can often be achieved through phrases such as "I understand that this incident is out of character with your usual high level of achievement in this area," or, "Since we all have aspects of our performance in which we'd like to do even better next year, I'd like to suggest that . . . " or, "One topic that I may be able to offer you some help on is . . . " Whatever you do, don't belabor a minor point to such an extent that it overshadows a highly favorable evaluation. Always ask yourself, "Is this criticism necessary?" and, "What do I hope to accomplish by pointing out this particular weakness?"

Questions That Should Be Asked Upon Reviewing Each Evaluation

Have I Been Forward-Looking Enough, Setting Clear Goals for the Future?

Frequently, we are so focused on past achievement in evaluations that we neglect planning for the future. To avoid this problem, use the evaluation process to recommend specific goals for the coming year. Doing so will be useful to you when you write next year's evaluation, because you will be able to talk about progress, or lack thereof, in attaining those goals.

You should never criticize a faculty member without including two items: 1) the specific observation(s) you made that led you to give this criticism, and 2) clear advice about what the faculty member should do in the future in order to improve. To make these goals as clear as possible, outline them with numbers or bullets so that they may be immediately understood by anyone reading the evaluation.

Have I Made My Overall Assessment Clear?

Never send an evaluation on the day that you write it. Always let at least a day go by—holding an evaluation for a week or a month is even better, if possible—between writing an evaluation and sending it to the faculty member. Before you send an evaluation, read it over carefully. Are all of your points clear *and* necessary? Can you still summarize your conceptual framework for this evaluation simply upon rereading it? One useful technique is to score each evaluation on a scale of 1 (extremely poor overall performance) to 10 (extremely good overall performance) immediately after you write the evaluation. Repeat this scoring when you reread the evaluation. Has your score changed significantly for any evaluation? If so, try to determine whether the language you use in the evaluation is as clear as you would like it to be. Also, be sure that you have really *evaluated* everything. A statement such as "Your scholarly activity for the year consisted of three presentations at regional conferences" does not make it clear at all whether you consider this to be an adequate level of activity. As you reread your evaluation, make sure that you have *assessed* all achievements, not merely listed them.

What Aspects of This Evaluation Are Most Likely to Be Challenged? Why? What Will Be My Response in Such a Challenge? Do I Have Evidence to Support My Position?

Finally, it is an all-too-real aspect of academic administration that evaluations will sometimes be challenged. Often these challenges will be informal, as faculty members want to meet with you to have you explain why you criticized them as you did. Less frequently, but more seriously, evaluations can lead to grievances or even legal challenges. For this reason, ask yourself how you would respond if any sentence that you wrote in a faculty evaluation were:1) challenged in a court of law, 2) read publicly at a faculty meeting, or 3) quoted in the local paper. Can you defend and give examples of every statement that you make? If you can, then you are probably on firm ground. If not, then you should go back and refine or omit the passage in question. In truly serious cases, of course, run the phrasing in question by the institution's counsel *before* it is sent to the faculty member or submitted to the next level of evaluation.

Conclusion

By asking these questions at each stage of your evaluation process, you'll have a clear idea of what message you wish to convey to each faculty member, how the message needs to be conveyed, and how you'll be able to guide your department forward through the advice that you offer.

REFERENCES

Edmonds, D. & Eidinow, J. (2001). *Wittgenstein's poker: The story of a ten-minute argument between two great philosophers.* New York, NY: HarperCollins.

Falcone, P. (1999). *101 sample write-ups to document employee performance problems: A guide to progressive discipline and termination.* New York, NY: AMACOM.

Furtwengler, D. (2000). *10 minute guide to performance appraisals.* Indianapolis, IN: Macmillan.

Max, D. & Bacal, R. (2002). *Perfect phrases for performance reviews: Hundreds of ready-to-use phrases that describe your employees' performance.* New York, NY: McGraw Hill.

National Council for Accreditation of Teacher Education. (1997–2004). Glossary of NCATE terms. Retrieved December 28, 2004, from http://www.ncate.org/search/glossary.htm

Neal, J. E., Jr., & Neal, J. E. (2001). *The #1 guide to performance appraisals: Doing it right!* Perrysburg, OH: Neal.

Swan, W. S. (1991). *How to do a superior performance appraisal.* New York, NY: John Wiley & Sons.

14

The Department Chair's Role in Assessment

While assessment at your institution is likely to affect nearly every office on campus, as a department chair your direct involvement in assessment is much more likely to be concerned with your discipline's own academic program than with other issues. In other words, even non-academic programs at your college and university are being assessed: the business office, residential life, student affairs, development, college relations. Any unit that exists at your school is doing a form of assessment that is appropriate to its structure, function, and mission. In a similar way, multi-departmental academic programs—the First-Year Experience, the honors program, the general education program, and the like—will be assessed in a manner that is appropriate for them. If you are asked to participate in any of these types of assessment that move beyond your individual department or discipline, you will almost certainly receive a great deal of guidance on what is expected from you by your institution's assessment office or whoever supervises these campus-wide efforts. Where you will probably be given a good deal more autonomy (and thus where you may feel that you may need more guidance) is in the area of assessing the effectiveness of your department and its proprietary academic programs (your major and minor programs, for instance).

In order for department chairs to play an effective role in leading the assessment process for their disciplines, they must start by knowing what assessment is and what it is not. Faculty members may sometimes tell you, "I don't know why we have to jump through all of these hoops on assessment. We're doing assessment all the time. We're assessing students in our courses by means of assignments, examinations, and final projects . . . and those assessment measures tell us that we're doing just fine." The problem is that such a perspective confuses *evaluation* with *assessment* and tries to draw a conclusion more appropriate for one of these activities from the means developed to accomplish the other. In other words, *evaluation* measures the success of discrete individuals, such as students, faculty members, and courses by determining whether these individuals reach some particular standard. *Assessment*, on the other hand, measures the effectiveness of combined units, such as programs or offices, by determining whether those units are producing particular results. There is an essential difference between these two types of measures.

For instance, the grading of students—one of the types of "assessment" cited by the imaginary faculty member above—is actually a quite appropriate means of evaluation, but a completely inadequate form of assessment. Consider, for example, this scenario: as an administrator, I tell a faculty member, "8 out of 30 students failed your introductory course last semester. From this, I'm concluding that your department is not successful, particularly since there's another department where *no one* failed the introductory course." In such a situation, the faculty member would certainly respond that my conclusion does not make any sense: it was not the department that failed or even the course that failed, I would be told, but rather those eight students. Perhaps they did not study or come to class. Perhaps they were not strong enough academically to be admitted to the college in the first place. Perhaps this is just a fluke, since most students have done well in the course in the past. And all of these points would be valid: The final exam in that course evaluated those particular students' progress in the course; it does not assess the effectiveness of the program at all, at least not in any useful way.

Similarly, your evaluations of individual faculty members indicate whether you believe that each individual has met the standard that you and the department have developed. They do not tell you anything useful about the success or effectiveness of your program as a whole. To learn this, we must rely on the procedure of assessment.

Mission, Goals, and Outcomes

So, if assessment is not the same thing as evaluation, what is it? To put it succinctly, *assessment is the process of determining whether academic programs (or other units of the institution) are meeting their stated objectives.* For academic programs, those stated objectives are placed in the form of *student learning outcomes.* In order to determine what appropriate student learning outcomes are for the individual programs in your department, it is best to begin with your departmental mission statement. To the greatest extent possible, you want there to be as much logical flow as possible from your departmental mission statement to your goals to your student learning outcomes to your assessment measures to the action plan you develop based on the results from those measures. Let's start, then, with your mission statement. While your departmental mission statement may be inspired, in part, by that of your institution as a whole and the larger units of which you are a part, you will want your departmental mission statement to reflect more specifically how that larger institutional philosophy is being interpreted in light of your discipline's approaches, methodology, and resources. For example:

As a service department within a public research university, the mission of the Department of X-ology is to contribute to the General Education Program of all students, provide support courses to other disciplines, and to produce a small but consistent number of highly accomplished majors. Secondary missions of the Department of X-ology are to assist the university in fulfilling its research mission by producing original scholarship within the discipline, supporting interdisciplinary courses in conjunction with other campus programs, and offering outreach to local schools in X-ology and related disciplines.

Rather than a generic mission statement that provides no guidance for making decisions, this mission statement specifies what the department is seeking to do, for whom, and why. It would be phrased completely differently if the mission of the department included a large major program, a highly popular minor, or a graduate program. It would also have been phrased quite differently if the department were serving a liberal arts college, a professional school, or a teachers' college.

One of the great advantages of developing a well-crafted departmental mission statement is that it makes it quite easy then to enumerate the *goals* of the department. What are departmental goals? *Goals are broadly conceived, general statements about what the program is trying to accomplish in order to carry out its mission in the future.* A program goal answers the question: What purpose are we trying to serve? Unlike student learning outcomes, goals need not be directly accessible or measurable. In fact, they need not even be particularly *attainable*, at least in the sense of providing you with indisputable evidence that you have attained them. In other words, goals are the sorts of things that your program will continue seeking year after year. *Perfection* is a goal:

Although it is something no program will ever completely achieve, that does not mean that it is not something worth striving for. One excellent illustration of how this principle might be applied in your department may be found in the very useful assessment planning guide developed at California Polytechnic State University (http://www.academics.calpoly.edu/assessment/assessplanguide.htm). Departments are urged to begin designing their goals by considering the following generic example:

Example: The Department of _____ will produce graduates who:

I) Understand and can apply fundamental concepts of the discipline.

II) Communicate effectively, both orally and in writing.

III) Conduct sound research.

IV) Address issues critically and reflectively.

V) Create solutions to problems.

VI) Work well with others.

VII) Respect persons from diverse cultures and backgrounds.

VIII) Are committed to open-minded inquiry and lifelong learning.

Your first response is likely to be that, indeed, these are worthwhile goals for any department. Your second response, however, may be more along the lines of "But how could I demonstrate to anyone that my students in our program really do respect persons from diverse cultures and backgrounds? And how could I prove that our graduates are committed to open-minded inquiry and lifelong learning?" The answer is that it is not important for you to assess your goals either easily or effectively. These are *aims* that your program is *striving for*, not *targets* that you expect to "*hit*" every time.

The ability to prove the attainment of an objective becomes much more important at the next level, when you make concrete the general goals of your program by phrasing them as student learning outcomes. *A student learning outcome is a concise statement of precisely what a student is expected to know, understand, or be able to do as a result of the goals that your program has adopted.* In other words, each learning outcome answers the question:

What will a student be able to accomplish after a particular unit, course, or program has been completed? Because it deals not with general aims for the future, but with specific tasks to be accomplished, each outcome *must* be assessable; the program must be able to demonstrate whether all students (or a specified percentage of all students) are able to perform the task in question.

As you move from your department's mission statement to its overarching goals to developing assessable student learning outcomes, it is probably useful for you to proceed by discussing the following questions with your colleagues in the discipline:

- What specifically do we want our students to know by the time they complete our program?

- What specifically do we want students to be able to do with this knowledge by the time they complete our program?

- What information, content, or skills do we want our students to retain long after our program has been completed?

- What should our students be able to do with that information, content, or set of skills?

- What competencies do we want students in our program to learn or develop?

- What observable behaviors will indicate to us that those competencies have been developed?

- Where—in which specific courses or through what specific experiences —do we expect students in our program to develop these competencies?

- Is there a certain acceptable level or threshold of achievement beneath which we will not permit a student to graduate from our program? If so, what is that threshold and where do we determine whether it has been crossed?

- Is there a certain percentage of students who, if they develop certain skills or competencies to a specified level, we would feel that our program is successful? (Remember the goal may be perfection, but how close to "perfect mastery" do you realistically expect to achieve?) What might we decide to do if our program failed to produce that desired percentage?

- In what kinds of higher-level thinking do we want our students to engage?

- Besides completing exams at the ends of discrete courses, how do we expect students to demonstrate what they have learned in our program and how well they have learned it?

- If an employer or the dean of a graduate school were to ask the students in our program what they have learned, how would we like them to answer this question?

By the time you and your colleagues answer these 12 questions, you should have a fairly clear image of what specific objectives your program is trying to attain and how someone would recognize whether those objectives actually are being attained. Your next step would then be to phrase your department's specific objectives in terms of measurable learning outcomes by using concrete and observable *action verbs,* such as "express," "critique," and "examine." An excellent list of suggested "action words" to get you started in phrasing your learning outcomes may be found at Abilene Christian University's center for teaching excellence web site: http://www.acu.edu/academics/adamscenter/resources/coursedev/syllabus/verbs.html. For instance, you might consider a structure for your student learning outcomes based on the following template:

> By [SPECIFIC POINT IN THE PROGRAM], [ALL or AN ACCEPTABLE PERCENTAGE OF] students majoring in [PROGRAM] will be able to [GENERAL ACTION PHRASE] by [PERFORMING SPECIFIC OBSERVABLE ACTIVITY].

Admittedly, that template may look quite awkward initially. Once you begin to use it in developing outcomes for your program, you'll see how flexible and useful this structure actually is. Consider the following examples built on this template:

- Upon completion of ITAL 350, 355, and 365, all Italian majors will be able to demonstrate mastery of intermediate language skills by having read an approved work in Italian of no fewer than 100 pages, discussing that work in Italian for no less than half an hour with no more than 5 grammatical errors, and writing a critical response to the work in Italian (entirely free of grammatical or spelling errors) of no fewer than 10 pages in length.

- Upon completion of any 100-level mathematics course, at least 90% of non-majors will have demonstrated basic quantitative competency by being able to:
  a) interpret core mathematical models such as formulas, graphs, tables, and schematics
  b) draw proper inferences from these core mathematical models
  c) represent sufficiently complex mathematical information symbolically, visually, numerically, and verbally
  d) use arithmetical, algebraic, geometric, and statistical methods to solve problems
  e) estimate and check answers to mathematical problems in order to determine their reasonableness, identify alternatives, and select optimal results

- By the time they are ready to begin the senior seminar, all history majors will be prepared to conduct independent and original research by having demonstrated that they can formulate appropriate and significant historical questions, use appropriate primary and secondary sources to determine information relevant to answering historical questions, organize historical information so as to formulate and defend a thesis, and present that thesis and its defense in an effective written form.

- Students who complete the minor in music performance will be able to communicate musical ideas effectively by demonstrating that they are able to perform on at least one instrument with a substantial level of understanding, provide a satisfactory oral summary of the nature of a performance career, demonstrate satisfactory acquaintance with a variety of music, styles, and cultural sources, understand basic compositional processes and styles, and develop and defend musical judgments convincingly.

The *general action phrase* allows you to tie each outcome to a particular statement in your department's goals; the *specific observable activity* allows you to indicate how that more general goal will be made operational in a student's academic development. The most important thing is that, unlike goals, these learning outcomes are always stated in ways that are measurable, at least measurable in the sense that one can readily determine whether students are achieving the outcomes that you have specified. Once your discipline has agreed on appropriate outcomes—congruent with your mission and goals—you are ready to plan your strategy for assessment.

Assessing Student Learning Outcomes

The means that you will use to assess whether students are achieving the outcomes you have set for your program will vary according to your discipline, its pedagogical methods, and the specific outcomes that you have set. For instance, in the case of the outcomes for the programs in Italian and history presented above, final projects or examinations might be constructed to include the activities required by the outcome. All of which might lead to the question: Earlier you said that examinations were techniques used to *evaluate* individual students; why are they now suitable forms of *assessment?* The difference comes in how an examination is constructed and in the use that is made of data resulting from the exam. For example, in the case of the Italian outcome mentioned earlier, the curriculum might be organized so that each student takes ITAL 365 *last* in the 300-level sequence. Then the activities specified by the outcome can be included as part of the final project for this course. This does not mean, however, that the instructor of ITAL 365 cannot also include other questions on the final exam or additional requirements for the final project. All of those elements—those required for assessment and those required by the specific material of that course—would then be used to evaluate the progress of each particular student. It is only the aggregate data—were all the majors in the course able to perform all the activities specified in the outcome—that is used to assess the program. What the outcome says, in other words, is, "We will consider our program to be fulfilling its objectives if all of our majors can do *this* by *that* point in the program. If they can't, then we have to determine how we can improve the program so that they *can*." In this way, individual course grades still evaluate the performance of each student; parts of the exam and final project are merely used to assess the program itself.

In other situations, different types of assessment measures—portfolios, surveys, exit interviews, employer questionnaires, and the like—may be more suitable for collecting the data that you need. For instance, in the case of the history outcome cited above, students might be required to accumulate a portfolio throughout their coursework indicating that they have fulfilled all of the criteria before being permitted to enroll for the senior seminar. In the case of the outcome for the music minor, a jury hearing might be structured in such a way that the elements of the outcome are required components. In each case, however, the important questions for your discipline to come to an agreement on are these:

- What are the specific "thresholds" or "trigger points" that would indicate to you whether the outcomes you have established are actually being achieved?

- What would your discipline's course of action be if the data suggested that one or more of your learning outcomes were not being achieved?

- How might you then document any improvement resulting from this course of action?

In other words, these questions will help your department to "close the loop," to use the insights gained from your assessment to improve your program continually.

It could be that, based on what your assessment reveals to you, you modify course content, alter the pedagogical methods used to cover certain material, alter course prerequisites or the order in which certain types of material are covered, introduce a peer mentor program for majors, spend longer time teaching skills that are regarded as higher priorities, provide supplementary materials to students on your web site, or introduce additional checks for competencies in lower-level courses. In certain circumstances, too, you may conclude that your outcomes need to be revised as you had established objectives for your program that are simply impossible for your department to achieve. However the members of your discipline decide to improve your program, you will be doing so now on the basis of clear and demonstrable data, rather than gut impressions or hunches. Remember that, unlike evaluation, there is no way to "fail" an assessment. If your assessment demonstrates that your program is fulfilling completely all of its objectives, you win; you now have data to demonstrate that you are accomplishing the very things that you set out to do. But if your assessment demonstrates that your program is not accomplishing all of its anticipated outcomes, you still win; you now have the information you need concerning how improvements can be made, and you may even have the proof you need to support a budget increase in an area of critical concern.

Assessment has now been in place for so long at so many institutions that there are a wide variety of resources available, so that no one needs to "reinvent the wheel." For instance, excellent examples of *program goals* include those developed by:

- Central Washington University's Department of Chemistry (http://www.cwu.edu/~chem/undergrad/goals.html)

- Wartburg College's Department of History (http://www.wartburg.edu/history/goals.html)

- George Mason University's graduate program in music (http://assessment.gmu.edu/programgoals/CVPA/music-MA/IGoals.cfm) Web sites devoted to further information on how to develop appropriate student learning outcomes include:

- The University of Western Australia's site on how to write statements of learning outcomes, developed by its Centre for the Advancement of Teaching and Learning (http://www.catl.uwa.edu.au/current_initiatives/obe2)

- The University of Washington's faculty resource site on developing student learning outcomes (http://depts.washington.edu/grading/slo)

- A site developed by the Office of Assessment at Kansas State University on how to write learning outcomes (http://www.ksu.edu/apr/Learning/HowTo.htm)

- The Learning Outcomes Assessment Planning Guide, sponsored by California Polytechnic University (http://www.academics.calpoly.edu/assessment/assessplanguide.htm)

- A survey of what learning outcomes are, how to write them, action verbs to include, and a bibliography of some basic resources, provided by the National Center for Geographic Information and Analysis (http://www.ncgia.ucsb.edu/education/curricula/giscc/units/format/outcomes.html)

RESOURCES

There are more books on assessment than any department chair has time to read. The following works should, however, be on every chair's bookshelf.

Allen, M. J. (2004). *Assessing academic programs in higher education.* Bolton, MA: Anker.

Angelo, T. A., & Cross, K. P. (1993). *Classroom assessment techniques: A handbook for college teachers* (2nd ed.). San Francisco, CA: Jossey-Bass.

Banta, T. W., & Associates. (2002). *Building a scholarship of assessment.* San Francisco, CA: Jossey-Bass.

Banta, T. W., Lund, J. P., Black, K. E., & Oblander, F. W. (1995). *Assessment in practice: Putting principles to work on college campuses.* San Francisco, CA: Jossey-Bass.

Brown, G., Bull, J., & Pendlebury, M. (1997). *Assessing student learning in higher education.* New York, NY: Routledge.

Diamond, R. M. (1997). *Designing & assessing courses & curricula: A practical guide* (rev. ed.). San Francisco, CA: Jossey-Bass.

Hernon, P., & Dugan, R. E. (Eds.). (2004). *Outcomes assessment in higher education: Views and perspectives.* Westport, CT: Libraries Unlimited.

Huba, M. E., & Freed, J. E. (1999). *Learner-centered assessment on college campuses: Shifting the focus from teaching to learning.* Boston, MA: Allyn & Bacon.

Suskie, L. (2004). *Assessing student learning: A common sense guide.* Bolton, MA: Anker.

Walvoord, B. E. (2004). *Assessment clear and simple: A practical guide for institutions, departments, and general education.* San Francisco, CA: Jossey-Bass.

15

The Department Chair and Post-Tenure Review

Institutions differ widely in their approach to post-tenure review. At some institutions, people say that there is no post-tenure review process at all. (Even at these institutions, however, tenured faculty members almost always receive at least some sort of review, even if it is only an annual performance appraisal or consideration for a merit increase.) At the other end of the spectrum, some institutions have elaborate, multi-layered systems in place for post-tenure review with special committees that conduct these evaluations and reports made to various members of the senior administration. Depending on where along this spectrum your institution falls, your precise contribution as chair to a faculty member's post-tenure review may well be specified by an official policy manual or set of operating procedures. Nevertheless, no matter what your institutional procedure may be, there are issues that will inevitably arise as to how you might mentor the faculty members who are undergoing this process, how you can make this procedure as constructive as possible for your program, and how you can provide more useful advice to senior faculty members than blanket, uncritical praise or bland and unhelpful statements that "some improvement is needed."

Unless your system requires you to be the sole individual responsible for deciding the outcome of a faculty member's post-tenure review, you might begin the process by sitting down with each faculty member who is scheduled to undergo the process and discuss, well before the deadline for submitting *official* materials, where the person stands relative to your own evaluation of his or her performance and what some of the likely conclusions of the process could be. Help the faculty member assemble the following materials, even if not all of these are required for your institution's official post-tenure review process:

- A draft of the application or cover letter that the faculty member intends to submit

- An updated curriculum vitae

- All official evaluations of the faculty member's performance that you or any other authorized groups and individuals on campus have written about the faculty member for the last five years

- Summaries of student ratings of instruction for all courses

- Representative student comments taken from evaluation instruments used in all courses

- Results of any peer evaluations that may have been conducted in your department or at your institution

- Sample course materials (syllabi, exams, and other items used in courses, including links to electronic materials)

- Representative publications

- Photographs, recordings, or summaries of creative works, if applicable

- A set of goals to be accomplished during the next five-year period

- A self-assessment of progress toward completing goals in teaching, scholarship, and service over the past five years

With these materials at your disposal, you can sit down with the faculty member and reflect candidly on areas of strength that emerge from your review of these documents, areas of weakness that are likely to be noted, and (most importantly) areas in which the faculty member has made significant contributions that are not made clear—or, at least, are not sufficiently highlighted—by the materials you have seen.

By reviewing these materials early, you still have time to reformat a curriculum vitae that is out of date, idiosyncratically presented, or organized in such a way that it does not highlight the faculty member's true strength. You will also have an opportunity to review syllabi and course materials with a new "lens," seeing them not merely in terms of how they might be effective in communicating with students, but also in terms of what they may suggest to the administrator or review committee about this faculty member's philosophy of teaching and methods of instruction. Your goal at this point should be to be as candid as possible in your assessment of weaknesses that you perceive. It is far better to identify a problem area now and try to remediate it before these same weaknesses may be noted by others who are acting in a more official capacity. Even in cases in which a faculty member's

cribe the areas in which you believe that serious weaknesses exist in order
prevent the faculty member from being blindsided later in the process
to allow time for an adequate plan for remediation to be developed.

does no one a real kindness for demonstrable limitations of a faculty
member's performance to be ignored at the departmental level. As a chair,
would be failing in your obligation to do everything you can to improve
formance in your department. As a mentor, you would have spared a fac-
member some discomfort in the short term only to set that person up
a major disappointment in the future. And you will have squandered the
e available to plan for appropriate actions to be taken.

he fourth category should be reserved for only the most severe cases of
ure to perform one's professional duties and for those individuals who,
whatever reason, are now proving seriously detrimental to your depart-
nt's mission of instruction, scholarship, and service. Although many peo-
in higher education believe the contrary, it is simply not the case that
ured faculty members can never be removed from their positions against
ir will. Nearly every institution has some sort of procedure allowing for
removal of tenure in extreme cases, and certain post-tenure review poli-
are actually connected to this procedure. Nevertheless, these proce-
es, when invoked, frequently cause a great deal of turmoil in the depart-
nts and institutions where they occur—resulting in negative publicity,
understandings by outside parties, and legal challenges. For this reason,
should be reserved for only those situations in which no other outcome
proved to be possible. If you regard termination to be at all within the
m of possibility for a faculty member undergoing post-tenure review, it
r better to discuss alternative "exit strategies" at the earliest possible date.
eassignment of duties might be possible. Your institution might have a
sed or early retirement plan that the faculty member could pursue. If
e are not options, a *willing* departure from the institution to take a posi-
elsewhere or to "pursue other opportunities" may preserve the individ-
s career in a way that outright dismissal would not. For faculty members
enough self-awareness to understand the nature and the severity of the
blem, these alternatives to being removed from their positions can be
active, face-saving options. Unfortunately, all too often the very reason
these faculty members are now in such extreme difficulty is because
lack the sort of self-awareness that would have caused them to modify
r behavior before the problem became unsolvable. In such cases, the dis-
sal of the faculty member will be one of the tensest challenges you may

weakness in an area is chronic and impossible to alter in the time that remains before the post-tenure review begins—if, for example, a scholarly record is so weak that there is no hope of improving it in the six months to a year that you have before the formal review begins—it is a kindness to point out in advance criticism that is likely to emerge, rather than allowing the faculty member to undergo the process with little inkling that there may be problems ahead.

As you review the faculty member's materials, try to view them with fresh eyes, ignoring the other aspects of the individual's performance of which you are aware and considering only the picture that emerges from the written documentation. Do those documents present a fairly accurate assessment of this individual's strengths and weaknesses? If there are aspects of the faculty member's performance that are very strong but that do not appear to be adequately reflected in the materials that you are reviewing, what additional information will it be necessary for the faculty member—or for you as chair—to provide to those who are conducting the formal review? If there are problems with the faculty member's professional contributions that are glossed over or distorted by the written materials, how can you, as the faculty member's supervisor, fulfill your obligations to the institution by providing a corrective?

As you are examining the packet of materials prepared by the faculty member, try to determine whether you can draw one of the following four conclusions from your review:

- The faculty member is fully meeting the institution's expectations for performance by a tenured faculty member, and no specific recommendations for improvement are necessary.

- The faculty member is meeting the institution's expectations for performance by a tenured faculty member, but there are several improvements that should be made.

- The faculty member is not meeting the institution's expectations for performance by a tenured faculty member, and there are several improvements that need to be made.

- The faculty member is performing at a level severely lower than the institution's expectations for performance by a tenured faculty member, and it is in the institution's best interest that this faculty member leave your employment.

Faculty members placed in the first category are those whom you regard as completely fulfilling your institution's expectations in all categories. In other words, their teaching is engaging, conducted at an appropriate level in each course, and designed to prepare students for success in later coursework or in their lives. They have remained active as scholars, not merely keeping up to date with your field, but contributing to the discipline at a level appropriate for the mission of your institution. In service, they are "team players," assuming their fair share of the business that is necessary for the efficient operation of your department and institution, making positive contributions at a level equivalent to their tenured status, and participating actively in the essential functions of your discipline. The percentage of your faculty members for whom you believe this category is appropriate will vary according to your institutional expectations and your department personnel. Nevertheless, it is the rare department for which more than approximately one out of every five or ten senior faculty members has absolutely *no* areas of weakness. While it may appear to be the easy option for a chair to conclude that nearly every member of his or her faculty falls into this first category, using this designation a bit more restrictively can actually be in the best interest of your department and of the faculty members themselves.

The second category is where most chairs will probably discover that a majority of their faculty members belong. In other words, this designation indicates that, although the faculty member is performing his or her duties according to the institution's expectations, there are one or two areas in which you would like to see some further development. Perhaps the faculty member has not been as aggressive as you would have liked in incorporating technology into certain courses or in updating his or her instructional techniques. Perhaps the burst of scholarship that led this faculty member to promotion and tenure has decreased below the level at which many departmental peers are performing. Perhaps teaching and scholarship are superb, but the faculty member is proving to be an obstruction in departmental meetings or reluctant to assume a suitable load of advisees. Since you are reviewing the faculty member's materials before the official post-tenure review is conducted, there may still be time to address some of these concerns or, at least, to develop an improvement plan that can be submitted along with the faculty member's other materials. Your advice to faculty members whom you believe belong in this category should always be constructive and forward-looking: remember that these are individuals whom you value and on whom the department depends. Your effort in making

recommendations should be clearly depicted as an ⸻ already strong record of performance, not to discou⸻ member who probably already believes that he or s⸻ extremely high level. Remind these faculty members ⸻ ing you, has areas of performance in which improv⸻ would be failing in your role as mentor if you did ⸻ obtain these improvements wherever possible.

For most departments, the chair will probably fir⸻ members who fall into the third category. Neverthe⸻ viduals for whom most institutions or systems ad⸻ review process. They are the faculty members who ⸻ over a number of years, sometimes precipitously ⸻ granted—ceased making the effort that led to their ⸻ their courses have not been updated in a number ⸻ tional methods are badly out of date. Students are f⸻ faculty member's courses because of an excessive re⸻ and other passive methods of instruction. Examina⸻ an appropriate level for the material or consist alm⸻ ple choice and matching questions even in smalle⸻ portfolios, and more complex projects are far more ⸻ dwindled to a trickle at best, and there is little or ⸻ ulty member has continued to grow in your field. ⸻ are either refused or made only with great reluctan⸻ hampering the smooth operation of your departme⸻ ted late or in a format that makes them unusable. I⸻ as it may be to do so, you may well need to set ou⸻ and objectively to the faculty member following yo⸻ her material. Wherever possible, try not to rely ⸻ anecdotal evidence. Provide clear data: what is ⸻ advisees, committee assignments, publications, con⸻ student projects assigned per tenured faculty me⸻ department or across the institution? How does th⸻ pare to others in terms of updating and improving⸻ pating in sessions to improve pedagogy, or volunte⸻ vice projects? In most cases, the improvements you⸻ members in this category are sufficiently substanti⸻ sible to complete them by the time the faculty mer⸻ review gets under way. Nevertheless, it will still ⸻

face as a department chair. The good news, however, is that you are unlikely to face such a challenge more than once or twice in your career, you are making your decision only for the good of your program and institution, and you will not be alone in recognizing that the faculty member's continued presence at your institution could be disastrous.

Another bit of good news is that the entire post-tenure review process, while occasionally revealing areas where improvement is needed, is far more likely to be a highly positive one for you and for the faculty member. It will reinforce for you just what a strong faculty you have, remind you of the numerous important contributions they have made, and give you an opportunity to congratulate the faculty member formally on his or her continued record of excellence in instruction, scholarship, and service. Particularly for faculty members who have already reached the rank of full professor, these opportunities for public reinforcement of their positive contributions tend to be relatively rare. By making the post-tenure review process a means to accentuate the positive and plan for continued growth in the future, you will be making a significant effort toward maintaining high morale in your program and expanding its reputation across your campus. Many institutions even have procedures in place for awards and recognitions that arise from highly positive post-tenure reviews. If your institution does not yet have such a recognition campus-wide, it might be worthwhile for you to explore the possibility of a departmental recognition for those who successfully complete their formal post-tenure reviews.

Once a faculty member's formal post-tenure review begins, your role in the process as chair is likely to change. You will shift from being a mentor and advisor to the faculty member (providing constructive, formative criticism) to being an evaluator of the faculty member (providing decisive, summative criticism). In some institutional processes, your role may be set out in great detail: you may be asked to submit a report that must contain certain types of information or be structured in a particular way. At other institutions, you may be asked to submit letters on behalf of your faculty members only in certain situations or if you desire to do so. In all of these cases, you should remember the gravity of your written report and its impact on the faculty member's career. Your formal evaluation is now no longer a matter of informal advice and observations made behind closed doors; it is part of the public record. It is a document upon which certain decisions will be made. At some institutions, your letter may even be the document rendering the outcome of the post-tenure review. For that reason, you must weigh your statements very carefully, recording only observations about which you are *certain* and for which you have data to support your conclusions. Avoid repeating innuendo or third-hand observations. Tie all of your remarks to specific indicators that can be verified. If deadlines were missed, what were those deadlines and what were the consequences of the faculty member's failure to meet them? If you have concerns about the faculty member's teaching, what were the student complaints, peer observations, or unsatisfactory course materials that gave rise to these concerns? If scholarship is an issue, how does the faculty member's scholarly productivity compare to those of colleagues in the department or in similar disciplines? Be as specific and data-oriented as you can. It serves the interest of neither the institution nor the faculty member for you to render a decision of "not good enough" without specifying your standard, the reason for its existence, and some targets for suitable attainment.

RESOURCES

Some of the best available sources on post-tenure review include:

Alstete, J. W. (2000). *Post-tenure faculty development: Building a system for faculty improvement and appreciation* (ASHE-ERIC Higher Education Report, 24[4]). San Francisco, CA: Jossey-Bass.

Licata, C. M., & Morreale, J. C. (Eds.). (2002). *Post-tenure faculty review and renewal: Experienced voices.* Bolton, MA: Anker.

Licata, C. M., & Brown, B. E. (Eds.). (2004). *Post-tenure faculty review and renewal II: Reporting results and shaping policy.* Bolton, MA: Anker.

Licata, C. M., & Morreale, J. C. (Eds.). (2006). *Post-tenure faculty review and renewal III: Outcomes and impact.* Bolton, MA: Anker.

16

The Department Chair's Role in Internal and External Program Review

Internal Review

In order to gain insight into the quality, viability, and institutional fit of their academic programs, colleges and universities frequently rely on a formal process known as *program review*. While a well-designed program review process examines far more than just *academic* programs, most department chairs play a limited role at best in the review of such offices as physical plant, the business office, and residential life. Also, while most program reviews address an institution's general education requirement, department chairs have far greater responsibilities in the processes that examine their own individual disciplines. For this reason, the following discussion uses the term "program" as equivalent to "departmental program" or, in other words, the curriculum offered by an individual academic department that, in most cases, leads to an academic degree.

When dealing with program review for the first time, many department chairs wonder how this process is different from such procedures as evaluation and assessment that they may already have in place, what sort of information is likely to be needed and analyzed in the course of each department's program review, and how they can help make the best possible case for their disciplines within the guidelines imposed by their institutions. The following overview of program review is intended to provide department chairs with clear information in each of these three important areas.

Evaluation, Assessment, and Program Review

The terms *evaluation, assessment,* and *program review* refer to three fundamentally different, though at times overlapping, methods of collecting and analyzing information. *Evaluation* measures the effectiveness of individual people, courses, or programs. It helps the evaluator decide whether the person or thing being evaluated is "meeting the grade" and, if not, how that individual performance may be improved. For instance, the grade and comments assigned by a faculty member to an individual student's project constitute an evaluation, as do the annual performance appraisals prepared for faculty members. That is to say, when a professor grades and provides comments on each student's course project, that professor is appraising that student alone and that specific assignment alone. The student's grade and the professor's comments tell us nothing at all about how much *all* the students in the course have learned, whether the faculty member was successful in designing the course syllabus, or whether the department's curriculum is appropriate for the purposes it is trying to achieve. Similarly, when the dean or department chair writes an annual evaluation of a faculty member, it is that individual alone who is being evaluated; the report that comes out of this process provides no information about the faculty as a whole, the quality of that institution's faculty development program, or the ongoing staffing needs of the department. In addition to students and faculty members, evaluation processes are frequently used for individual courses (peer evaluations, student evaluations, external reviewers' evaluations), individual program curricula, or individual administrators. In all of these cases, one learns the answer to: "How successful was this one individual at the task in question and how can improvement be made?"

Assessment is the process by which entire programs are examined to determine whether they are succeeding in accomplishing a clearly established set of goals and outcomes, and, in those cases where standards are not being met, how the *program* (not the performance of individual students, faculty members, or administrators) should be modified. In order to conduct an appropriate assessment of your program, you should first begin with your discipline's mission statement (a document that is usually based on the mission statement of the entire institution), develop goals that reflect the substance of that mission statement, refine those goals into *measurable outcomes,* and then measure the degree to which those outcomes are achieved. Failure to achieve specific outcomes should lead to consideration of clear steps for improvement. In other words, is there a better sequence in which students should take their courses in this program? Should the syllabi of courses at various levels of the program be modified and, if so, how? Was the curriculum designed with clear enough goals that the students can reasonably accomplish what you believe to be necessary at various points in their academic careers?

Program review is a process that is far broader than either evaluation or assessment, particularly in terms of what type of considerations are involved in the process. Evaluation and assessment provide information only about the *quality* of what you are examining: Did this individual perform up to expected standards, or did that entire program achieve our stated outcomes? Evaluation and assessment do not tell you whether the program itself is viable in terms of student enrollments, the size of its budget, or likely demands for graduates in the future. Nor do they indicate how important the program is to the institution's overall mission and strategic plan. To provide this more comprehensive look at an institution's programs, colleges and universities frequently rely on a periodic process of program review.

A solid program review process *includes* information obtained from evaluation and assessment, but it also requires additional perspectives and sources of data. For instance, in determining the quality of instruction, some institutions require departments to provide aggregate scores on student course evaluations in order to compare these overall averages to median scores in other related disciplines and to those of all disciplines at the institution. They may also require the submission of external reviews developed by accrediting agencies or peer programs. Almost certainly, institutions require that departments either provide or respond to data about enrollment trends, numbers of majors, graduation rates in the discipline, the size of externally funded grants received, placement of students in graduate school or professions closely related to the major, and trends in faculty scholarship, research, and creative activity.

What Information to Gather

If your institution already has a clearly established program review process in place, it should be fairly easy to determine what type of data you need to collect and in what form your institution wants that information reported. If your discipline has not yet had to submit a program review, ask to see examples of successful documentation submitted by departments as similar to yours as possible. Then use these other reports as a model for your own collection of data. If, on the other hand, your institution is relatively new to program review or if your reports are allowed to be more "free form," the task that you face will be more challenging, since you will need to determine *what* you should report and *how* you should present this information so that it makes your department's strongest case. One good place to begin is to ask yourself such questions as:

- What are my department's strongest assets, the features that make it distinctive from other departments at my institution and from other departments similar to mine at other institutions?

- What weaknesses might others see in our program, and how can I account for these areas of vulnerability so that even someone not familiar with our field will see the larger picture?

- If I were examining a program that I did not know very well, what information would demonstrate to me that students were learning what they needed to know, that faculty members were producing scholarship or creative activity of the appropriate quality, that the program was sustainable for the future, and that the program as a whole was an essential part of what we do as an institution?

The answers that you provide to these questions will tell you a great deal about what type of information you may wish to collect and how you might wish to present it.

If your institution permits you some flexibility in the program review process, you may wish to assemble data in any or all of the following categories:

Quantitative indicators consist of data that are "countable" or at least measurable in some consistent, reproducible manner. Quantitative indicators may be raw numbers, percentiles, rankings, averages, or other similar types of information. The most useful types of quantitative indicators at most institutions tend to be ratios, since they place a raw figure into at least a partial context. For instance, a raw figure such as "Over the last five years, an average of eight graduates each year were admitted to their first-choice post-baccalaureate program," while it may be interesting, is ultimately meaningless for review purposes. Is eight a high figure or a low figure? Presented in isolation, the number alone gives the reader no way of making this judgment. Presented as a ratio, however, the figure begins to take on meaning and to be incorporated into a larger context: "Over the last five years, an average of eight out of eleven (72.7%) graduates each year were admitted to their first-choice post-baccalaureate program, while our overall institutional placement rate is only 53.1% and the rate within our closest peer disciplines is 65.5%." Similarly, presenting raw numbers of student credit hours generated per term or per academic year may be requested at some institutions, but this information really only becomes useful when it is calculated in terms of some other relevant factor, such as the number of full-time equivalent (FTE) faculty members who produced those credit hours.

Qualitative indicators include sources of information that, while not specifically measurable in and of themselves, are nonetheless helpful in providing a more comprehensive picture of a program. Because they tend not to result in specific scores, qualitative indicators almost always require more interpretation than do quantitative indicators. Nevertheless, they can demonstrate aspects of a department's success, viability, or unique mission in a manner that proves to be far more compelling than sheer numbers. Perhaps the most commonly used type of qualitative indicator for program review purposes is the portfolio. For instance, representative portfolios of student work provide a valuable impression of the level of work achieved by students and their rate of growth during the program. In much the same way, faculty portfolios of teaching, scholarship, service, and administrative contributions can provide a much more balanced view of the faculty than can mere scores on student evaluations or the number of refereed articles published. The ground-breaking work of Seldin (2004) in *The Teaching Portfolio: A Practical Guide to Improved Performance and Promotion/Tenure Decisions*, now in its third edition, is a good place to begin for information on assembling this type of material, followed by Murray's (2000) *Successful Faculty Development and Evaluation: The Complete Teaching Portfolio*. Moreover, Seldin has recently begun exploring other types of professional portfolios in such works as *The Administrative Portfolio: A Practical Guide to Improved Administrative Performance and Personnel Decisions* (Seldin & Higgerson, 2001), and the possibilities exist for using the portfolio approach to document faculty professional contributions in such areas as scholarship and service as well.

Indicators of quality are, as their name implies, factors that suggest to an observer how good a program is or the level of success that the program has had in achieving its goals. Indicators of quality may be either quantitative or qualitative and may draw upon data dealing with students (e.g., five-year graduation rates, placement rates for graduates, alumni portfolios of scholarship in the discipline, etc.), faculty (e.g., percentage holding a terminal degree, number of refereed publications per FTE faculty member each year, teaching and administrative portfolios, etc.), support staff, access to information resources, and other such elements that contribute to the overall quality of an academic program.

Indicators of viability are those factors that indicate whether a program is likely to be sustainable in the future. Quantitative indicators of viability include such things as enrollment trends, estimates of probable demand for graduates in the discipline over the next five to ten years, additional sources of program revenue such as grants and sponsored programs, and ratios of tuition generated by the program to expenditures made in such areas as salaries, benefits, and operating expenses. Qualitative indicators of viability might include a discussion of factors that are likely to affect demand for graduates within the foreseeable future, a listing of honors or achievements attained by alumni, and a statement of the advantages accruing to your program from your institution's location or the uniqueness of your curriculum. One quantitative indicator of viability that disciplines occasionally overlook is the correlation between enrollment in one or more of the department's courses and retention at the institution. Frequently, courses that have a clear mentoring or experiential component—for instance, studio art, lab science, or applied music courses—produce students who are more likely to persist at the institution because they develop closer bonds with faculty. By demonstrating a differential between the retention rates of students who have enrolled in your department's courses and the retention rate of the institution as a whole, you can provide a perspective on viability that your college or university may find particularly compelling.

Indicators of centrality to mission are those types of information that suggest the degree to which your department is essential to your school's fundamental purpose, strategic plan, and vision for the future. For instance, at a research university, the ratio of books and articles, grants received, patents obtained, or academic recognitions won per FTE faculty member helps to suggest the vital role your department is playing in advancing your institution's mission. At a liberal arts college, the connection you can make between your discipline and the traditional liberal arts goals of developing critical thinking, improved communication, and aesthetic appreciation is likely to assume greater significance. Church-related schools, professional schools, community colleges, comprehensive institutions, and schools adhering to the model of the "New American College" are each likely to have distinctive missions and goals for the future to which you will need to relate your mission as a discipline. In each case, however, it is likely to be *outcomes*—what students and, under certain conditions, faculty members *produce*—that will be the most important and compelling as sources of evidence, rather than "*inputs*," such as faculty credentials, SAT/ACT scores of incoming students, or the number of volumes relating to your discipline in your institution's library.

How to Make Your Case

Inevitably, every institution's program review process will be based on its own set of core values and assumptions. As a department chair, you will need to determine what underlying values and assumptions have been in order to know how you can make the strongest case for your discipline. For instance, does the program review process at your institution primarily focus on the number of majors in each program or on your discipline's overall production of student credit hours? If you find that most of your school's questions tend to deal with the number of majors in your department, then it is clear that what your institution values most is recruiting students to your program, graduating them on time, and placing them in graduate school or employment closely related to your field. Departments that, for instance, do not generate a large number of majors will then need to put this information in its proper context: can you demonstrate that, even though your major itself may be small, you provide a vital role in supplying service courses to other majors and offer a number of important courses in the general education program? If, on the other hand, most of your institution's questions tend to deal with student credit hour production, then the overall focus appears to be on general productivity and efficiency rather than the size of the major. Programs such as business administration, which may be required by their accrediting agencies to have majors take a substantial amount of coursework outside the department, may need to clarify this situation for reviewers who might not understand the context in which your discipline is compelled to operate.

Similarly, are you ever asked in your institution's system to differentiate your student credit hour production into upper-level as opposed to lower-level courses or according to courses that satisfy the institution's general education requirements as opposed to courses that are usually taken to satisfy major requirements? If not, and this distinction is integral to your department's mission, try to find a way in which you can make this distinction, clarifying the data for the individual or the committee that will be reading your review. Also, at many institutions, the revenue produced by a department is calculated by a formula similar to the following:

department revenue = discounted tuition generated − (salaries + benefits + operating expenses)

If your discipline is also contributing to your institution's overhead through significant grant activity or sponsored programs, and this is not reflected in the revenue formula adopted by your college or university, be sure to cite this added resource as an important factor in your department's ongoing viability.

Above all, be sure to consider assets of your program that are not easily quantifiable or that do not lend themselves to the reporting format required by your institution. Are your faculty or the students who take courses from your department demonstrably more diverse than elsewhere in the institution? If so, then this may be an asset in enhancing your college or university's diversity plan that may not be visible from the data *required* by your institution's program review process. Consider, too, whether a larger percentage of your faculty members or students would have had a significant international experience compared to their peers across the institution. Or do your faculty members or students help improve your institution's diversity in terms of gender or socioeconomic background? Either of these factors can add value to your discipline in a way that may not otherwise be clear from the review format required by your institution. It may also be that your discipline is attracting an exceptionally large number of first-generation college students to your institution, a factor that you can present as enhancing the school's mission to reach out to traditionally under-represented groups. If your faculty's scholarly output appears low in terms of the number of refereed publications or the total number of pages of work appearing in books and journals, can you document that these works were commonly cited by other scholars in your field or that your department's scholarship tended to appear in extremely selective journals? If so, you will need to introduce this information in a discussion of "quality versus quantity," even if your review format does not specifically request this information.

Finally, remember that a score or ratio alone, without the benefit of interpretation, rarely tells the entire story. For instance, the incoming SAT or ACT scores of your majors may be significantly higher or lower than those of students in other disciplines. Either one of these results may be an asset to your institution, depending upon the interpretation that is made of it. High standardized test scores may indicate that your department's recognized level of academic excellence is attracting exceptionally strong students. On the other hand, low standardized test scores may nevertheless result in high rates of student success after graduation, demonstrating the life-transforming nature of your program. By making your case in this manner, therefore, you will be much more likely to create a review of your program that casts your achievements in the best possible light, places vulnerable areas within a more comprehensive context, and guides your department as it continues to make progress in the future.

External Review

As part of the program review process at many institutions, departments may be encouraged—or even required—to obtain some sort of external evaluation. In many cases, this external review may be conducted by an accrediting agency specific to that individual discipline. In other cases, it may follow a process set forth by the institution itself. Or, it may be left up to the individual department to propose the most appropriate form for this review to assume. In the last of these cases, the department will find itself having an incredible amount of flexibility, but the chair may also be left wondering *how* best to conduct this external program review, *what* should be included in the review, and *how* the information should be collected and analyzed. Sometimes, chairs may not even be sure which questions they should ask or even where they should begin. To assist in these cases, it is frequently helpful to have a general framework for what the chair's role is likely to be in the most common type of external program review, what information will be most beneficial for the chair to obtain, and how to make the strongest possible case for the department undergoing external review.

If you are scheduled to participate in an external review of your department, you may be asked to select (or at least to recommend) a partner institution for an external paired assessment. In this case, you will want to recommend an institution that has a program reasonably comparable to your own, that is not located so far away that visiting the other campus is needlessly expensive, and that stands to benefit as much from the external review project as your institution will. When looking for a comparable institution with which to share program reviews, try to consider not only such matters as the size of each program and the overall similarity of the two institutions' missions, but also such factors as entering student SAT/GPA scores, size of endowment, and the condition of the physical plant used by each department. Failure to consider variables of this sort can result in a forced "comparison" of two departments that are in reality so different that meaningful results will end up being all but impossible to obtain.

Even while you are still locating a comparable program with which to conduct this review, you should begin thinking about what instruction you will give faculty members who themselves may never have participated in such a review before. What types of observations are they likely to find most useful? What sort of information should each team examine in order to develop a realistic assessment of and worthwhile advice for the other program?

In situations where the institutions themselves do not provide any standard set of guidelines or templates for external program reviews, department chairs might begin by instructing the faculty members on each review team to examine the following nine areas.

1) Learning Goals

First, try to determine the adequacy of the learning goals adopted by the department that you are reviewing. Have goals been written at the appropriate level for each of the following types of students: majors (where the department offers its own major), minors (again, where this is an appropriate question), and non-majors/minors? Where specifically in the curriculum is each of these learning goals addressed? How does the department assess its effectiveness in attaining these goals? What has this assessment process suggested about the program's effectiveness to date? What improvements has the department made on the basis of the results of its assessment plan?

2) Curriculum

Next, using these learning goals as your guide, assess the adequacy of the program's curriculum as a whole. Consider its overall structure. Does it flow in a logical sequence? After examining catalog offerings and syllabi, members of each review team should consider whether, in their professional judgment, there are noticeable "holes" in curricula, course offerings, or course content. Conversely, are there areas of exceptional strength, distinction, or innovation? What recommendations can you give your peers in terms of improving their course offerings, content, and rotation?

3) Student Achievement

Then, looking beyond the program's formal program of assessment, try to gauge a sense of how effective the department has been in helping students to develop their knowledge and skills in the discipline. One of the best ways to do this is by examining a representative sample of student projects. For instance, the Association of American Colleges and Universities (2004) states that

> There should be periodic evaluation by external reviewers of the goals, the proficiency standards, and work samples submitted by students to meet standards. Such external reviews provide validation of both the goals and standards. A representative sample of student performances in different fields will provide sufficient evidence for external feedback. (p. 12)

In performance-based disciplines such as art, music, and theater, ask to attend an actual jury, performance, or exhibition. In research-oriented disciplines, try to review a selection of senior projects or at least of significant coursework done for upper-level courses. In your professional judgment, is the discipline "taking students to the level they need to be?" If not, what suggested improvements can you recommend? Ask to see examples of what the department considers to be its best student products. Then ask to see the same number of examples of minimally acceptable (and even unacceptable) student projects. The difference between these two sets of coursework should indicate for you the expected standards of the department and provide you with a touchstone by which to compare student achievement at your own institution.

4) Faculty

Consider the number, credentials, and achievements of the faculty members in both departments. Adjusting for FTE, calculate how many full-time and how many part-time faculty members are serving how many students. To get a more accurate sense of comparison, you may need to calculate this figure several different ways. For instance, first compare FTE faculty to the total number of students enrolled in any of the department's courses, then to the number of majors (where applicable), then to the number of students in introductory courses, and finally to the total number of student credit hours generated by the department (or in some disciplines, such as the natural sciences, to student contact hours). If the total number of student credit hours varies significantly from year to year, you may find it useful to develop a three- or five-year rolling average. How do the two institutions compare in terms of teaching load, average numbers of students in a discipline's courses, the maximum number of students allowed to enroll in a course, the number of advisees per faculty member, and the average number of students served by each faculty member? Where there are striking differences, begin to see if you can determine why those differences exist. How do the two institutions compare in terms of expectations for scholarship and service by faculty members? In which professional organizations are the faculty members of the two institutions active? Are these at all comparable? Over the past five years, how many publications and how many conference presentations have the faculty members of each program produced on a per capita basis? In cases where there are reviews or referee reports related to these publications, try to gauge a sense of how successfully the scholarship of the two faculties was received by the academic community. Did the publications of each program tend to occur at the highly competitive presses and most selective journals in the field or in less distinguished venues? At institutions where there is aggregate data on student ratings of instruction, how did the department fare relative to the rest of the institution? How did it fare relative to other disciplines that are similar to it (i.e., that are in the same college or division or that logically seem comparable to one another)? Aside from retirements, what has been the rate of faculty turnover during the past ten years? If it appears to be high, ask for the reasons why this turnover may have occurred.

5) Staff

Evaluate the adequacy of support staff in fulfilling the department's mission. Again, adjusting for FTE, calculate how many full-time and how many part-time staff members are being called upon to serve how many students. Remember to think of support staff in the broadest possible sense: In addition to departmental secretaries and administrative assistants assigned to each area, be sure to include laboratory assistants, audio-visual technicians, staff accompanists, costumers, curators, editorial assistants, and other staff. What is the breakdown of administrative staff—chair, co-chair, and assistant chair—per FTE student and student credit hour generated? Compare the ratio of administrative to teaching assignment of all members of the administrative staff and then relate this figure to the number of FTE students and student credit hours generated by each department.

6) Departmental Mission and Vision

Examine any internal documents generated by the institution's own planning and review processes. What do these items reveal to you about points of similarity and contrast between the department that you are reviewing and your own? How has the department that you are reviewing attempted to develop a distinctive mission and identity? In your professional judgment, is that mission and identity appropriate for the number and level of students that the institution is enrolling, the expectations of its faculty for teaching and scholarship, and the resources that the department has available? Are there constructive suggestions you might make about how the department's mission or vision for the future might be clarified? Are there ways in which each department may want to revise its mission or goals after learning from the other?

7) Program Support

Examine the operating budget of the program, prorated by FTE faculty member and then prorated by the total number of student credit hours generated. Compare travel funding and other sorts of faculty development support at the two institutions. What resources are available for faculty members who wish to present a paper at a national conference, hold an office in a professional organization, or complete additional coursework to advance their knowledge? Take a look at the professional organizations in which faculty members serve and where they actively participate: In your professional judgment, are the faculty members active in the *appropriate* organizations and at the most suitable conferences for their department's mission?

8) Facilities

Do the classrooms, office space, laboratories, practice rooms, gallery space, rehearsal rooms, and so on appear to be meeting the needs of each department in terms of its size, mission, and focus? Do instructional spaces have a level of technology that allows them to achieve their pedagogical mission or are they hampered by facilities that are obsolete or in a poor state of repair? If you can obtain it, try to gain a sense of the cost of deferred maintenance for the facilities most used by the department; how does this figure compare with the amount of deferred maintenance of the institution as a whole?

9) Overall

As you review all of these areas, where are there areas of noticeable strengths? Where are there weaknesses? If you were a prospective student or faculty member being recruited by the program, what would most attract you to it? What would concern you? What are the three to five greatest successes of the department that it should be featuring in all of its contacts with prospective students, donors, and administrators? What are the three to five things that ought to be improved if resources were available? As you review the information you have received, remember that the most important factors to consider are always the *results*: What has the department *done* with the human, physical, and monetary resources that it has? Those resources will be interesting in offering points of comparison for discovering where the two programs are similar and where they are different, but they cannot tell the whole, or most useful, story alone.

By examining the information in these nine categories, you will begin to learn several important things about the department that you are reviewing and its areas of success and weakness relative to your own program.

- You should gain a clear sense of how the department you are reviewing is similar to your own and how it operates in ways that are simply not comparable to the practices of your department. Understanding these similarities and differences is an important part of the external review process for one very important reason: *Simply because two programs are different in some way, it does not mean that one of the two departments is flawed, inadequately funded, or poorly designed.* You may discover, for instance, that the department you are reviewing has a much larger budget in some area—or even in many areas—than your own. You cannot immediately assume that your department is underfunded. It is possible, of course, that the other department is *overfunded,* but it is even more likely that you will learn this difference in funding exists because of an underlying difference in mission, size, or focus between the two programs. Use, therefore, distinctions between your department and the program you are reviewing to begin asking why those distinctions exist. Don't immediately assume that they indicate a problem.

- You should develop a good sense of what the expectations or standards of the department have been. You know the prestigious journals in your field. You know the conferences where it is difficult to get an abstract accepted and those where virtually everyone who applies to be on the program is successful. You know the level at which students should be performing by the time that they complete upper-level coursework in your discipline. Are faculty members and students at the institution you are reviewing performing at those high levels? If not, should they be doing so in light of the department's size and stated mission?

- You should be receiving a clearer sense of whether the department is meeting its own stated goals. Do the learning goals expressed by the department have any real meaning—for instance, are they actually reflected in the design of the curriculum—or have they been suggested as a mere exercise? Is there any systematic assessment of these goals being conducted? Can the department point to anything that it is doing differently now than it was doing five or ten years ago because it has gathered data about its effectiveness, given serious consideration to those data, and made a deliberate attempt to improve in those areas where it has not been as successful as it would like? Is the department *intentional* about the learning that occurs under its supervision or does it appear not to have much insight into how it is achieving success?

Common Mistakes

Finally, there are several mistakes that are commonly made by faculty members who do not have much experience with external program reviews. The following are common "rookie" mistakes that must be avoided if the review is to be valuable.

"Log-rolling." The problem of "log-rolling" develops when the express or tacit operating principle of each review team is, "You tell us we're wonderful, and we'll tell you you're wonderful." Or, at the other extreme, "log-rolling" can occur when the operating principle is "You tell us that we desperately need what we say we want, and we'll do the same for you." This type of providing mutual favors between the review teams is unethical and degrades the reviewing process. Moreover, as a strategy, it never really works. There is no ploy easier for an upper administrator to see through than this type of mutual back-scratching. After all, if an external review does not contain candid and substantive reporting of programmatic strengths and weaknesses, it will end up being dismissed out of hand, and the department that did not push for more objective analysis could easily suffer as a result.

Excessive fault finding. External reviews that are nothing more than long lists of extra faculty positions wanted, facility improvements needed, reductions in workload required, and budget increases sought are unlikely to be given serious attention by anyone outside of the department. Whenever needs or recommended changes are included in a report, they should always be carefully prioritized, not simply "dumped" as a laundry list of requests. What needs to be done most immediately? *What is likely to happen if this action is not taken?* How does that priority rank compared to the other competing needs of the department (e.g., scholarship support, salary increases for faculty and staff, improvements of technology, renovations in facilities, etc.)? If a recommendation is regarded as extremely urgent, what expenditures ought the department to defer or what reductions in its budget are permissible in order to make this recommendation possible?

By helping your faculty members to understand these guidelines, you will be taking an important step toward developing a valuable review of an external program . . . and of receiving a more useful review from that program. By going over these guidelines with the external team assigned to review your department, you are more likely to receive a final report that contains accurate, reliable observations and that is clear in its guidance about how you can improve your program.

REFERENCES

Association of American College and Universities. (2004). *Our students' best work: A framework for accountability worthy of our mission.* Washington, DC: Author.

Murray, J. P. (2000). *Successful faculty development and evaluation: The complete teaching portfolio.* San Francisco, CA: Jossey-Bass.

Seldin, P. (2004). *The teaching portfolio: A practical guide to improved performance and promotion/tenure decisions* (3rd ed.). Bolton, MA: Anker.

Seldin, P., & Higgerson, M. L. (2001). *The administrative portfolio: A practical guide to improved administrative performance and personnel decisions.* Bolton, MA: Anker.

17

What Every Department Chair Needs to Know About Fundraising

The financing of higher education is so complex that every department chair should have at least some familiarity with the basic principles of fundraising. Even if there is already a well-established development office at your institution—*particularly* if there is a well-established development office at your institution—there might be a time when some highly desirable opportunity for your department can only be pursued through the acquisition of external funding. Perhaps there is some special project—a scholarship in your discipline, a distinguished lecture series, a conference, a new or expanded facility—that would help you advance your program's goals but for which your regular, internal sources of funding are insufficient. On the other hand, it is also possible that you will someday find yourself approached by a donor who has some particular interest in making a contribution to your area. Whatever the situation may be, you will need to know at least the basics of fundraising and understand what your role in this process could potentially be. As a result, here is a very general primer of fundraising, outlining a few basics that *every* good department chair needs to know.

The Importance of Careful Preparation

Fundraising projects largely fall into two categories: those that originate at the institution and for which external funding is sought and those that arise from the interest of a donor who approaches the institution with a desire to make a contribution of some kind. The first of these two types is significantly more common than the second and, in order for these projects to be successfully planned and implemented, they require a great deal of planning, research, and preparation. Even in situations that arise out of a donor's interest, however, where the donor may feel a great deal of urgency, it is important for the chair to be certain that proper steps are taken and the appropriate plans are made before the project gets too far under way. Failure to prepare properly can leave the institution vulnerable to unanticipated costs at a later date, alienate a once enthusiastic donor, and doom what could have been a highly successful project. Careful preparation for every fundraising gift should always include the following steps.

Include an Appropriate Amount of Professional Support From the Institution's Development Office

In any fundraising venture, make use of your institutional advancement staff sooner rather than later. These individuals are more likely than most department chairs to understand immediately the legal and long-term financial implications of a gift proposal. They are likely to understand options that can simultaneously be of greater benefit to the donor and the department than an outright gift may be. They are likely to have some sense of the larger picture of the institution's financial plans and thus may be able to use your current project to leverage even greater support for your department in the long run. Members of the development staff are your strongest and best allies in the area of fundraising for your department; it is always a mistake to exclude them from your discussions, even at an extremely early stage in your planning.

Create an Appropriate Case Statement That Will Help You Guide Your Project and Elicit Contributions to It

A *case statement* is a concise summary of your department's mission. It should specify whom the department intends to serve, your program's specific need in terms of the project that you are proposing, and your department's potential to fulfill its mission more effectively, better serve its constituents, and satisfy your established need through the completion of the current project. A good case statement should not be wordy; a reader should be able to digest it quickly and easily. It should represent a clear plan that will seem important to the reader, inspire that person to become part of the solution to the problem you have outlined, and supply a sufficient amount of evidence that the project you are proposing is realistic and significant.

Build the Prospective Donor's Ties to Your Department as Well as Your Institution

One of the fundamental principles of fundraising is that "People give money to people more than they give money to causes." The *cause* may seem to you to be the most important thing, and perhaps it is; but a potential donor is unlikely to invest in that cause unless there is trust in your ability to steward resources properly and to use them in the most effective way possible. For this reason, the more time you are willing to invest in cultivating a potential donor, making that person feel an important part of your program and your future, the more successful your project is likely to be in the long run. Even if the prospective donor has made the initial contact with you and has proposed the project that is being considered, you should spend as much time as you can learning about what is important to that person. Try to identify connections between the values of the potential donor and the unique mission of your department. Listen to the potential donor's story and, when possible, find connections to your *department's* story. Remember that you are not ultimately seeking an isolated gift but, wherever possible, a new advocate for the goals, values, and aspirations of your program.

The Value of Teamwork

Too often department chairs feel that they ought to make their development calls all on their own. Either they do not want to distract the other members of the department from their critical duties in teaching or scholarship, or (more ominously) they are hoping to take full credit for the entire project. In many cases, however, chairs may choose to "go it alone" simply because they do not understand the valuable contribution others can make to the success of the proposal. Whatever the motivation, attempting to initiate, develop, and close an entire fundraising proposal by oneself is rarely successful and deprives the chair of the expertise that the following individuals might bring to the project.

Development Officers

A development officer has a great deal of experience in making contacts with donors, potential donors, and other supporters of the institution. He or she is much more likely than the department chair to have detailed knowledge about the financial and legal implications of different types of gifts, the vocabulary that tends to motivate or reassure potential donors, and the often complicated steps that the institution may require in order for a gift to be accepted, recorded, and acknowledged.

Faculty Members

A faculty member may be able to describe the impact of a gift in a manner that is far more eloquent than anything the chair alone might say. Particularly if the potential donor is a graduate of your institution, a cherished faculty member can help remind the donor of the important role that your department played in his or her life and intensify already close emotional ties to the institution.

Students

A student can help make more immediate the impact of a potential gift. The donor will be able to visualize more readily the sort of person that his or her gift may help. A carefully selected—and rehearsed!—student can speak personally about the importance of your program in the lives of students today, its success in improving students' career opportunities, and the type of needs it has for fulfilling its vital mission for the future.

Other Donors

Another donor can help the prospective contributor feel part of a larger and extremely important activity. Potential donors may feel more secure when they encounter other existing donors who are like them or whose opinion they respect. Current donors help keep the purpose of the development call as "pure" as possible; in other words, *they* are not the ones who will be benefiting from this new gift. Rather, they have been people who have caused similar benefits in the past. Current donors can also say things such as "Join me in making this important dream a reality" in ways that can be extraordinarily powerful and much more effective than when the same words are spoken by the chair.

The Effectiveness of the Personal Touch

Potential donors respond more effectively to *results* than they do to any vague statements you may make about your department's outstanding qualities and past achievements. They want to know *whom* they would be helping and how. They will be interested in understanding *why* the constituents of your department will not be served as effectively if the project you are proposing does not include their support. As a result, prepare a clear summary of all the ways in which the project you are proposing will provide a genuine and demonstrable benefit to people. Try to identify the type of person who is most likely to be helped by the idea that has been developed. Will all the students at the institution be better off because of the new facility/scholarship/lecture series that you are trying to create? If so, how? How will this endeavor help your institution attract and retain a larger student body or students who are more likely to succeed in your program? Are there underprivileged students who have not been able to benefit from your department's work because of the high cost of tuition, laboratory expenses, or private instruction? Is there a larger need in society that is likely to be filled through the research that will result from this project? Are there external constituents who could benefit from the type of work conducted in your department if only the web site, library resource, television program, or lecture series that you are proposing were in place? Make these potential beneficiaries of the proposal as vivid as possible in the mind of the donor—find areas of commonality between those who would gain from the project and either yourself or, even better, the donor—and help make the project's importance seem more tangible to the donor by making its benefits seem as personally significant as possible.

The Significance of Strong Departmental Support

Potential donors are much more likely to contribute to your department if you can say something like, "Our program is so important to our faculty members that every single one of them contributes each year to the annual fund." Even better, imagine the impact of being able to say, "100% of my faculty have already contributed seed money to this project. *That's* how much we all believe in it." The individual contributions of the members of your department need not be huge—it is the contribution *rate* that will matter more than the total amount you have raised—but it should be as broadly based as possible. In the case of the most recalcitrant members of the department (and make no mistake: these individuals exist everywhere), try to point out to them the importance of even a $5 or $10 annual gift that could help produce many times that amount in new contributions. Even before you approach potential donors with a large request, increasing the participation rate among members of your department can begin paying dividends. You can use any improvement in contribution rate that you can document ("We raised our departmental contribution rate by more than 35% in only one year") in order to help promote similar higher rates of contribution from alumni, parents, and friends of the department. Then, when you are ready to begin cultivating a potential donor for a larger project, you can approach that individual with an established record of fundraising success and a history of effective use of these increased contributions for the benefit of your department.

The Role of Having the Proper Attitude Toward Fundraising

Too often academics feel that the whole process of fundraising is slightly unsavory. Seeking external support smacks of asking for charity or implying that one's program has not been receiving its appropriate level of support from the institution and therefore is not seen as important. The fact of the matter is, however, that contributing to an academic department is a form of making a financial investment, not unlike the other types of financial investments that all of us make every day of our lives. Either we make investments because we believe we are likely to receive a greater return or because there is a particular product, service, or experience that we wish to obtain. A contributor is actually investing in the quality of your program and in its future growth. The return that donors will see on their investment is the satisfaction they will derive from knowing that they have played an important role in helping to solve a problem, serve a new generation of students, or improve the lives of others. What we sometimes forget is the amount of satisfaction that people derive from their own generosity. By requesting a gift to your department, you are helping potential donors focus their natural desire for serving others toward a particular, tangible project from which they can derive pleasure and satisfaction. People, particularly people who have amassed a great deal of wealth, are rarely offended when they are asked—appropriately and with the right amount of planning on your part—for a substantial gift. In fact, if your request is *too* large, they are more likely to be flattered that you considered them capable of making such a sizable contribution than insulted by the amount of the gift you are seeking. The important thing to keep in mind, however, is that any contribution you are requesting should be worth the investment the individual is expected to make. Your request should include a clear plan of how the gift will be used, how the impact of the project will be measured, and how the benefit produced by the project will be made known to others. The only time potential donors are likely to be offended by a gift request is when they feel that you have not thought through your proposal sufficiently and thus are wasting their time, insulting their intelligence, and not respecting the effort they exerted is acquiring their assets to begin with. Only in such a case are you better off never to have made any request at all.

Important Terms

In addition to these general principles of fundraising, there are also a few terms that every department chair ought to know since they are likely to arise in discussions of various kinds of fundraising and donor calls.

Gift Agreement. A document that sets forth the terms under which a gift is offered by the donor and accepted by the institution. Gift agreements usually specify the donor's charitable intent, what would happen to the gift if the original purpose is no longer appropriate for the institution at some point in the future (or, in the worst case scenario, if either the department or institution ceases to exist), who will be responsible for making certain decisions about the gift, and any other operating procedures that may be necessary for the successful completion of the project that has been proposed.

Endowment. The transfer of money or property to an institution for some particular purpose. In most cases, the endowment of a college or university is a corpus of funds, the interest of which (or some portion of, usually 4–6%) may be used for operation of the institution while the principal remains intact.

Bequest. A legacy or gift of personal property that comes to the institution through the terms of someone's will.

Trust. A right of property that an individual or institution holds on behalf of (and for the benefit of) another.

Lead trust. Also called *charitable lead trust*. A trust in which the income (or some specified portion of the income) created by the corpus is donated for charitable purposes but then, at some particular time in the future (such as the death of the donor), the corpus reverts to the donor's beneficiaries. Lead trusts are frequently attractive to individuals who want to reduce their tax liability for a set period. At the present time, they have an added advantage in that the federal government taxes only what they project the *likely* value of the principal will be at the end of the trust period. If, as is often the case, the value of the principal increases *beyond* what the IRS has calculated, that additional increase can pass to heirs free of transfer taxes.

Remainder trust. Also called *charitable remainder trust*. In many ways the opposite of a lead trust. A remainder trust occurs when the income of a trust is distributed to beneficiaries until some particular time in the future, after which the trust is donated to the specified charity. Remainder trusts are frequently attractive to donors who wish to reduce the amount of tax that will need to be paid from their estate or who wish to provide a guaranteed income to a beneficiary, while also achieving a second charitable goal at a later date.

Gift-in-kind. A gift made in some other form than cash. Tangible gifts-in-kind may consist of either property or services. Intangible gifts-in-kind may consist of rights (such as patents or copyrights) that have the potential of providing value at some future time.

Booking a gift. The official recording of a gift's receipt and incorporation into the institution's resources. Institutions have very specific accounting rules regarding when a gift may officially be booked (such as, "gifts must never be booked before a formal agreement has been signed by both the donor and institution") and the way in which the value of the gift must be calculated. The determination of a gift's value is subject to restrictions set forth by the U.S. Internal Revenue Code and by either the Governmental Accounting Standards Board (GASB: for public institutions) or the Financial Accounting Standards Board (FASB: for private institutions).

RESOURCES

There are a number of excellent resources that every department chair needs to have on his or her bookshelf when dealing with issues of fundraising. Some of the most valuable resources are:

Buchanan, P. M. (Ed.). (2000). *Handbook of institutional advancement* (3rd ed.). Washington, DC: CASE.

Elliott, D. (Ed.). (1995). *The ethics of asking: Dilemmas in higher education fund raising.* Baltimore, MD: The Johns Hopkins University Press.

Hopkins, K. B., & Friedman, C. S. (1997). *Successful fundraising for arts and cultural organizations* (2nd ed.). Phoenix, AZ: Oryx Press.

Panas, J. (2002). *Asking: A 59-minute guide to everything board members, volunteers, and staff must know to secure the gift.* Medfield, MA: Emerson & Church.

Rhodes, F. H. T. (Ed.). (1997). *Successful fund raising for higher education: The advancement of learning.* Phoenix, AZ: American Council on Education/Oryx Press.

Tromble, W. W. (1998). *Excellence in advancement: Applications for higher education and nonprofit organizations.* New York, NY: Aspen Publishers.

Worth, M. J. (Ed.). (1993). *Educational fund raising: Principles and practice.* Phoenix, AZ: American Council on Education/Oryx Press.

Worth, M. J. (Ed.). (2002). *New strategies for educational fund raising.* Westport, CT: Praeger.

Five Fundraising Mistakes . . . and How to Avoid Them

An active record of development has increasingly become the expectation for all levels of college administration. While college and university presidents have long been expected to serve as "fundraisers-in-chief," it is no longer uncommon for deans, directors, and department chairs to be expected to demonstrate some success in fundraising, at least in enhancing the support of their own programs. Moreover, department chairs who seek higher administrative positions will need a portfolio of successful development experiences to cite during interviews. Yet even department chairs who have no ambition to serve as a dean or provost can help the students and faculty members in their disciplines become more successful by knowing a thing or two about fundraising.

Chairs who have never given much thought to development activities are frequently concerned about where they should begin, and they are anxious about making mistakes in an area in which they have very little training and even less confidence. Department chairs are likely to make at least one of five common "rookie mistakes" when they contact external sources about potential contributions to their programs. By avoiding these five common errors, you will be far more likely to be successful in closing the deal and far less likely to feel out of your depth when meeting with a prospective donor.

The five mistakes all chairs should be certain to avoid when raising funds for their departments are:

Not Being a Team Player

Since many department chairs don't know precisely where to begin in the area of fundraising, they just begin. The problem with this approach is that they deprive themselves of the help that their institution's development offices can provide and increase the likelihood of stepping on someone else's toes. More than one chair has reported to a dean or president their joy in just having been promised a $500,000 gift from an external source only to be severely reprimanded because it will damage the institution's chances to receive the $5–$50 million that it was planning to ask of this same candidate. Forgetting that your department is part of a larger enterprise is one of the worst mistakes that the chair can make when seeking external funding.

To Avoid This Mistake

Never go it alone when planning your department's development strategies. As soon as you feel that you have the time to begin pursuing some external support for your department, tell your dean and your institution's chief development officer. Be sure to state the reasons why you are developing this interest. What specifically are you hoping to accomplish through your activity? If you wish to pursue a particular facility, piece of equipment, or curricular enhancement, they will need to guide you in how this project relates to the institution's other priorities. If you have a list of possible donors, be sure to share them with your development office. Find out which potential donors are already active prospects for other endeavors at the institution and be prepared to back off from them. One other aspect of being a team player is remaining flexible about what sort of funding you are willing to pursue. Gifts that are budget relieving for the institution may be particularly desirable for the school's financial officers. Can you combine a proposal that helps raise funds for a new project that is important to your discipline with an opportunity to redirect some money currently being spent by the institution on salaries, supplies, faculty development, or equipment? Could your project be redesigned to benefit the college as a whole? Could you enlist the support of and help provide assistance to other disciplines or programs?

Not Doing Your Homework

Individuals with the resources to make substantial contributions to your program tend to have extraordinarily busy schedules and limited amounts of time to discuss your pet projects. Even those who are retired or who appear to have a great deal of leisure time are frequently committed to other time-consuming projects or charitable endeavors. As a result, potential donors will expect your calls and visits with them to be fully worth the time that they are spending with you. A vague idea that has not yet been fleshed out, a proposal that contradicts the donor's own interests and values, or a proposal that has already been presented to this person, can immediately alienate the individual whom you want to cultivate as a supporter of your program. By not doing your homework and thinking through all of the things you will need to discuss with the donor, you are making a serious, potentially career-threatening mistake.

To Avoid This Mistake

Work closely with your college's development office long in advance of the actual donor visit. What do they know about this particular donor's interests, habits, and dislikes? What proposals, if any, were previously presented to this individual? Of those that were received favorably, what aspects of the proposal did the donor particularly like? Of those proposals that were declined, what aspects of the project did the donor find least attractive? If the prospective donor is a graduate of your institution, contact your alumni office to find out what they may know about the donor's particular interests, level of activity at college functions since graduation, and anything else useful that may be in the files. Alumni offices frequently survey their constituents and maintain records on their activities since graduation. This information can guide you in how best to explain a project to an alumni donor. If an alumnus had a particular professor who was a favorite or who served as his or her mentor, perhaps this faculty member will be willing to serve as a liaison to the potential donor. If the professor is deceased or has left the institution, perhaps the potential gift can be constructed as a memorial or honor to this individual.

Never request funding for a project unless you can outline very specifically how the project will function, when it will begin, what benefits will accrue, and how various decisions will be made along the way. If you embark upon your proposal unable to answer the numerous operational questions that the donor is likely to ask, you are almost certainly not going to be successful in your request. Even worse, you may leave the impression that individuals at your institution don't know what they're doing.

Not Considering All Options

Of course, thinking through all of the details is not the same thing as developing a proposal so inflexible, narrow, or restrictive that it can only function in one way. Interesting potential donors in departmental projects should never be a take-it-or-leave-it proposition. Nevertheless, it is not at all uncommon for a department chair to be so focused on one desirable scenario for an anticipated new program, building, or improvement to facilities that any deviation from that plan seems to betray the project's original purpose. This approach is bound to be counter-productive since prospective donors will almost certainly have their own points of view about how they want their contribution to be used and how your proposal would best be implemented. For instance, you might approach a donor about a new graduate program, but find that he or she is interested in enhancing undergraduate education. Or, you might want to discuss a new facility, but discover that the donor has a strong sentimental attachment to the current facility and fervently resists any plans to replace it. Adhering too strongly to only one way in which a goal can be accomplished can turn a likely contribution into a failed opportunity. Even worse, it could sour the potential donor on the institution as a whole, transforming a consistent contributor to the annual fund into someone who no longer makes any contributions.

To Avoid This Mistake

Work out multiple game plans with your development office as part of the preparation for your visit. Consider possible responses to the proposal that you are making and how you should best address each response. Realize that very rarely are requests granted in the full amount and exactly in the way that the original proposal is made. Be sure to develop clear strategies for various options. How would the proposal develop if the contribution were stretched over a longer period than you had anticipated? Are there ways to achieve your goal besides the method that you are proposing? What must you do if the contribution is given to you in the form of a trust or challenge grant? It is far better to be able to say, "We've thought of that, and while that could be one avenue toward accomplishing our goal, here are the drawbacks that we foresee if we proceed that way . . . " than, "I never thought of that. I guess we could give it a try." Whenever possible, approach the potential donor with a solid and detailed primary proposal in mind, but with several other equally well worked out scenarios just in case the conversation goes in a direction that you do not expect. It often will.

Not Listening Carefully

As advocates for our individual areas, we are sometimes so fixated on our own needs and programs that we fail to listen to the verbal cues that a potential donor provides to us. You may approach a prospect who graduated with a degree in science from your institution, had a distinguished career in medicine, and previously supported a number of small science projects. This person seems to be a logical candidate to fund a new lab or underwrite a new science center at your institution, but perhaps all the donor wishes to speak about is a spouse's interest in the arts or a newfound commitment to ethical issues. Failure to comprehend that this individual's priorities have changed can lead to a situation in which you repeatedly return to a topic that the potential donor has already set aside. Not listening carefully enough to a donor can also mean missing the key phrases that motivate this particular individual.

To Avoid This Mistake

Remember that you are meeting with the prospective donor to learn about his or her interests and to help this person accomplish something that would lead to his or her personal satisfaction. Your task is not to sell a preconceived product that the potential donor will have no role in shaping and no pride in making succeed. Keep alert to issues that the donor returns to and make a mental note of what aspects of your discussion he or she tends not to mention, describes differently from how you have presented them, or simply does not respond to with enthusiasm. Repeat several of the individual's key phrases and priorities in order to make sure that you understand them. Write them down. If you notice, for example, that the potential donor continually directs the conversation toward the life-changing nature of the courses that he or she took in an area completely different from your own, this may be a signal that the person's interests have changed. The donor may be more responsive to a proposal advanced by a different discipline. Listen carefully. Try to understand as much as possible of the prospect's concern. Afterwards talk privately and candidly with a development officer about possibly putting the chair of a more appropriate department in touch with the candidate. Handing off a prospective donor in this way may help you build good relationships with your colleagues elsewhere in the institution, reward you when they know of prospective donors interested in your area, and prevent your institution from alienating an important contact who has developed new interests and areas of philanthropic concern.

Not Following Through

There are times when an institution is so excited about receiving a major gift and so focused on the new activity, building, or scholarship resulting from it that it tends to forget the person who made it all possible: the donor. After having been the center of attention while the institution was trying to obtain the gift, donors sometimes feel forgotten once the contribution has actually been made. They learn about new developments at your institution only from the newspaper. They fail to receive invitations to important campus events associated with their contribution. And sometimes they simply become annoyed because, after weeks or months of frequent contact, the phone-calls and visits stop. Not following through adequately after a gift has been made can turn a friend of your institution into one of its most bitter opponents. It can also cost you other fundraising prospects in the future.

To Avoid This Mistake

Keep in mind that the stewardship of a gift is as important as obtaining the gift itself. Excellent stewardship of gifts leads to further gifts from the original donors or from their friends and associates. As a department chair, you are in the perfect position to steward a gift in the best possible manner. Because you have fewer major contributors to track than any of the major gift officers in the development office, you can handle things much more personally—with a visit or an extended phone call—than many of the professional fundraisers. You have the information at your fingertips to tell the donor what he or she really wants to know: the lasting impact of their gift on the lives of the students and faculty members of your department. It should be your role, therefore, every time an activity occurs on campus that is in any way connected to this gift, to be sure that the donor is contacted, informed well in advance of what will occur, and invited to participate in an appropriate way. As a department chair, you are used to being an advocate for your discipline. Part of this advocacy must now include remembering the needs of your donors as well.

Conclusion

Like so many other aspects of departmental administration, fundraising is a skill that gets easier the more that it is practiced. Very few academic administrators come to their profession with formal academic training in philanthropy. Fundraising is something that most of us learn on the job. If you have not yet had any significant prior exposure to fundraising, contact your development office and ask if they offer formal training to people like you who want to do more for the institution. Offer to tag along with a more experienced fundraiser on a call to a prospective donor in order to get the feel of how it is done. Ask the alumni office for the names of graduates who may have expressed an interest in remaining involved with your area. Check with the development office to make sure that these individuals are not already being cultivated elsewhere at your institution and, if not, make some phone calls to talk with them about how they may be able to assist your department in a way that they would find personally satisfying. Understand that many people will volunteer their time before they consider contributing their money. Start out small and avoid the five common mistakes outlined in this chapter, and you will be on your way to successful fundraising for both your institution and your department.

18

What Every Department Chair Needs to Know About Budgeting

The responsibilities that department chairs may be assigned in the area of budgeting can vary widely. While some chairs serve as the primary budgetary authority for their units and take full responsibility for every expenditure, other chairs (particularly those in smaller departments or at smaller institutions) have little direct authority in this area. They may simply track the expenses incurred by the members of their faculty, or, in certain cases, serve as a conduit for budgetary information, while the actual decisions are made at other levels of the institution. Nevertheless, despite the level of budgetary authority you may have as a chair, you will perform your responsibilities better if you understand at least certain aspects of how college and university budgeting tends to be done, why decisions are made as they are, and how this knowledge can best serve your discipline and its constituents.

While it is possible to divide the budgetary process into any number of different components, for simplicity's sake it is useful for chairs to think of budgeting as having two primary parts: the planning phase and the implementation phase. The planning phase consists of all of those activities—beginning a year or more before the onset of an institution's fiscal year—by which anticipated sources of income are identified and initial strategies for allocation and expenditure are developed. The implementation phase occurs during the fiscal year itself (when actual expenditures are made and allocations are modified, as necessary, either within or among budgetary units) and concludes when the institution's budget is formally audited by an external, objective agency. Because the chair's role in these two budgetary phases is likely to be significantly different, it is useful to explore each of them individually.

The Planning Phase

During the planning phase of budgeting, goals are set for the institution's income and expenditures for a pre-determined period, usually a *fiscal year.* A fiscal year is any regular twelve-month period over which an institution plans and tracks the use of its funds. While for some institutions, fiscal years are identical to calendar years, most institutions find that some other twelve-month division—such as July 1 through the following June 30—fits their academic calendars, state legislative cycles, and student enrollment habits better. It is traditional to denote a fiscal year through the abbreviation FY, followed by two or four digits indicating the *calendar year* in which the fiscal year *ends*. Thus, most institutions use the designation FY15 or FY2015 to indicate a fiscal year that begins in 2014, but concludes on a predetermined date in the year 2015. Nearly every state institution and many private institutions require that budgets be closed out in each fiscal year. That is to say, funds and deficits cannot be carried over from one fiscal year to the next. In these systems, on the last day of the fiscal year, all unexpended monies must be spent and all unreconciled deficits must be covered. This practice leads to the possibility of "year-end funds" that will be addressed later.

In planning for the budget of each fiscal year, institutions have several options. They may practice *zero-base budgeting*, in which all budgetary sources and allocations are reestablished every time that a new budget is set, or they may practice some form of *historical budgeting*, in which a past record of income and expenditures is used to help plan for the future. The advantages of zero-base budgeting are that it is extremely flexible, helps free institutions from budget patterns that no longer make sense, and causes every single goal in the budget to be developed with a clear and defensible rationale. The disadvantages to this system are that it is extremely time-intensive, can exacerbate divisiveness within an institution, and frequently does not result in budgets that are terribly different from a more historically based approach. The advantages of historical budgeting are that it is quicker to implement, gives institutions an initial plan that they can adjust according to their needs, and has the merit of having been tested by the experience of previous years. The disadvantages of this system result from the practice of having each year's budget based (at least initially) on that which was used the previous year. As a result, it can be extremely difficult to change poor practices that are well entrenched; it is also relatively easy to overlook poor budgetary plans since every category of income and expenditure tends not to be justified each time the budget is set.

At most institutions, the budget planning process tends to be hierarchical. That is to say, departments submit plans to colleges, colleges to the university, and the university to the university system. Even at small institutions, private colleges, and autonomous state institutions the budgetary planning process, while it may differ in specific details from the structure just outlined, follows some sort of hierarchical design: Plans and proposals move from smaller units to larger units (bottom to top); budgetary decisions are passed from larger units to smaller units (top to bottom). The precise manner in which your department will be asked to submit its plan to your division, college, or institution is likely to be different from that expected of your colleague at another institution. Some colleges have established formats for budget requests; others do so quite informally. ("Get me a list of your most critical needs for the coming year by [DATE].") Some institutions have formal budget hearings at which proposals for the coming fiscal year are made, discussed, and debated before the budget is finally set. Others leave this process to a committee, to the president's cabinet, or even, at certain institutions, to the discretion of the chief financial officer.

Regardless of the specific planning process in place at your institution, there are certain principles to keep in mind as you prepare your budget proposals each year:

Tie All Requests to Your Institution's Strategic Plan

The general rule that "at institutions with well-designed strategic plans, the budget is guided by the plan; at institutions without well-designed strategic plans, the budget *is* the plan" proves itself each year during the planning process. A request for an expenditure that is not supported by planning and data is unlikely to be taken seriously by the individuals making decisions at your college or university. *Every* budgetary request should be tied convincingly to the fulfillment of the strategic plan.

All Requests Should Have a Clear Priority Order Based on the Institution's Mission and Plan

Budgetary requests that are not made in a clear and compelling order based on established institutional values are mere "wish lists" that will ultimately prove ineffective. If a specific item must appear in a priority order that may initially surprise a reader, then that item should be given more extensive and compelling justification. This will help individuals who are unfamiliar with your discipline understand why that item serves to advance the fundamental mission of your college and university. For instance, if you are requesting research equipment at an institution that has just reaffirmed a "Teaching First" philosophy in its mission statement and strategic plan, you may need to explain that the primary purpose of this equipment will be pedagogical, permitting a type of student-directed experiential learning that is not now possible.

Keep in Mind That Budgets Have Two Components: Income and Expenditure

Most department chairs are fairly good at recognizing where money needs to be spent in their disciplines; relatively few chairs are equally knowledgeable about how that money is to be raised. Chairs weaken their cases considerably in making budgetary proposals that appear to imply that additional sources of funding will emerge if they merely state their needs in sufficiently compelling terms. They need also to be aware that, for every additional dollar allocated in one area, a different need of the institution will receive less funding. Is there a way, therefore, for your department to come up with a funding source for some or all of the money requested for an item? Can a fee be established, admission charged for a popular departmental event, external donations be solicited, a foundation be approached for seed money, or existing funds be redirected from a low-priority item in your department to this new higher priority? As an exercise, you might try redirecting on paper 5% of your operating budget to give more funding to the highest priorities of your discipline. You may be surprised to discover what you can do internally simply by refocusing your priorities.

Be Aware of the Difference Between One-Year Expenditures and Continuous Expenditures

Not all spending is alike. An extra piece of equipment that is purchased affects a single year's budget. A new faculty line, a permanent increase in scholarship aid, or the start of a distinguished lecture series requires ongoing support year after year. A surprising number of academics confuse these two types of expenditures, saying things like "Well, we just won't get the new copier next year and use that money to expand our part-time position to full-time." As a chair, you cannot afford to make this type of mistake. At best, you will undermine your credibility with others at your institution who deal with budgeting on a daily basis. At worst, you may inadvertently commit your department and institution to an ongoing expense that cannot be sustained.

The Implementation Phase

Once budgets have been set for a fiscal year, the department chair's duties largely shift from planning what income and expenditures *should* be made to those costs and allocations that actually *are* made within the discipline. Each institution has its own system for tracking the budgetary activity of its departments. At most institutions, this information is available electronically and is updated continually; at some institutions, paper budgetary statements are still sent, listing income, transfers, and expenditures according to each budgetary category.

Object Codes

The most common system used for tracking activity within budgets is to tie each transaction to a specific *object code* or category that indicates the precise location and type of transaction that has occurred. Institutional systems of object codes vary from the mildly to the extraordinarily complex, depending on the nature of the institution, its organizational structure, and the manner in which it is following the practices required by its board of accounting standards (the Governmental Accounting Standards Board or GASB for public institutions and the Financial Accounting Standards Board or FASB for private institutions). In most cases, the object codes used by institutions are nine or more digits long, with each digit or group of digits providing such information as the specific campus on which the transaction took place (in multi-campus systems), the source of funding (e.g., education and general, foundation, and sponsored programs), the unit responsible for the transaction (e.g., college, division, department, or program), and the precise nature of the income, transfer, or expenditure. This can include a vast array of types such as full-time salaries, part-time salaries, casual labor, benefits, postage, telephone: local, telephone: toll, subscriptions, memberships, equipment over a certain amount, equipment under a certain amount, travel, food, lodging, and office supplies.

Transferring Funds

Since institutions almost always allow at least some types of transfer among these various funds, your general approach should be—unless otherwise instructed by your business office—to tie each transaction as closely as possible to its *actual* object code, not simply to any account that happens to have sufficient funding remaining. For instance, in a year where your department's small equipment account has already been depleted, you may be tempted to fund the purchase of an additional item of small equipment through your department's postage account or account for supplies and expenses. Nevertheless, it is almost always desirable—and at many institutions it is required—for you to fund the purchase from the proper account, even though it is depleted, and then to submit a one-year transfer of funds from another account to cover that expense. Not only does this procedure make it much easier for departmental accounts to be reconciled and audited, it also provides you with a far more realistic picture of your needs when you review each budget year. If you notice that you are transferring funds from operating supplies to small equipment several years in a row, you may decide that it is preferable to realign these accounts permanently. On the other hand, if you are chronically short of funds in one account and must repeatedly cover those expenditures by piecing together remaining bits from several accounts, you may use this as additional support for a request that the underfunded account be increased by your institution.

Transfers among certain accounts may not be possible at your institution. There may be restrictions on transfers between personal services accounts (i.e., accounts used to pay for salaries and benefits) and operating supplies accounts that limit whether you can transfer unexpended salary funding to such accounts as travel, photocopying, and equipment. Other institutions may have restrictions on whether institutional funds (the type of accounts usually known as "Education and General Funds") may be used for such purchases as student travel, entertainment, or food and alcoholic beverages. Your institution's business office or chief financial officer can give you an overview of the restrictions that may be in place in your system. In cases in which restrictions on transfers or expenditures exist, be sure to ask about *permissible* ways to achieve your ultimate goal. Restrictions on institutional funds may not apply, for instance, to funds overseen by a college's foundation. It is possible that the foundation may either be willing to cover the cost itself or to "swap" a cost with you, paying for some item or activity that is permissible for them while you absorb an equivalent expense that they were going to pay but which your institution would allow to be charged to your department. In other cases, it may not be possible to transfer the *funds* in one direction, while it is perfectly permissible to transfer the *cost* in the other direction. It may be a long while for you to discover all the intricacies of your institution's operating procedures in terms of its budget. The basic point is simply not to assume that there is only one way of accomplishing a budgetary goal. If you are informed that a certain type of purchase or transfer is not allowed, be flexible in your response. Say something like, "Well, this is essentially what I need to do. What are the ways you can explore with me that would allow me to accomplish that same goal within our existing operating procedure?"

Salary Savings

Unexpended funds on salary lines are commonly referred to as *salary savings*. Salary savings may occur in a number of different ways. For example, if a faculty member is earning $80,000 and either retires or otherwise leaves the institution, a replacement hired for $50,000 results in a salary savings of $30,000. (The resulting savings in benefits can make the actual gain somewhat higher.) That $30,000 in savings is of great interest to the institution since it is continuing money rather than a one-time expenditure—it is money that remains in the budget year after year, even increasing in years when raises are allocated. For this reason, it is likely that your institution has standard procedures for how salary savings are allocated. They may revert to the general budget to aid the "bottom line," they may be absorbed by the upper administration (presidents, provosts, and deans frequently combine pools of salary savings to create new positions), or they may remain with the units that generated them. Whenever you are replacing an individual in your department and salary savings are likely to result, you should always inquire about the institution's plans for those funds. If the amount is large and your department is severely understaffed, you might inquire into the possibility of splitting one faculty line into two or using the savings for an additional lab assistant, student worker, or secretarial support. If the amount is small, you might inquire into the possibility of shifting the savings into a permanent increase for one of your accounts that you frequently deplete early in the fiscal year. You should by no means expect that you will be successful every time that you make one of these requests. Nevertheless, success will be all but impossible if you do not approach each opportunity with a clear and compelling plan.

Shadow Budget

No matter how much budgetary information your institution provides, most department chairs find it useful to maintain their own *shadow budget* in an electronic spreadsheet. Items are occasionally coded incorrectly at other levels of an institution, and shadow budgets can help you detect discrepancies when you are either charged for something that should have been charged to a different unit or not credited with funding that should properly be yours. It is often the case, too, that official institutional budget reports lag actual activity by a substantial period. Preserving records in a shadow budget prevents you from accidentally spending the same money more than once, resulting in a deficit at the end of the year. You can think of your shadow budget as something similar to the check record you keep in your checkbook: Reconciling this record with your bank statement helps you spot errors and avoid overdrawing your account. It also assists you in identifying funds that you have already encumbered or promised to use for a particular purpose.

On both your shadow budget and official budget one figure that you will wish to track is the percentage of each account expended versus the percentage of the fiscal year expended. If your institution does not calculate this ratio for you, it is easy to set up a spreadsheet formula that does so. For instance:

(AMOUNT EXPENDED ÷ ORIGINAL AMOUNT) x 100 = the percentage of that account expended to date

(DAY WITHIN FISCAL YEAR ÷ 365) x 100 = the percentage of the fiscal year that has passed to date.

After you have tracked this information for several years, you will learn the particular budgetary patterns and rhythms of your department, thus understanding the red flags to watch for in your budget. Thus, an account that is 98% expended with only 35% of the academic year gone may or may not be an area of concern. This could be an equipment account that only supports one or two purchases each year or the account could cover the type of supplies or services that are regularly needed at the start of the academic year, but rarely again afterwards. On the other hand, a photocopying account that is depleted too rapidly may leave your department vulnerable when final exams must be copied at the end of the semester. Your own familiarity with the needs of your discipline, coupled with a healthy dose of common sense, will guide you in determining which percentages are problematic and which are not. (You may need to explain your department's spending patterns to budget officers outside of your department who may not know your discipline's rhythms as well as you do.)

Year-End Money

One aspect of academic spending patterns that may occur at your institution—and that you may need to plan for—is the phenomenon of *year-end money.* Year-end money occurs when institutions need to "zero out" their budgets at the end of each fiscal year, covering all deficits and depleting all other accounts. In years where there is funding remaining in an institution's budget at the end of the year, it may be required to spend it in order to bring its books to a zero balance. There are frequently restrictions on *what* may be purchased with year-end money—supplies, but not equipment, or equipment only if it has been priced according to a preexisting contract— and you will need to know what these limitations are at your institution. But the possibility of year-end funding can, if it is permitted, be an important part of your funding strategy. You may be able to stock up on supplies at the end of a fiscal year, thus transferring funds from operating supplies to another critical area during the new fiscal year. You may be able to purchase a piece of equipment that exceeds the equipment budget of your individual department, pooling your own funds with year-end money from other areas.

Cost Accounting

Another budgetary item that you may wish to track is your unit's cost vis-à-vis other departments at your institution and other similar departments at other institutions. How much does it cost to produce, for instance, one student credit hour of instruction in your discipline at your institution compared with similar programs at other institutions? Frequently, the business office of an institution has a system already in place to calculate these figures. If your institution does not do so, you can determine at least a crude approximation of cost by adding all of your department's expenditures in salaries, benefits, and all categories of operating expenses (being sure to include travel funding and other accounts that may not be controlled within your department itself) and dividing that figure by the number of student credit hours your discipline produces in the same fiscal period. The reason why the resulting figure is crude is that it does not account for overhead and other institutional expenses, such as your department's share of the salaries paid to your president, provost, and dean as well as librarians, support staff outside your department, or the registrar. On the other hand, provided that you calculate rates for other departments in precisely the same way, you will get a good general sense of how expensive your program is to maintain. If you discover that it costs significantly less to produce one student credit hour in your department than it does in other departments at your institution or in similar disciplines at other institutions, you may be able to use this information to argue for your program's efficiency and sustainability. If you find that your costs are much higher, you can be proactive in identifying some of the actions that you can take internally to help reduce those costs. In either case, this type of very basic *cost accounting* can only be to the benefit of your institution. You might even begin using it to determine the cost-benefit ratio of making certain types of equipment purchases.

There is certainly no need for every department chair to become an accountant or to master every detail of an institution's fiscal procedure. The more you do understand about budgeting, however, the better you will be able to help your program tie resources to priorities and to make its most compelling case for institutional support.

Five Case Studies in Budgeting

One of the most effective tools department chairs have for improving their skills at making decisions and setting priorities is the consideration of case studies. Case studies compel us to make decisions, choose among various competing "right" decisions, and express our reasons for following a particular plan of action. The following five case studies for department chairs all deal with various aspects of budgeting.

Many of the issues involved in budgeting are really questions about setting priorities. These case studies do not present right or wrong answers, merely difficult choices that you may handle differently from another chair because of your individual leadership style and your institution's unique situation. Try discussing these case studies with other chairs at your institution to see how they might handle the various challenges outlined below.

Case Study 1: Past Practice Versus the Strategic Plan

You chair the Department of Aeronautics and Aerobics, a department that contains two largely independent subdisciplines. Both areas, aeronautics and aerobics, have roughly the same number of faculty members, majors, and student credit-hour production. Neither area has been particularly active in securing external funding and, as a result, both depend almost exclusively on the annual budget assigned by your central administration. Before your arrival as chair, aeronautics and aerobics were independent departments, with the aerobics program funded at a significantly higher level than the aeronautics program. After reviewing the budget, you have come to believe that aerobics has been over-funded while aeronautics has been under-funded. Your attempts to provide greater equity in funding have met with resistance from faculty members in aerobics who have come to expect high levels of institutional support for travel and equipment. Recently, however, your institution's new strategic plan has declared that aerobics will be a major focal point for the university, while you cannot find that aeronautics has a direct and obvious tie to the strategic plan. The bud-

Case Study 4: Transfers in a Tight Budget

The fiscal year has just begun and you, as department chair, are meeting with your dean to discuss priorities for the coming year. Your dean has asked you whether you might want to transfer funds among your existing accounts in order to meet your department's needs more efficiently. You know that any one of your non-personal services accounts could use help, but you're not sure where to get it. For instance, you could transfer funds out of your equipment account and hope to buy any new equipment with funding that may become available at the end of the year when the budget is closed out. On the other hand, relying on yearend funding is rather risky, and you are badly in need of several major equipment upgrades. You could transfer funds out of your travel account, but you have a large number of younger faculty members who desperately need to travel for professional development. You could transfer money out of your supplies account, but you barely made it through last year because of the high cost of toner, paper, and other routine expenses.

- What additional information do you need in order to clarify your priorities?

- Since you seem to be stretched thin in every category, can you think of a reason why you might still want to transfer funding and thus strain one of your accounts even further?

- How do you go about getting your faculty members to be more proactive in controlling costs and thus making better use of the budget that you have?

- Does it ever make sense to defer equipment purchases or faculty travel from one year to the next?

- What strategies can you suggest for not just making it through the year, but for making your department stronger for the future?

Case Study 5: The Dean's Great News

While attending a faculty meeting in your department, the dean has just announced "great news": For next year, your travel budget will be increased $10,000 because of the dean's longstanding commitment to faculty development. As soon as the dean leaves, however, an argument breaks out among your faculty members about how this money should be spent. Carla

Marx wants all faculty members in the department to benefit equally. Since your department has 25 members, she suggests that each faculty member be given an additional $400 travel allowance. M.N.S. Greeze rejects this idea, saying that those faculty members who are more active professionally should receive more money. It doesn't make sense, he argues, for people who haven't been going to conferences or presenting papers to receive the same increase as "serious scholars" like himself who have long been nationally known. Barry Jung counters by saying that this new funding is just the thing to help junior faculty members like himself get tenured and promoted. He argues that the $10,000 be set aside for the development of newer faculty members. May X. Plode attempts to restore peace in the department by suggesting that a new faculty committee be formed which would allocate the new money on the basis of travel proposals submitted by faculty members. Secretly, you wish that the dean had told you about the new money privately since faculty travel is, in your opinion, not your department's greatest need.

- How do you go about weighing the four competing proposals suggested by members of your department? Is there a fifth, better idea?

- Is there any one of the four proposals that makes more sense than the others?

- In light of your own feeling that travel is not your department's greatest need (and in light of your dean's "longstanding commitment to faculty development"), has the dean left you any options for finding common ground?

19

Finding Your Administrative Style

Department chairs do not come in just one size, shape, or personality type. That degree of diversity is actually a very good thing, since different departments and different institutions need different types of administrators to achieve the various missions they have set for themselves. In fact, different departments and different institutions need different types of department chairs at different *times* in their developments. For instance, a relatively new department might need someone who is skilled as a creator. More established departments might need someone who has more expertise as a builder, sustainer, or consolidator. Departments that have grown stale might need a change agent. Units that have been through chaos or turmoil might need a calming influence or a counselor. And there are many other types of administrators, all of whom have their proper places in different types of units at different times during their development.

As a department chair, you may find a good deal of relief in the knowledge that academic administrators do not all have to be alike. It is not at all an unusual phenomenon for a chair to think that *all the other chairs* at his or her institution are more gregarious, detail-oriented, imaginative, forceful, well-organized, or dynamic than he or she is. Nevertheless, the fact of the matter is that, despite what you may think and what all the self-appointed experts may tell you, *there is no single type of personality or administrative style that makes for a perfect department chair.* Nearly *any* sort of person can be a successful chair, as long as you know what it is you need to do and who you are.

So, who are you?

Each of us comes to our administrative positions with varying degrees of self-knowledge, but there are a number of things that you can do—in fact, that you *need* to do—in order to discover what your own administrative style tends to be, to develop an approach to departmental management that builds on the strengths of that style, and to create a departmental team in which your weaknesses (and we all have them) are counter-balanced by someone else's unique strengths. The first thing you need to do is to learn a few rules.

Rule #1: You Can Only Lead Others If You Know Where You're Going

Now, this first rule may seem absurdly self-evident. How, after all, can you lead anyone anywhere if you have only the vaguest notion where it is you wish to lead? When we are planning a trip, we do not immediately leave the house and walk off "in all directions at once," as the old saying goes. Any trip that sets out without a destination ends up being merely a stroll. That kind of aimless wandering can be good exercise, and we might enjoy it as a pastime, but it is hardly the sort of *intentional* model that we should borrow for good departmental administration. As the aphorist Doug Horton has said, "If you don't know where you're going, any road will take you there." In other words, as effective chairs, we have to know our objectives. Once we do, we can sit down and map out the various ways to reach those objectives.

To return to the image of planning a trip for a moment, when we are going somewhere at some distance from home, we tend to ask ourselves various questions. Is time of the essence so that we should seek the most direct route possible? Are we more interested in scenery and adventure along the way? Is it likely that we will have to make detours once we have started, with the result that it is prudent to have several contingency plans? These are similar to the questions that we must ask ourselves as department chairs. Where is it that our disciplines need to go? Can we get there rapidly or will there have to be time for resources to be obtained and for people to adjust to new ideas? What aspects of my plan is it best to delegate to others, even if that means that what results will not be precisely as I envisioned? What sort of contingency plans will I need for those situations when, inevitably, events do not develop as smoothly as I had intended? Your department will benefit immeasurably from this sort of planning. In the worst of scenarios, if you don't have any clear-cut notion of what it is that your department can achieve (either in the short term or in the distant future), then you are likely to convey to your faculty members merely a sense of drift or indecision. They will become frustrated, and their morale will plummet. Their distress will be caused by insufficient attention being paid to . . .

Rule #2: Most Faculty Members Would Rather Feel That the Department is Moving in the Wrong Direction Than Feel That It Is Moving in No Direction at All

The first two rules of finding your administrative style probably represent thoughts that you have had many times since you first learned that you would be chairing your department. On the other hand, the *corollaries* to Rule #1 and Rule #2 tend to be far less self-evident to most administrators.

Rule #3: You Can Only Tell How to Get Where You're Going If You Know Where You Already Are

Rule #4: You Only Really Know *Where* You Are if You're Honest With Yourself About *Who* You Are

Let's return to our metaphor of the trip. Just as a map will do you relatively little good unless you know where your current position is on the map, so is it difficult to take your department anywhere unless you know its current position, its budget, its status within your institution, its role in the strategic plan of your college or university, and its overall history including producing majors, bringing in grants and sponsored programs, conducting research, generating student credit hours, and serving other disciplines. Similarly, it is difficult to get anywhere—even with the best of maps and a thorough knowledge of your current position—if you haven't taken stock of the means of transportation available to you. Will you walk, drive, sail, or fly? If you don't know what type of vehicle you have (or if you don't even know whether you *have* a vehicle available), you're not going to get very far. Again, it is much the same with departmental leadership. If you don't take stock of your strengths and weaknesses, your preferences and strong dislikes, you won't take your department very far, and you'll probably end up annoying yourself and your faculty in the process.

Determining Your Administrative Style

The path to self-knowledge can involve some pretty serious business, and it has been the province of philosophers for nearly as long as philosophy has existed. For instance, in ancient Greece, the Delphic doctrine of "Know thyself," often attributed to Thales of Miletus, was usually interpreted as meaning "Know your limits." In chapter 12, verse 4 of the Dhammapada, it says, "Self is the lord of self, who else could be the lord? With oneself well trained, a person finds a master such as few can find." And one of Muhammad's aphorisms that appears in the hadith concludes, "He who knows his self knows his Lord." In other words, the difficult part is that knowledge of who one is has to include knowledge of one's imperfections, of the fact that one is *not* always the lord and master of every situation. And coming face-to-face with one's flaws can be mighty unpleasant, even if it *is* a time-honored tradition.

Personality Assessment Tools

So, how can you best attain this difficult and sometimes painful knowledge of who you are and what self-awareness can mean for your personal administrative style? One approach that many department chairs have found useful is to begin with one of the many personality type inventories that are currently available. These "pre-packaged" inventories have a great deal of research and literature behind them, provide results that are widely recognized even outside your institution, and offer a good beginning for administrators who want a candid external opinion of certain aspects of their personalities. A few of the more common personality tools and inventories include:

- *The Myers-Briggs Type Indicator®,* or MBTI, probably the most famous and widely used of the personality assessments currently available. The MBTI dates back to the 1940s when Katharine Briggs and her daughter, Isabel Briggs Myers, began exploring ways of putting central concepts of the psychologist Carl Jung (1875–1961) into a format that ordinary people—particularly employers and prospective employers—could readily use and understand. The MBTI assigns each individual four letters, indicating which of two traits among four pairs a person appears to possess in greater abundance. The four pairs and their key letters are: Extroversion/Introversion (E/I), Sensing/iNtuition (S/N), Thinking/Feeling (T/F), and Judging/Perceiving (J/P). After the MBTI is scored, the person taking it receives a four-letter code (such as INTJ or ESFP) that provides a short-hand summary of his or her dominant quality in each of the four pairs. The MBTI is a registered trademark of Consulting Psychologist Press, Inc., which publishes and distributes instruments for taking and scoring the inventory.

- *The Keirsey Temperament Sorter®* (http://www.keirsey.com) is an online personality inventory that classifies those taking it by four major tem-

peraments: Rationals, Idealists, Artisans, and Guardians. These four
temperaments can then be then sub-divided into sixteen "role variants":
Composer, Crafter, Performer, Promoter, Protector, Inspector,
Provider, Supervisor, Healer, Counselor, Champion, Teacher, Architect,
Mastermind, Inventor, and Field Marshal. One then emerges from the
test with a brief identifier (such as Guardian Inspector or Idealist
Counselor) that provides guidance into one's temperament and one's
style of relating to others.

- *The DiSC Personal Profile®* is based on the work of William Moulton
  Marston (1893–1947), the psychologist who is probably most famous
  for his creation of the character Wonder Woman. The DiSC inventory
  provides each person with scores in four central areas known as "styles
  factors"—Dominance, Influence, Steadiness, Conscientiousness—and
  then indicates more precisely which personality pattern the taker tends
  to exhibit. The sixteen personality patterns assigned by the DiSC
  Personal Profile are Developer, Result Oriented, Inspirational,
  Creative, Promoter, Persuader, Counselor, Appraiser, Specialist,
  Achiever, Agent, Investigator, Objective Thinker, Perfectionist,
  Practitioner, and Pure Style DiSC. The DiSC personality test is available either online (http://www.discprofile.com) or in paper format, is
  backed by years of extensive research, and provides a great deal of information about using one's personality style to meet the needs and
  strengths of others.

One instrument that department chairs are sometimes tempted to use,
but that is really not suitable for this purpose, is The Minnesota Multiphasic
Personality Inventory® (MMPI). The MMPI was developed at the
University of Minnesota in the 1930s, thoroughly revised in 1989, and is
not particularly adaptable to simple self-testing and analysis of results. As a
pathology-oriented inventory, it is far more useful in detecting severe psychological aberrations than for common workplace personality issues, and
its results should *always* be interpreted by a trained professional. (In fact,
many department chairs may not be aware that the MMPI actually requires
a clinical license for purchase.)

An important proviso to keep in mind when using any of these personality inventories is that they indicate only where your individual personality
traits tend to lie along a spectrum; they do *not*—and never can—tell you
whether you adhere to some "perfect personality type for department

chairs." There simply is no such perfect type. You may hear it said that "all academic administrators need to be ENTJ leaders" or that "introverts have no business leading an academic unit" or that the "best department chairs are Idealist/Champions." All of these generalizations are really nonsense. Aside from misinterpreting what the introversion/extroversion scales of personality tests actually indicate—the taker's tendency either to "think out loud" or to process information internally, to seek personal renewal in public settings or in quiet and privacy—they provide extremely little insight into the degree of one's "people skills" or whether one enjoys the company of others. Blanket statements of this kind miss the fact that all *types* of people are successful as administrators. Just remember that the point of taking the test is not to determine *whether* one can chair a department, but rather to gain a clearer image of one's own personality type in order to be able to balance it better with those having *other* dominant traits on committees and in other working relationships. Also, by knowing how you tend to approach situations, you'll find that you're more aware of the working styles of others and can adapt your strategies accordingly.

Finding Your Administrative Style Using Your Own Inventory

While, as we have seen, well-established personality inventories have the advantage of relying on significant research providing widely-recognized results, they also have several major disadvantages. They are not specifically focused on the needs and duties of college administrators. Moreover, you gain more from them only if you have their results interpreted by trained professionals. Finally, even when you do go over their results with a trained (and, at times expensive) consultant, you still may not end up with the type of information on which you can readily act to improve your departmental leadership.

A second possibility for finding your administrative style, therefore, would be to forego these prepackaged personality inventories by (or, at least, to supplement them with) taking a highly focused, nonscientific, very individualistic inventory of your own. Begin by asking yourself, as candidly as possible, a series of questions directly related to your job and its responsibilities.

- What is your greatest strength that you bring to your administrative position?

- What is your greatest weakness?

- Which aspects of your position give you the greatest personal satisfaction when you do them well?

- Which aspects of your position are you willing to tolerate because they "go with the territory," even though they provide you with relatively little personal satisfaction?

- If you could hand off three of your regularly occurring tasks and never do them again, what would they be?

- If you were compelled to take one aspect of your current work and do it all day long, week in and week out, which one would you choose?

To get started in making this sort of personal assessment, it might be helpful for you to take the following informal test. Look over the list of the following 20 activities that a department chair may be required to do, and then number them from 1 to 20 on the basis of which of them you would *rather* do. Let #1 indicate the activity that you find most personally interesting, satisfying, and productive. (Answer honestly, not on the basis of how you think you *ought* to answer or how others might *want* you to answer.) Let #20 indicate the activity that, all things being equal, you would do, although you would really prefer *not* to. To make it easy to keep track of the twenty activities as you rank them, each of them has been assigned a unique letter. Would of the following activities would you prefer to do?

A) Speak in person with the parent of a student who is having a problem in one of the courses offered by your department

B) Write a letter to the alumni of your program, outlining some of the plans you have for your department over the next several years

C) Speak to a group of 300 prospective students about the courses offered by your department and the career opportunities available in your field

D) Write a report for the chief academic officer setting new learning goals based on data you've seen that indicate certain areas where students have had difficulty in your discipline for the past several years

E) Block out several hours of quiet time in your schedule so that you can review and reconcile the expenditures made in your department over the past year

F)   Present ideas at a small faculty gathering about how the institution's new strategic plan might be implemented in your area

G)   Answer an email sent to you by another department chair who is criticizing the section size that has been common in your department's courses since you have been chair

H)   Begin outlining and writing an academic article in your discipline

I)   Prepare a spreadsheet to help you improve the course rotation in your department

J)   Attend a committee meeting outside of your discipline

K)   Write a position description for a new faculty line in your department, basing your description on specific curricular weaknesses cited by a discipline-specific accreditation report, alumni surveys, and departmental exit exams

L)   Meet with the dean (or the president of your institution) in response to his or her request to go over some particular issue or problem with you, even though you will not learn the nature of the issue until the meeting occurs

M)   Answer a phone call from a parent who is concerned about remarks made by a lecturer you had recently invited to campus

N)   Write a survey of recent scholarship done by members of your department for publication in the newsletter of a local service group (Rotary, Kiwanis, Lions, Optimists Club, or similar organization)

O)   Polish the current draft of an academic article that you have nearly completed for publication

P)   Prepare your budget proposal for the coming year

Q)   Conduct the annual in-person review session with a faculty member in your discipline

R)   Start developing a draft proposal for a new academic program in which your department will play a lead role

S)   Represent your department at a full meeting of your Board of Regents or Trustees

T) Serve on a panel that will interpret the likely effect a new state law will have on the General Education program offered by your institution

Once you have organized your list of all twenty activities into the best order that you can determine, with those duties that you would most enjoy doing at the top and those that you would really prefer not to do at the bottom, look at your top five activities and then look at your bottom five activities. Do you notice any overall patterns in either of these groups? In other words, do you tend to favor activities in which you:

- Deal more with *"the big picture"* (B, D, F, K, P, R, S) or with *particular details* of day-to-day academic administration (A, E, G, I, L, M, N, Q)

- Spend time developing a *plan for a new activity* (B, D, H, K, P, R) or *implement plans* that are already made (C, F, G, I, N, Q, T)

- Work with others through *direct, face-to-face communication* (A, C, F, J, L, Q, S, T) or more *indirect forms of communication* (B, D, G, H, I, K, M, N, O, P, R)

- Interact with *large groups* (C, J, S, T) or *small groups* (A, D, F, G, L, M, Q)

- Focus your attention on *those to whom you report* (D, L, S, T) or *those who report to you* (A, B, C, F, M, Q)

- Start endeavors from the very *beginning* (B, D, H, I, K, P, R) or deal with matters that are already well *under way* (E, G, J, N, O, Q, T)

- Take the *initiative for action* (B, H, R) or *react to the needs* of others (A, G, J, L, N, Q, T)

- *Analyze information*, moving from *concept to detail* (D, F, H, K, P, R) or *synthesize* information, moving from *detail to concept* (B, I, T)

You are unlikely to discover patterns in your responses that apply to all eight of these major differences in administrative style. Nevertheless, you should find at least two or three of these pairs in which you can begin to detect a clear difference in administrative preference. For instance, you may discover that your style is to maintain a focus on "the big picture," while you also prefer direct, face-to-face communication with smaller groups. Or you may discover that your attention tends to be directed more toward those to whom you report, while you also prefer to react to the needs of others and to move from detail to concept. As in the case of the nationally normed personality inventories mentioned earlier, there are *no right and no wrong answers* to this informal personal inventory. What it will tell you is *what* your administrative style tends to be, not *whether* you are a capable administrator.

Then, once you know your style, you will be in a better position to balance your strengths and weaknesses when you make committee assignments, build a team to pursue a project of importance to your discipline, or appoint those with whom you will work closely (such as an administrative assistant or assistant department chair). If you prefer to work on tasks that are already well under way, you may need to balance your skills with someone who prefers to be an initiator. If you are comfortable speaking before large groups, but dislike small talk or interacting with others one-on-one, you may wish to delegate these responsibilities to others who already have these strengths. Conversely, you may wish to pursue additional administrative training to build your skills in areas that you discover do not come to you as naturally as you might like.

RESOURCES

There are a large number of resources that will help you to continue discovering and refining your individual leadership style. The five best of these resources are:

Beck, J. D. W., & Yeager, N. M. (1994). *The leader's window: Mastering the four styles of leadership to build high-performing teams.* New York, NY: Wiley.

Diamond, R. M. (Ed.). (2002). *Field guide to academic leadership.* San Francisco, CA: Jossey-Bass.

Glanz, J. (2002). *Finding your leadership style: A guide for educators.* Alexandria, VA: Association for Supervision & Curriculum Development.

Kippenberger, T. (2002). *Leadership styles.* Minneapolis, MN: Capstone.

Leaming, D. (2003). *Managing people: A guide for department chairs and deans.* Bolton, MA: Anker.

Three Case Studies in Departmental Leadership

While many colleges and universities are either beginning or expanding leadership programs on their campuses, relatively few department chairs have ever had any formal leadership training. Department chairs are usually appointed directly from a position in teaching and research—having excelled at coursework in an academic field, not in higher education administration—and are typically expected to "demonstrate leadership," even though they may have only the most rudimentary sense of what "leadership" means. Many of us attempt to lead our departments by imitating the leaders whom we most admire, either in our own academic careers or from other aspects of our lives. Only gradually do we begin to develop our own style of leadership, based on our unique personalities, talents, and views of the world.

The following three case studies are intended to help chairs determine their individual leadership style and assess how they might respond in moments of stress or crisis—the touchstones of any leader. All three situations are hypothetical but based on the sort of dilemmas that most chairs will inevitably face. There are no right or wrong answers in hypothetical situations, only answers that are more or less appropriate depending on your personality, institution, and leadership style. After determining your approach to each situation, discuss the case studies with other chairs at your institution to see how they may have handled the various challenges.

Case Study #1: The Parent Trap

Near the end of the academic year you receive a telephone call from an extremely angry parent. You try to calm your caller down for several minutes, listen to what appears to be the problem, and attempt to sort through various accusations of bias, incompetence, and professional malfeasance on the part of one of your faculty members. The caller is the parent of a student enrolled in one of your department's courses, and this student has just received a failing grade on a major project. You attempt to explain that one poor grade frequently can be counterbalanced by an otherwise good record, that you would need to hear more about this particular situation from the faculty member involved, and that grades should not be misinterpreted as reflections of the student's worth or likely success in the future. But the parent will simply not listen: "You've got to understand, this grade wasn't even close to passing. And when asked about it, the professor was rude and completely unprofessional. Your faculty member humiliated my child in front of the entire class, saying things like, 'Of all the projects I have ever received from a student, yours was the absolute worst; you didn't even *begin* to follow my directions,' and 'You can forget about graduating from *our* department next week because, take it from me, that's just not going to happen.'" As you hear these remarks, you realize that they are not entirely out of keeping with the personality of this particular faculty member. In fact, you can easily imagine this person saying precisely these things. You also know that the student in question is not particularly strong and probably is incapable of completing a major project that is anything better than minimally acceptable. Nevertheless, the parent accuses the professor of having made many other dismissive remarks in the same vein, publicly humiliating the student for mistake after mistake that was allegedly made. The caller is outraged by your faculty member's professional insensitivity and demands that the following steps be taken immediately:

1) The professor must apologize to the student during the course's only remaining class period.

2) This apology must be made in as public a manner as the student was humiliated.

3) The student's project must be reevaluated by you as department chair, because the parent does not believe that the professor has been fair or impartial.

4) As the professor's supervisor, you must give your personal assurance that nothing will occur to prevent the student's graduation next week because of your faculty member's "unprofessional and unwarranted" failure of the student's project.

You know that you cannot agree to this because your institution has a grade appeal policy already in place. According to the existing policy, the final grade in the course must first be submitted by the instructor, reported to the student, and then formally appealed by the student in writing. When the parent says, "Does this mean that graduation next week really may not be possible?" you reply by saying that while that is possible, you certainly hope that will not occur. "The best thing for me to do," you say in an attempt to conclude the telephone conversation, "is to look into this matter as fully as I can in order to find out exactly what happened. I know I've heard one side of the story, and I can understand why you're upset. Nevertheless, I have a responsibility to balance the rights of both the student and faculty member, and I need to learn all that I can." Despite your attempt at a comforting tone, your last statement makes the parent even angrier. "I didn't waste my time calling you," the parent says, "just because I wanted you to 'look into' anything. You already know what happened. I *told* you what happened. Now I'm telling you to *fix* this problem. You're the supervisor here, and I'm holding you personally responsible for taking care of this situation." In closing, the parent informs you that your supervisor and the parent's attorney will be contacted by 9:00 a.m. tomorrow if you do not solve this problem.

As you stare at the phone upon hanging up, what is going through your mind? How do you transform this situation from merely management of a problem into an opportunity to demonstrate leadership?

1) Suppose that the faculty member cannot be reached. What else can you do or whom else can you call in an attempt to resolve this situation in the best possible manner?

2) Based solely on what you know so far, with which person involved in this situation (besides yourself, of course) do you find your sympathies lying?

3) Which person involved in this situation do you initially believe to be at greater fault?

4) Suppose that your entire schedule between now and the parent's deadline of 9:00 a.m. tomorrow is already scheduled with some activity that your dean or president regards as of the highest priority.

- Do you cancel that activity—which in the long run may be extremely important to your institution—or do you attempt to deal with the crisis at hand?

- Do you try to accomplish both goals by delegating either the crisis at hand or the other important activity to someone else in your department? If you choose to delegate one of the two, which one do you choose to delegate and why?

5) In this case study, the gender of the parent, the student, and the faculty member is not indicated. As you read the case study, which gender did you assign to each individual?

- Was there anything about the situation that led you to make those particular assumptions? What does this suggest to you about your preconceptions?

- If any or all of those genders were different from what you assumed, would you respond any differently?

6) Would your handling of this situation be any different if any of the following were true?

- You had personally witnessed the faculty member engaging in behavior almost identical to that described by the parent with another student.

- The student in question is the weakest student in your program and you believe that this student should never have been admitted to your institution.

- This is the fourth call that you have received this semester from this parent, each time with a different complaint about a different faculty member who "victimized" the parent's child.

- The faculty member in question is one of your stars with a solid reputation for student-centeredness, and this accusation is entirely out of character.

- The faculty member and the student were of different races and the parent either implied or explicitly stated a belief that the professor's actions were racially motivated.

- You know that the parent is a(n):
  - Attorney
  - Member of the Board of Trustees/Regents
  - Close friend of your direct supervisor

- The telephone call had come directly from the student rather than from the parent.

Case Study #2: Old Blindsides

Just before the start of a department meeting you are told that your application for a major grant has been approved, provided that your institution can increase the amount of the guaranteed match that had been part of your original budget. Since faculty morale has been extremely poor recently—there have been no salary increases for four years, several of your faculty members have been denied promotion or tenure, and a long-awaited decrease in teaching load has been postponed by the upper administration—you decide to share this bit of good news with your faculty. Ever cautious, you make certain that everyone is aware of the challenges that still lie ahead: Budgetary constraints mean that the institution may not be able to provide the increased match, you have not yet seen the amended budget figures in writing so you don't know whether the new budget will be feasible, and any number of other problems could still arise. You remind your faculty that all of this information is still "purely confidential," thank them for their excellent work in completing such a successful grant application, and adjourn your department meeting early so that you can inform the dean of the grant's approval. In your conversation with the dean, however, you are told that the proposed increase in institutional match is out of the question; the same budgetary constraints that have made salary increases impossible for the last four years will continue next year, and expenditures will need to be reduced, not increased, even in such critical areas as servicing this grant. You quickly make a phone call to the agency sponsoring the grant, and your worst suspicions are confirmed: Without the increase in match, your department cannot possibly be awarded the grant.

You are still disturbed by the implications of losing such an important opportunity a short time later when you arrive at your last commitment for the afternoon: a meeting of the full faculty of your institution. You can hardly concentrate on the mostly minor business that comes up during this meeting, but one turn of events suddenly grabs your attention. A senior member of your department rises to announce to all the faculty of your college the "great news" about the new grant. Not only will this opportunity finally make possible the long-awaited reduction in teaching load, but it will also bring some welcome recognition to your department. "I tell you," the faculty member concludes, "this is really going to put us on the map. And I think that we all ought to recognize the person whose leadership has made this all possible: the chair of our department." You find yourself receiving a loud round of applause from your institution's faculty—some faculty members have even risen to their feet—and you notice that they all turn to you expectantly. You notice that the dean is present, but looking your way with far less delight and approval than are the others. You suspect that the dean may be assuming you encouraged your faculty member to make the announcement about the grant. The room gradually quiets and you are expected to speak. What do you say? What is the best way to demonstrate leadership in such a situation?

1) Do you embarrass your faculty member by contradicting what the rest of the faculty has just been told?

    • If you do this, do you mention that you had told your faculty that the pending grant approval was supposed to be confidential?

    • Do you accept any public responsibility for "jumping the gun" on this announcement?

    • How do you feel it would be best to deal with the faculty member's very public breach of your instructions at the department meeting earlier that day?

2) Do you try to find a way out of the predicament by saying something like, "Of course, we don't want to be premature. There are still many hoops that we need to go through, any one of which might make acceptance of this grant impossible. For one thing, we would need to increase our institutional match substantially and, frankly, I doubt that that's going to be possible."

    • Would you find taking this position questionable since you already know that it will not, in fact, be possible for the institution to accept the grant under the conditions required?

    • Would you be concerned that such a ploy would put the dean, your direct supervisor, on the spot by encouraging the faculty to ask whether an increased match might be possible?

3) Would your handling of this situation be any different if any of the following were true?

    • You believe that the chronic budgetary shortages at your institution are due largely to the dean's inability to manage the budget.

- You are aware that substantially more than the required institutional match for your grant has tentatively been allocated for projects that you regard as of relatively low priority.

- The faculty member who blindsided you at the faculty meeting has a history of revealing confidential information, has been warned about this behavior in the past, and could be subject to disciplinary action for this conduct.

- The faculty member who spoke at the faculty meeting was a dearly beloved senior member of your department who probably believed that your instructions to keep the grant "purely confidential" did not apply to telling other members of the faculty.

Case Study #3: No Good Deed Goes Unpunished

A student comes to see you during the first week of classes. The student needs to complete a course offered by your department in order to graduate at the end of the current term. In fact, this course is the only requirement standing between the student and graduation. The problem is that the course needed by the student is already vastly overenrolled. You know that the number of students already admitted to the course significantly exceeds the number of seats available in the classroom, and the professor told you that, because of limited amounts of essential course materials, the course could not possibly accommodate even one additional student. You explain all of this to the student, who replies, "But that's the very professor who *sent* me here. I was told that all I needed to get into the course was your signature. It wasn't explained to me where there's room in the course, but there is. Maybe someone else dropped, and so there's a seat available now. The professor knows that I need this class to graduate and told me specifically to come here to get your signature."

Not feeling particularly comfortable granting an override without talking to the professor, you try making contact by telephone and, when that is not successful, you walk down to hall to the faculty member's office. Since the professor is still not available, you tell the student that you really cannot sign the form without speaking to the professor first. But the student replies, "This is the last day to add the course. The registrar told me that if I don't get into this course *today*, I can't graduate. Besides, I've already told you: The professor told me that it's okay. All I had to do was get your signature." At this moment, another faculty member comes into your office to drop off a budget report. You ask whether this professor knows anything about the situation and are told, "Yeah, I think it's okay. I heard a couple of students were dropping that course, so the story sounds right. If it were me, I'd go ahead and sign the form." You try one last time to contact the professor and, trying to exert some active leadership, you sign the form admitting the student into the course.

When you arrive at your office the next morning, you find the professor of the course waiting for you by your door, positively seething. "Why'd you allow that student into my course? You *knew* I didn't have room for the students who were already signed up for it. I specifically *told* you that I couldn't take anyone else. You said you wouldn't do it, and then I find this morning I've got one more student for whom I've got no materials and no space in the classroom." When you explain that you had tried to contact the professor several times and that the student was adamant that the professor was satisfied and that all that was needed was your signature, the professor responds, "What I told the student was that I couldn't let the student into the course; a couple of students have dropped it, sure, but it's still overenrolled. Adding one more student to the course would take your signature, and I sent that student to you knowing that you would have to say no. After all, that's what you told me you were going to do." Despite your best efforts to calm your faculty member, you are told, "I don't care. This is going to be reported to the dean, and it may even result in a grievance."

How do you begin to resolve this situation? You review your actions—did you do anything wrong? How can you regain control of the situation, while setting an appropriate example for both the student and the faculty member and demonstrating good departmental leadership?

1) Do you start by speaking to the student again? If so, what do you say? Do you include the faculty member in the conversation this time?

2) Do you contact the registrar and have the student withdrawn from the course, even though it means that the student will not graduate this semester? If so, do you do this before or after speaking to the student?

3) Is this a situation to which you would alert your immediate supervisor? If so, would you do so:

   • To keep that person informed?

   • To ask that person's advice?

- To involve that person in making the decision?

- To defer this particular decision to that person?

4) Would your handling of this situation be different if any of the following were true?

  - Your institution had a strict honor code to which all students were compelled to subscribe.

  - The student in question was the child of your institution's president.

  - Your institution was unionized.

  - You checked the registration records for this course and discovered that not just a few but a significant number of students had dropped the course during the first week and there was now room in the course.

  - The student had a 4.0 GPA.

  - The student had a very low GPA.

  - The faculty member in question was a newly hired, untenured faculty member.

  - The faculty member in question was your own mentor in the department, a distinguished and widely admired scholar who had won numerous awards for excellence in teaching.

  - The faculty member teaching the course was your dean.

20

Career Planning for Department Chairs

As rewarding a position as it may be, one's stint as department chair doesn't last forever. Either there is a fixed term after which one returns to the faculty or seeks another assignment, or the position is open-ended and the chair and the institution have the right to decide when another chair should be appointed. In either case, however, it is natural and appropriate for the chair to begin considering "what next?" at some point during his or her tenure in the position. Depending on how you answer that question, there are different choices that you will need to consider now as a department chair in order to keep your options open and to increase the amount of success you'll have in pursuing your future plans. Let's consider several possible choices individually.

Return to the Faculty

The vast majority of department chairs eventually return to the faculty. They may do so immediately after completing their term as chair or they may choose this option only after filling a number of other positions. Nevertheless, since serving as a rank-and-file faculty member again is a highly likely outcome for most chairs, there are several things you should keep in mind during your period as chair. To begin with, as difficult as it may be, it is highly advisable to maintain an active scholarly agenda throughout your administrative appointment. With all of the pressures of time that arise as part of administrative assignments, too many chairs cut back on active scholarship as a way of freeing up their schedule. This is unfortunate because they then may find that, upon their return to the faculty either at their own or at another institution, their record of scholarship is significantly smaller than many of their peers who continued their faculty positions all along. Even worse, scholarly activity, once it has diminished, is notoriously difficult to resume. Changes have occurred in the field that one needs to catch up on. One's network with other scholars in the discipline may have weakened. (At times this occurs because the chair is obliged to devote limited travel funds to attend conferences for chairs and other administrators rather than participating actively in disciplinary meetings.) Nor is it likely a chair's research, which may take several years of collecting data, will result immediately in publications or major conference presentations; one will have to "gear up" a research agenda again, and that can require a substantial amount of time.

For this reason, as difficult as it may be, it can be extremely important for the department chair to remain active in scholarship, research, and creative activity in some way even during the administrative appointment. Perhaps you can join a team of scholars who are jointly working on a project, contributing time and ideas whenever possible; even being third or fourth author on an article is far preferable to a large gap in your publication record. Perhaps you can segue temporarily to research the scholarship of teaching in your discipline or curricular planning in the field. While published works in these areas were long seen as less prestigious in many academic areas, that attitude is changing as a result of broader views of scholarship, such as those presented in Boyer's (1990) *Scholarship Reconsidered;* Glassick, Huber, and Maeroff's (1997) *Scholarship Assessed;* and Braxton, Luckey, and Helland's (2002) *Institutionalizing a Broader View of Scholarship Through Boyer's Four Domains.* Work done on the scholarship of teaching can open up an entirely new field of research for the chair; it can also help you to "keep your hand in" until you resume your previous line of research upon your return to the faculty.

The second common mistake that chairs can make before their return to the faculty is not teaching sufficiently or not teaching sufficiently *broadly.* Because of the pressure of time, chairs may frequently teach only the minimum required by their contracts. In certain large departments, the chair may not be expected to teach at all. The difficulty arises then when one must return to teaching—sometimes after a gap of many years—with updated information, new teaching methods, and means of engaging a new generation of students. Even teaching a course or two a year can be detrimental if the chair simply "cherry picks" the most desirable sections: the advanced seminar for majors, the orientation course that only meets once a week, the online course for graduate students. In the worst scenario, selective teaching is counterproductive since it can provide a distorted view of the full range of students that the program is attracting. For this reason, team teaching a course, teaching a unit within a larger course, and rotating widely the levels at which one teaches (introductory, intermediate, senior-level seminar, graduate course) are superior strategies to teaching too little or too narrowly. Not only will such continued breadth of teaching help your transition back to the faculty, it will also make you a better chair by providing you with a better overview of your program.

Another Chair Position

Some chairs enjoy the opportunities and challenges of being a chair so much that they begin to look for opportunities either to make a lateral move as chair at another institution or to progress to a larger or more prestigious college or university. If this is your situation, you should complement your own experience as chair with a broad range of issues involving best practices, curricula, and challenges in your field. It is all too easy to fall into the practice of thinking, "Well, that's not the way we did it back at my old institution," since that tends to be one's immediate frame of reference. The difficulty with such an approach, however, is that it tends to limits one's thinking, narrowing it to what one has actually experienced. To the greatest extent possible, you should keep up with how different programs in your field are structured. How are their curricula organized? What courses are required and what prerequisites are enforced? How do they promote scholarship in the discipline and what do they tend to regard as the most significant contributions in the area of scholarship, research, and creative activity? By knowing this, you will increase your dossier of ideas to bring to a new institution and even gain some new perspectives for your current department.

If you are thinking about moving to another position as chair, you should have at least one contribution that you can call your own as an example of your leadership and initiative. What courses were you instrumental in developing or revising? Have you developed any new emphases or tracks within your major? Did you inaugurate a lecture series, discussion group, or teaching circle? Did you establish a departmental office of your campus's center for teaching and learning? Did you author a new policy manual for your discipline? Achievements such as these will help to demonstrate to your new institution that you haven't just been an effective manager of resources: You've also been responsible for the sort of initiatives that they are looking for to help their program move forward.

Another Mid-Level Position

Some chairs discover that they not only enjoy but also have a talent for academic administration; however, they are not yet prepared for the very demanding challenges of a deanship or position in upper administration. Instead, they may be attracted to other mid-level positions, such as assistant or associate dean, director of a center for teaching excellence, or honors program director. To begin career planning in this area, you will need to amass skills at coping with highly detailed information and develop a thorough understanding of the office in which your new position will be. Mid-level administrative positions tend to involve managing tremendous amounts of information, completing reports, being certain that deadlines are met, keeping large numbers of people apprised of developments, handling stress effectively, working quickly with short turnaround times, and many of the less glamorous aspects of academic administration. These positions can be great training grounds or wonderful careers for certain people, but they tend not to be appropriate for individuals without good computer skills, organization, and attention to detail. In particular, the positions of assistant or associate dean, provost, or vice president require individuals who can effectively implement someone else's initiative without taking undue credit for the effort or pursuing their own initiatives. As a department chair, therefore, you need to be certain that you have demonstrated, not mere success in meeting deadlines and supplying information accurately, but *excellence* in this area.

You should also be fully acquainted with the needs and operations of the office to which you will move. You are unlikely to be successful in your application to serve as director of the honors program, for instance, if you have demonstrated only a modest amount of interest in honors programs and recruiting students of high ability during your term as chair. Gaining broader knowledge of campus programs and offices can be essential for any mid-level move that you are attempting to make—without neglecting your primary departmental responsibilities. For this reason, try to seek opportunities that enhance your knowledge while benefiting your department. What sort of programs can you offer in conjunction with the center for teaching excellence? How can you better promote their workshops among your faculty? Are there opportunities for participation in the honors program that your discipline has not yet pursued? If you are already heavily involved in honors education, how can your discipline improve the experience that it is providing for these students? Are you able to launch a targeted recruitment weekend for students who might be interested in your major, coordinating this activity with some office about which you would like to learn a great deal more? Any of these initiatives will make a major contribution to your program, while also enhancing your network of contacts across campus and teaching you much that you need to know about the operation of other offices.

Dean

Many department chairs find that the taste of academic administration that they have developed through their responsibilities as chair has given them the hunger for still greater challenges, such as serving as dean of a college. There are many good reasons for wanting to be a dean, such as a passion for making a difference in the academic program of an institution, a desire to serve as an advocate for a broad but related group of disciplines, and the belief that one's talents for motivating people and getting things done are appropriate for fulfilling the many functions of the dean's office. There are also many wrong reasons for wanting to be a dean, such as the false belief that the work involved is actually easier than teaching and research, a mere desire for the income and privileges that come with the position, and any sort of hidden agenda (a plan to promote one's discipline at the expense of others, to settle old scores, or to undermine senior administrators). Deans who assume their positions for the wrong reasons may do a disservice to their colleges and end up failing at their tasks. If money is your motivating factor, you may find it far easier (and more lucrative) to develop grant proposals, teach overloads, or write a popular textbook. If advancing your own discipline is your goal, there are less destructive ways of doing this than by holding back other departments. Deans need to have a sincere interest, not just in their own academic fields, but in all the fields that they are representing. They need to become intimately acquainted with how scholarship is performed in a variety of disciplines, how successful and engaged learning occurs across the college, and how to inspire others whose perspective on the world may be significantly different from their own. They also need a great deal of patience for sitting in meetings and the ability to handle even more constituencies than they encountered while serving as chair.

If your career plans are leading you toward a deanship, you need to develop a reputation for being able to see "the big picture" of a college's needs. Offer to serve on college-wide committees, such as those dealing with curriculum, tenure and promotion, and long-range planning. Gain experience collaborating with other disciplines, perhaps through promoting interdisciplinary approaches in your department's courses or through initiatives that involve representation from different departments. Gain as much expertise as you can in planning and defending budgets; be sure that you have a record that does not include overspending your own budget but that does include innovative approaches to bringing in grants and sponsored programs. Attend lectures, art openings, concerts, plays, and other cultural activities outside of your area; if you find that these activities are ordeals to be endured rather than new tastes to be cultivated, then you are unlikely to be happy in a dean's role. Offer to represent your institution at conferences and symposia that bring together faculty members from a number of disciplines. Be certain that you have not only made "the hard decisions," but that you have made the right decisions and can defend them. When you make mistakes (and you will), always try to find a way to learn something positive from the experience in order to avoid making similar mistakes in the future. As a dean, you will have the opportunity to make even more mistakes than you have now, and it is highly beneficial to develop the sort of approach to your work that allows you to grow from them.

Upper Administration

Some chairs believe that their administrative careers are likely to lead them (perhaps by way of a deanship) to an upper administrative position such as provost, president, or chancellor. If this is your career path, then in addition to the other administrative experiences you will need to amass as chair, it will be very important for you to begin early to develop a successful record as a fundraiser. Your development efforts may include the successful submission of grants, the creation of new sponsored programs, the receipt of contributions from individuals or corporations, or the inclusion of your department into an individual's planned gift, such as a bequest or a trust. Increasingly, upper administrators are expected to have expertise in all of these areas, and your applications for upper administrative positions will be far stronger if you can document a solid record of achievement in at least one of these areas.

You may wish to start a few fairly small development efforts and to progress from there. Offer your services to the campus phonathon or other types of solicitation efforts that are being made. Seek opportunities for applying for grants that correspond well with your department's mission and bring indirect funding to your institution. Contact your development office and let them know that you are willing to accompany anyone on donor visits if the prospect has an interest in your academic field, majored in your area, or had a close connection to one of your faculty members.

Once you attain some record of success in these smaller areas, you'll be able to formulate more ambitious plans for such things as an endowed chair or lecture series in your area, external funding for enhancement of your facilities, or increased faculty development funding in your area. Just be certain to make all of these efforts in close cooperation with your development office. You'll need to know that you are not contacting donors that have already been identified for some other purpose by the institution and that your overall efforts correspond with the goals of your institution's strategic plan and its chief executive officer. In other words, if your goal is to be a president, you need to begin seeing how, even now, your activities within the department may be viewed from the presidential level.

Retirement

One final career path for many chairs may be to retire from academic life altogether. Planning for this step in your career is rather different from others outlined in this chapter. In addition to continuing to advance the interests of your department, you will also be preparing for the new opportunities that will be awaiting you after your retirement. How closely will you want to maintain your ties with your institution, your academic discipline, and your professional organizations? Will you want, at least occasionally, to teach a section of a course as an adjunct faculty member or to serve as a consultant to a new chair who could benefit much from your expertise? Are there opportunities that you have not been able to pursue in your discipline that you may wish to explore now that you have time—travel to other campuses or to parts of the world intimately related to your field, offices in professional associations, or publications that you never found time to write? Remember that, while you will want to give the new department chair a chance to make his or her own name by bringing fresh perspectives to the position, it is rarely necessary for retirement to sever entirely your relationship with your institution. Offer your services to the extent that you feel comfortable doing so, and expect that the institution will take you up on your offer only to the extent that it is comfortable doing so. For most former chairs, retirement consists neither of complete abandonment of their discipline nor full-time service to the extent that they previously worked. As in so many aspects of life, a balance is to be found that promotes both the good of the college or university and gives the retiree the satisfaction of making a much-needed contribution in the area of his or her expertise.

Whether they are conscious of it or not, all chairs do *some* sort of career planning. The more intentional you make your efforts, the greater the likelihood of being successful. Remember that it is never wrong to keep an eye on where you are going after your term as chair ends, as long as that is not the only focus of your attention. Properly perceived, career planning can provide many advantages to the department even as it helps bring you closer to your ultimate professional goals.

REFERENCES

Boyer, E. L. (1990). *Scholarship reconsidered: Priorities of the professoriate.* Princeton, NJ: The Carnegie Foundation for the Advancement of Teaching.

Braxton, J. M., Luckey, W., & Helland, P. (2002). *Institutionalizing a broader view of scholarship through Boyer's Four Domains.* (ASHE–ERIC Higher Education Report, 29[2]). San Francisco, CA: Jossey-Bass.

Glassick, C. E., Huber, M. T., & Maeroff, G. I. (1997). *Scholarship assessed: Evaluation of the professoriate.* San Francisco, CA: Jossey-Bass.

21

Chairing Small Departments

Serving as the chair of a small department brings challenges that are either not faced, or not faced to the same extent, by your colleagues in larger departments or bigger institutions. Chairs of small departments tend to have different relationships with members of their faculty than do chairs of large departments. They may not have their own administrative support, frequently sharing a secretary with one or more other departments or only having clerical help for a few hours a day. In small departments, chairs may receive little or no release time for their administrative duties; they may be expected to teach a full load while still tending to the needs of their departments, frequently receiving a stipend or release from a committee assignment as compensation. Chairs of small departments tend not to have the buffers available to their colleagues in larger programs. They are more likely to answer their own calls or receive their own visitors, which at any moment could be a dissatisfied student, an angry parent, a potential major, an alum, an administrator with a crisis, or a colleague needing some immediate guidance. Chairs of small departments may not supervise budgets as large as other chairs, but their days tend to be equally as diverse and challenging. They are simply diverse and challenging in different ways.

Issues Arising From Intra-Departmental Relations

Chairs in smaller departments tend to find that, in most cases, their departments are less hierarchical and more collegially organized than are large departments. The chair of a small department is less frequently the "boss" in a top-down manner than a colleague who is willing to provide some organizational support to the unit for a fixed period. The chair of the small department is unlikely to be the individual who evaluates members of the department and makes recommendations for salary increases. The chair may not even be the person who establishes the course rotation or schedules classes for the unit. These decisions may either be made by consensus or they may be deferred to a dean or registrar. But this relatively flat organizational structure creates its own challenges for the chair. How, for instance, do you "make" someone do something when the nature of your position provides you with extraordinarily few "carrots and sticks?" How do you require a faculty member to embark on a course of action when that person is unwilling (and is likely to serve as the department chair someday, perhaps in the very near future)? And, most challenging of all, how can a relatively young—and possibly untenured—chair relate to a senior department member who seems unwilling to accept the chair's authority and who may soon be voting on the chair's promotion and tenure?

While there are no perfect solutions to these challenges that will work in every situation, one or more of the following strategies may be effective in your situation, depending on the history of your department and the personalities of the individuals involved.

Communicate One-on-One

One of the best ways that you can help improve communication within your department—particularly if you are dealing with colleagues who are senior to you in rank—is to go out of your way to communicate with them as individuals. Go to their offices, sit down, and have a frank but cordial chat about how you see things in the department and what you hope to accomplish. Be clear about explaining your hopes and visions, but be a good listener as well. One of the most valuable things you can receive from these conversations is a genuine understanding of the perspectives brought to issues by various members of the department. If you hold these face-to-face conversations often enough, you will begin to break down boundaries and perhaps even resistance to some of your ideas. Don't simply meet with these faculty members once a term or so as a sort of obligation. Take them out to lunch or for coffee. Get to know them and allow them to get to know you. You may be pleasantly surprised to learn that what you had been viewing as resistance to you personally or as hostility to new ideas actually stems from other concerns. These concerns may be out of your control or, in fact, better addressed simply by reaching out to members of the faculty as individuals.

Meet Formally

As important as these casual, unscheduled conversations may be, they should never take the place of formal meetings as a department—even if there are only two of you in the department. It is very important for clear communication and for the professionalism of your unit that there be a regular, recurring time for a department meeting. These sessions need not be long—many small departments can wrap up their business within half an hour—but they need to be consistent. Find a pattern that works for your unit's needs and complexity: once a week, once every other week, once a month. The precise scheduling is less important than the fact that you are gathering to discuss issues in common, with a set agenda, tasks to be completed before the next meeting, and an anticipation of reports and updates on progress towards meeting your unit's goals.

Create Alliances

Creating alliances within your department should not be regarded as the same thing as collusion. In other words, you should not be working behind people's backs for the purpose of advancing a hidden agenda or overcoming another faculty member's serious resistance to an idea through keeping its continuation secret. What you should be doing, however, is working openly to foster alliances of faculty members who might assist you in completing the essential work of the department. For instance, suppose you have a three-person department (yourself and two colleagues), one member of which regards your proposal to work closely with admissions to recruit incoming students to your program as a waste of time, while the other has relatively little interest in your initiative to pursue a major new grant for your program. While perfect consensus would be highly desirable, in the real world it can sometimes not be obtained. Rather than causing progress on your initiatives to grind to a halt until "everyone is on board," you can form two alliances to work openly on these projects, freeing the faculty member who opposed them from direct involvement. In time, success can encourage individuals who initially did not see the value of a proposal to "jump on the bandwagon." Also, if your alliance contains at least one respected "opinion leader" in your program, enthusiastic updates about progress in this area at department meetings might well serve to quell open and destructive resistance to the idea.

Seek Support

Particularly if you are a junior faculty member placed in the position of chair of one or more senior faculty members, you are going to want extra-departmental support for advice, counsel, and (in extreme cases) sheer *gravitas*. Another more experienced department chair—usually from another discipline but sometimes a senior respected former chair in your own discipline—may be able to give you invaluable advice on how to contend with some of the personalities in your discipline. (Frequently these individuals have a long history with senior members of your department and find them a good deal less intimidating or threatening than you do.) Sharing your concerns with the person to whom you report—not in a whining or despairing way, but simply stating the objective facts—can also be extremely valuable. Your dean, provost, or academic vice president may be able to help you formulate useful strategies for interacting with these senior members of your discipline. It may even happen that this individual can set your mind at ease by explaining the protections that your institution or system has in place for you should such an individual seek to block your tenure or promotion on inappropriate grounds or because of your decisions *as chair*, as opposed to your contributions *as a faculty member*.

Offer Exchanges

Just as "creating alliances" is not the same thing as "creating collusion," so is "offering exchanges" not the same thing as "cutting deals." By offering exchanges, you are simply recognizing that every individual has different needs, interests, and ambitions at different stages of his or her career. Based on your conversations with individual faculty members, you will probably understand a good deal about the day-to-day likes and dislikes of members of the department. One faculty member will find the submission of textbook orders under your institution's system to be excessively onerous. Another will find formatting travel reimbursements particularly irksome. Still others will feel that they are never the ones who are selected for choice committee assignments or to represent the discipline at conferences. With a little bit of creativity, you will discover that there are relatively easy ways in which you, or any clerical support you can obtain, will be able to assist these faculty members find relief from "where the shoe pinches." Naturally, the exchange you offer should never be anything that you would not, in similar situations, offer any other faculty member. You wouldn't, for instance, unilaterally reduce a faculty member's teaching load, waive the requirement for conducting student course evaluations, or excuse a person from holding required office hours. But you may well find a number of small, perfectly permissible ways to make the faculty member's life easier. Then, as part of the exchange, you might ask for participation in some project that is of great importance to you and the department. For instance, you might say, "Well, look then, if I could perhaps find a way to get those travel reimbursements prepared for you, do you think you might at least be willing to run an eye over our grant proposal when we get it ready and give us one or two constructive suggestions on how to strengthen it?"

Issues Arising From Inter-Departmental Relations

Sometimes the greatest challenges faced by chairs of small departments do not come from within their own ranks. Particularly at institutions where other departments may be significantly larger, small departments may feel like they are not given equal respect. While you certainly don't want to "protest too much," there are several steps that you can take in order to avert the Too Small (to be a) Department Syndrome.

Use Data to Your Advantage

Regardless of a department's size, there is almost always some way in which its distinctiveness is measurable. Perhaps your discipline produces very few majors, but you have high enrollments in service courses, courses that are a critical component of the general education program, or courses that serve as prerequisites for other disciplines. Perhaps your cost to produce a student credit hour is the lowest at your institution (or in your college, school, or division). Perhaps faculty members in your department score the highest in your institution on student ratings of instruction. Or, perhaps your department brings in the highest amount of external funding for any unit in your institution or generates the most student credit hours with the smallest number of full-time faculty. Calculating data that demonstrate a few of the ways in which your unit's superior contribution may be measured can be important to develop pride and esprit de corps within your department and to help it gain respect across campus. Having this information ready and continually updated will allow you to say such things as, "Well, yes, we're small as a discipline, but only in terms of full-time faculty lines. Don't forget that, per capita, we serve more students than any other department in our division. We also placed a higher percentage of our majors in graduate school and published more articles last year per FTE faculty member than any other undergraduate department at the university. So, I think we're doing a pretty good job."

Highlight Your Unique Mission or Methodology

Your discipline is unlikely to have achieved its "independence" as a stand-alone department if there were not compelling reasons of mission or methods that distinguish your field from other areas. It may be time to update your departmental mission statement to highlight all the ways in which what you are trying to do sets you apart from other fields of study and how your methods are unique and important. For instance, some members of your institution might not understand why your Department of Classics— or Physics, Philosophy, Germanic Languages, or Art History—should not be consolidated with other "similar" disciplines until you make the case effectively that your area possesses a distinctive mission and approach to learning that sets it apart from other fields. Even more important than serving as a defensive document, however, your updated mission statement can reinvigorate your department by clarifying for everyone your continued uniqueness, importance, and relevance. It is a good starting point for your continued discussions with prospective students about why they should consider taking courses in your field and possibly even completing your major. By keeping your rhetoric fresh, you will be able to tie initiatives in your department more readily into the changing needs of your student population, perhaps eventually building your small department into a unit that is not quite so small.

Become an Early Adopter

One of the great advantages that small departments have over their larger counterparts is that they can be nimble and responsive. For this reason, they can take advantage of fresh opportunities much more readily than can more cumbersome units. As new technology becomes available, as your institution seeks programs to participate in pilot projects, and as volunteers are sought to advance part of the strategic plan that is important to your president and provost, your department can quickly proceed with a proposal or offer to participate while other units are still debating the merits of the idea. If your unit is truly small, a hallway conversation—or perhaps a telephone call or two—may be all it takes to develop consensus that the opportunity ought to be pursued. The advantage of being an early adopter is that your department will be recognized for its entrepreneurial spirit and for being a good team player. You will increasingly look indispensable to your dean and provost if your area is always the first to step forward when a significant contribution is needed. Your department will discover that it has created a whole cadre of supporters (among those who valued the project and even among those who didn't want their unit to have to take it on). People who matter will start saying things like "I don't care how small they are. They're always the first ones there when we need something done for the university."

Chairing small departments can thus be an art in and of itself. Although chairs of larger units may be called upon to deal with the complexities that arise from larger budgets (and there are complexities, not just benefits, that go with larger budgets) and more cumbersome course rotations, chairs of smaller departments deal more frequently with inadequate resources—both human and financial—to provide a program of the highest quality. At the same time, they must struggle for recognition in the institution's priorities and deal with the greater informality that tends to occur in departments of fewer than ten individuals. The chair of a small department is required to be guardian of the budget, personal mentor, solver of all problems, first resort whenever a question arises, and last to receive credit when some great achievement occurs. It is a position of great challenge and few, if any, rewards. Nevertheless, chairing a small department well can be absolutely essential to the overall academic program of any institution.

22

Chairing Large Departments

The nature of the department chair's position changes substantially depending on the size of the department. Despite what one might initially believe, chairing a large department is not inherently more difficult than chairing a small department; it's simply *different.* The dynamics of how one interacts with members of the faculty are different. The role that one plays relative to the rest of the institution is different. And the nature of some of the tasks that one performs is different. In addition, there are certain aspects of the chair's position that, while not essential elements of larger departments, are more likely to be the case for chairs of large departments. For instance, chairs of large departments are much more likely to have:

- Line authority over department members

- More of the job description devoted to administrative duties than to duties in teaching and research

- Been hired in as chair, rather than as a faculty member first who was later selected to be the chair

- An open-ended rather than a fixed term for the position

Of course, there are plenty of exceptions to all of these. Sometimes in large departments, the position of chair rotates—either explicitly or informally by tradition—among all the members of the department. Sometimes, too, there is a departmental election of the chair for a fixed term; these positions may be renewable or, at some institutions, one cannot succeed oneself as chair. Or, the department chair might not be given authority as an entry-level administrator, but rather merely serves as first among equals among the faculty in the discipline. Nevertheless, despite this great variety, there are certain challenges and opportunities that arise for chairs of large departments resulting both from their unit's greater size and from these common, though not universal features of large departments.

Issues Relating to Line Authority

At one time, the presence or absence of line authority was the distinguishing difference between *department heads* and *department chairs*. Departments heads were the boss: Faculty members in the department reported through them to the upper administration; they conducted performance reviews of the faculty, perhaps the only sort of performance review that was conducted except in cases of promotion and tenure decisions; they set salaries, including allocation of merit increases; they assigned courses and adjudicated differences in faculty workload; they played a lead role in all faculty hires, perhaps equal to or greater than that of the search committee; and they were usually the ones who initiated non-renewals. Department chairs, on the other hand, were considered much more to be managers of departmental resources than bosses; like committee chairs, they were catalysts for organization and the efficient operation of departmental activities; in all important matters, however, the chair's vote carried no more weight than that of any other faculty member. The chair was regarded as the collegial solution to departmental organization. The department head smacked of top-down management and rigid, authoritarian structures.

Now, however, this once clear distinction has largely been blurred. Just as the term *university* is now commonly applied to institutions that at one time would have been regarded as *colleges,* it is now common practice to refer to individuals as department chairs even though their responsibilities are far closer to those of a true department head. This tends particularly to be the case in large departments. Faculty members tend to prefer the collegial tone of the term department chair, even if the structure of the institution is such that the chair really does need to have line authority over his or her colleagues. The institution may be so large that annual performance reviews simply cannot be conducted in depth at the dean's or provost's level. The budgeting may be sufficiently complex that salary recommendations may need to be initiated at the chair's level in order for it to be completed in a timely manner—although subsequently approved or altered by the upper administration. For whatever reason, regardless of the nomenclature in use at individual institutions, even chairs of large departments are far more likely to have line authority over their faculty members than are their colleagues at smaller institutions or in smaller departments.

Possessing line authority creates a special challenge for the chair. You will find that you constantly need to be changing hats. At one moment you will be acting primarily as just another member of the department, at another as the boss, as your unit's mentor or coach, or as the buffer between your department and the upper administration. Because of this complexity, you may be at risk of sending mixed messages unless you take precautions to clarify the various capacities in which you are acting. At times, you may find it necessary to say, "I'm speaking now just as a member of this department," or, "I'm speaking now as your supervisor." If you do not take these additional steps toward clarifying your role at that moment, statements that may seem extraordinarily clear to you may end up being misinterpreted by members of your department. Your statements of support that you made as a mentor and friend in order to create a positive atmosphere, good morale, and much-needed encouragement may be read as an endorsement of a level of performance that as an administrator you believe still needs improvement. Having line authority thus complicates some of the relationships you will have with your colleagues (particularly if you are in a situation where the chair rotates and someday soon they will end up having line authority over you). You may need to edit your comments a bit more scrupulously than you would if you were not the chair. Above all, don't let your position relative to the members of your department go to your head. It's a slight bit of eminence that you have right now, but it's more a position of responsibility than one of grandeur, and it must always be seen as such.

Issues Relating to Delegation

Regardless of the size of your department, it is useful and desirable to delegate certain responsibilities. Even in the smallest department, there is no reason why the chair should take and distribute the minutes for every departmental meeting, be solely responsible for proofreading every departmental document, or plan the four-year schedule of each student who majors or minors in the program. Delegation of certain responsibilities allows the work of the department to be conducted much more efficiently. It also helps protect the chair from burnout as a host of duties, running the full spectrum of administrative significance, falls on one set of shoulders. Moreover, delegation is quite beneficial to the faculty members who assume some of these responsibilities. It gives them a sense of empowerment in the activities of the department, provides them with documented evidence of service that they can use in applications for major personnel decisions, and prepares them for other administrative assignments that may come their way. Another benefit of delegating responsibilities is that it helps increase the level of trust that faculty members place in you, since you are dealing with departmental issues in a transparent manner. For instance, delegation helps prevent the appearance that you are withholding information or "colluding with the administration." You can increase this transparency further by sharing with the entire department summaries of meetings you hold with those to whom you have delegated responsibilities when their content is relevant to the operation of the department.

In larger departments, delegation is far more necessary and complex than it is in smaller units. The delegations that you will seek will range from the very informal (e.g., "Say, can you give me a hand with this report for a second?") to the extremely formal (e.g., appointing assistant department chairs or departmental committees that are empowered to make important decisions). Certainly any academic department that contains 20 or more faculty members requires a significant amount of delegation. Any situation in which a person must supervise more than 10 or 12 direct reports stretches the ability for careful, closely detailed management to the limit. The more people there are in a unit, the greater the likelihood of interpersonal and intergroup conflicts; the chair is going to need time to deal with those as they arise. Larger units also tend to be responsible for more students, bigger majors, and larger section sizes, all of which can add to the chair's challenges. By delegating day-to-day or routine matters, you will enable yourself to focus on those issues for which *only* the chair can intervene, and thus you will improve the efficiency of your department.

Nevertheless, when delegating responsibilities, there are three cardinal rules that you must follow:

- *Delegate responsibilities that are reasonably performed by another person or group; don't just delegate the responsibilities that you don't like.* Don't view delegation as merely an opportunity to pass tasks you don't like onto others. Doing so makes faculty members cynical about your management approach and reluctant to assume responsibilities when you offer them. Besides, it is far more efficient to delegate a set of responsibilities that can reasonably and effectively be performed by others than those which, while they may be unpleasant, are really central to your position.

- *Remember that when you delegate tasks, you surrender a certain amount of control.* The product or result that you receive may not be precisely what you had envisioned or performed precisely as you would have done. Unless the product that you receive has serious problems with quality or the result is utterly unacceptable in some serious way, loss of having it your way is one of the things that goes hand-in-hand with delegation to others.

- *Even when you delegate to others, stay in the loop.* Delegating an assignment is not the same thing as forfeiting responsibility. The group or individual performing the task is still doing so in your name. Therefore, without micromanaging the situation, take steps to be informed. Know the results of their process, the steps that took them there, and the reasons why they followed those steps.

Issues Relating to Workload

The larger your department, the more challenging your task will be in balancing your workload. But the key word here is *balancing* your workload. The temptation is always to direct more attention to situations that are critical rather than those that are important. Critical issues tend to be those with looming deadlines, faculty members or students who want answers immediately, and simply the latest predicament that has arisen. But critical issues are frequently less *important* in the long run than other matters. They may seem more pressing because emotions are high right now, but in the long run they may pale in comparison to improving the structure of your curriculum, putting more thought into the design of a new building, or submitting a grant proposal that could make your department's reputation for a decade or more.

Nearly every department chair has been in the situation of returning from several days away from campus to several urgent email messages from a faculty member or student saying "Please contact me at once. I have an emergency!" However, once the chair tracks the person down, the faculty member or student says, "Oh? That? When I couldn't get a hold of you, I took care of that myself a couple of days ago." Not every crisis is like this, of course, but it does indicate how different the urgent may be from the truly essential.

In balancing your workload, you want to be sure that you are devoting as much time as possible to the truly important and essential tasks that you face as chair. Although you may have been hired in primarily as an administrator with relatively few teaching obligations, you may discover that teaching more than your required amount—and at all levels, not just the choice upper-division and graduate courses—tells you more about your department's needs and the quality of the students in its courses than can stacks of memos and reports. You may find meetings with architects excruciatingly dull, and yet they may be the most important thing that you can do to secure the facility needs of your program. The goal, therefore, must always be to identify the range of truly productive activities that you can pursue for the benefit of your program (even those that aren't your favorite academic experiences), balance them, and delegate what you can of the less significant responsibilities that remain.

Issues Resulting From Being Hired In

It is far more common in larger than in smaller departments for someone to be hired in as chair from outside of the institution. If this is the situation that has brought you to your current position, you are facing certain challenges that are not shared by your colleagues who have been hired from within. For one thing, you are stepping into a set of group dynamics that every other member of your department may understand better than you do at the moment. Every department has a history, and your department members may know far more than you do about who has quarreled with whom, who was once married to or dated whom, who is generally considered to be the brightest star or weakest link, or who has a strong (but perhaps unwarranted) reputation with the upper administration. You can make all the statements you like about the past being the past and the present moment being a new beginning, but such platitudes are partially effective at best. Your primary responsibility at first must be to keep your eyes and ears open, asking a few discreet questions where necessary, and learning as much as you can. Above all, avoid the temptation to take sides from the start and don't put too much credence too soon on any one person's perspective. Inevitably, there will be one or more faculty members with whom you feel a special rapport—perhaps they were even members of the search committee, so your relationship with them is of slightly longer standing than it is with other members of the department—or who impress you more at first. The temptation is to see things through this group's eyes or to put stock in the information they give you. Resist this impulse. We all have agendas, frequently not even being aware of them ourselves. If you allow yourself to be co-opted by a particular faction or member of the department, it can quickly destroy your credibility. Many chairs report that one of the first mistakes they made was taking advice from someone in the department who at first seemed reliable and well respected, but who later turned out to be advancing an unsubstantiated opinion.

Sometimes new chairs worry that they may appear nosy if they begin asking too many questions about past practices and events. This should not be a concern: It is the chair's obligation to learn as much as possible in order to avoid being blindsided or acting on inadequate information. Feel free to explain to anyone who asks that being a chair requires you to act on the best information possible, and you can't do that unless you ask questions sometimes. Just be certain to ask sufficiently broad questions so that you are not relying on a selective view of the department's history. Collect multiple accounts. Weigh them against other facts and your own perceptions. Then rely on your own judgment.

Remember, too, that while you will want to make changes to reflect your own philosophy, management style, and vision for the department, it is the rare department—particularly the rare large department—that got where it is by being incompetent. Be generous with your praise and recognition. Acknowledge publicly and often the positive accomplishments of your predecessors. If you give the impression, even unintentionally, that you are there to "save the department" or that you have a lot of fixing to do, it is ultimately your reputation—not your predecessor's—that will suffer. Make changes quietly and give a great deal of attention to how you are building on your program's established strengths. This approach will serve you far better in the long run.

Issues Resulting From Departmental Elections

In departments in which the chair is chosen by election, larger departments are far less likely to have unanimous elections than are small departments. The challenge for the chair in these cases is that there will need to be some fence mending done in the department from the very beginning (particularly when the discussions leading up to the election have been contentious or the vote was very close). It is important that all serious issues discussed by the other side be acknowledged and dealt with as openly as possible. Remember that, even if you won the election by only a single vote, you are the chair of the entire department, not merely the faction that supported you. It may have been a competing vision or stance on a major policy matter that led to your election; in such a case, you will need to follow through on any commitments you made or initiatives that you advanced. But this does not mean that you cannot be sensitive to the genuine concerns on the other side of the issue. Are there any ways in which you can incorporate some of the good aspects of their position while still attaining the goal that caused you to be elected? Even if this is not possible, it may bring about more departmental unity—and help you achieve other goals in the future—if you acknowledge other positions rather than allowing them to be passed over in silence. Saying things like, "I know we haven't all been in agreement on this issue, but one of the things that I'm sure we can all agree on is . . . " demonstrates that you are sensitive to other points of view, unwilling to sugarcoat constructive conflict, and yet eager to achieve consensus wherever possible.

One of the first things you should do after being elected as chair is to have at least a short conversation behind closed doors with every member of the department. At times, you may want to begin these meetings with an agenda, saying something like, "I'd just like to have a brief conversation with each member of the department so that I can feel up to speed on . . . " At other times, just a general conversation "to get further acquainted" is sufficient. How you handle this depends on how well you feel you know your colleagues and whether the department's pending issues are already clearly defined for you. Either way, you can learn a great deal from these discussions. You will learn how much of each person's public stance was grandstanding and how much was personal conviction. You will learn how much public disagreement stemmed from different perspectives and philosophies and how much stemmed from personality conflicts. And you will learn that you probably have a great deal more support and good will in the department than you may originally have thought. You may not be able to win everyone over, but you can go a long way toward understanding the motivation of the members of your department, and this knowledge will help you better address the dynamics of your unit in the future.

While communication is an essential quality for any department chair, *superb* communication skills are particularly desirable when chairing the large department. You will regularly need to share information, "rally the troops," improve morale, focus the attention of diverse individuals, and lead (not merely manage) a highly complex unit within your institution. Though the size of your department may be large, so will be the degree of satisfaction you receive from leading it well.

23

Five Case Studies in Decision-Making

The following five case studies, all based on hypothetical situations, introduce several important issues that department chairs are asked to face on a regular basis. Since these cases are not real, there are no completely right or wrong answers; the specific decisions that you make—and the approaches that you take in reaching those decisions—depend on your institution, your experience, your discipline, and your leadership style. More important than any particular choice you make as you read these case histories will be the reasons you develop for preferring a particular course of action. One recommended approach is to read through each case study, choose one possible decision, and then discuss that case study with another department chair at your institution. What can you learn from one another's strategies and the questions you find yourselves asking as you examine one another's decisions?

Case Study #1: The Office Dilemma

There has been some new construction and, as a result, your department has just inherited a corner office that abuts a small workroom. You are very glad to be assigned this new office since the space is better than any faculty office you now have. Perhaps more importantly, you're acquiring the new office just in time to accommodate a new faculty member who will begin working in your department next fall. Since this is the first time your department has obtained a new office in anyone's memory, you have no established policy on how the space should be allocated. The dean wants you to take responsibility for making this decision and, because the dean has only arrived at your institution within the past several months, how you handle this decision will be one of the first opportunities you have to show your new boss your leadership style. Almost immediately after the news is out about the extra office, you begin receiving advice.

- Faculty member A says that the faculty member who currently occupies the largest office now should be given the new office: "That way all of us can move up a notch and everybody gets something. The new faculty member will receive the smallest of the old offices, and that's fair in terms of seniority."

- Faculty member B pleads with you not to be disruptive by forcing everyone to move, but simply to make it as easy as possible by letting the new person have the new office.

- Faculty member C says that choice of offices should be done on the basis of seniority. This will require some wholesale reassignment of office space, since some senior faculty members may want to swap offices with those who arrived at the institution more recently.

- Faculty member D agrees with Faculty member C, but insists that seniority should mean "years in the profession, not just years at the institution." This would require a different ranking of preferences.

- Faculty member E disagrees with Faculty Member D, saying that rank is a more effective reflection of "true merit than mere seniority," and, "I don't want some unproductive associate professor having first choice over me in office space just because that person's been here longer."

- Faculty member F says that the attached workroom makes the new space more suitable for the journal (s)he is editing, and "appropriateness of function simply has to be a more important consideration than anything else."

- Faculty member G insists that "a lottery is the only fair way to decide this."

- Faculty Member H recommends using the same principle in assigning office space that the college uses in setting the line of march for commencement, "whatever that principle is."

After discussing this matter in a department meeting for some time, you realize that a consensus is simply not possible.

- What factors do you consider as you make your decision?

- Do any of the positions advanced by members of your faculty appear to have particular merit? Can you rule out any of these positions immediately?

- Are there any possible solutions that the members of your department have not yet suggested?

- What is your final decision in this matter? On what basis did you make that decision? How do you go about selling it to the members of your department?

Case Study #2: The Great Compression

You have just accepted a position as department chair, having joined your new institution after a national search. Because starting salaries in your department have increased faster than salaries for continuing faculty members, you have inherited a department with extremely severe faculty salary compression and inversion problems. Congratulations! You have already noticed since you started your term as chair that this salary situation is having a detrimental effect on faculty morale. When March comes, you're assigned a 4.5% salary pool to use for raises—cost of living adjustments, merit increases, inequity adjustments, or whatever you like. You are tempted to apply some of this funding to address the inequity problems in your department, but you notice that your predecessor as department chair, although given this option, never decided to pursue it. Is it a wise idea to use part of this year's salary pool as an equity adjustment?

Suppose you do plan to use the 4.5% salary pool as an equity adjustment:

- What risks do you run by adopting this plan?

- Is it better to attempt a radical fix all at once (at least to the extent that is possible within a 4.5% salary pool) or to seek an incremental solution over several years?

- How do you make the most compelling case to your dean? To your faculty members?

- After announcing your decision, one of your newer faculty members shows up in your office outraged that you are "balancing the budget on the back of the junior faculty" and shifting his or her "hard-earned money yet again to the good old boys." How do you reply to this accusation?

- Would your decision be any different if you know that the majority of the faculty members who are suffering from salary compression and inversion will be retiring in a year or two?

- Would your decision be any different if the salary pool were higher or lower than 4.5%? What might you do, for instance, in a particularly lean year when you had only .5% to allocate? Is it wiser to "raise all boats" or to address a few of the most critical cases while others receive little or no increase? In a very different year, what might you do if you were given a "one time only" salary increase pool of 10% in an environment where the raise pool usually varies between 3% and 5%?

Case Study #3: Loose Cannon Wars

You chair a department that contains four related but independent programs. Each of these programs has its own director possessing signature authority over his or her own program-specific operating expenses. It is early in the fiscal year, and one of your directors has just blind-sided you with a serious problem: He or she has just spent a significant part of that program's annual operating budget on a single piece of equipment. While according to your institution's procedure it was within that director's prerogative to make this decision, you believe that it was unwise to do so and you are concerned that the program will not have sufficient funding to eke out the remainder of the fiscal year. Worse yet, you discover that the order for the piece of equipment cannot be canceled. When you call the director into your office and ask why you were not consulted about this decision in advance, you are reminded that the director was doing no more than he or she was authorized to do. Further, the director argues that he or she was hired to make "tough decisions" that would improve the program, the institution's budget officer had been duly notified of this pending purchase, and the piece of equipment would have cost more if not purchased during a fairly narrow "window of opportunity" (which conveniently occurred while you were away). When you insist that, even though the cost of the item may go up, it would have been prudent to wait until later in the year to make this purchase, you are reminded, "We tried doing that for the last two years running. And because of mid-year budget cuts, we merely lost the money we had been setting aside. It was my professional judgment—the judgment I'm paid to make—that we should spend the money now, rather than lose it later." When you finally ask, in exasperation, what the program will do for money if it exhausts its entire budget before the year is over, the director replies, "Well, the institution will just have to find more money somehow. After all, if you penalize us, you're really just penalizing the students."

- What options do you have in solving this problem? Is there a way to hold the program director accountable without penalizing the students in his or her program?

- Is it ever appropriate to address this problem by working with part of the budgets of the other three programs in your department? What conditions would have to occur to make you willing to consider this option? How might you make this solution more palatable to your other program directors?

- Do you replace this program director? If so, do you do so immediately or only if the program actually does create a shortfall for the year? (Remember that the director technically had the authority to make this decision.) What is the issue that prompts you to make your decision: the lack of proper consultation with you, the error in judgment, or something else?

- Is this a problem that you take to the dean or do you try to handle it internally?

Case Study #4: Allegations Con Brio

One morning, Professor Klatschmaul enters your department, closes your door, and tells you there is a certain "very serious matter" the two of you need to discuss. Then for the third time this month Klatschmaul begins to detail the shortcomings of Professor Cossard, another member of your department. The first time Klatschmaul came to see you it involved a complaint that Cossard was spending too much time conducting personal business on the phone or over the internet, frequently requiring Klatschmaul to assist Cossard's students. The second time Klatschmaul accused Cossard of begging off a departmental committee, citing an excessive workload, even though "everyone knows" that Cossard has the fewest students in the department and is not the discipline's most productive scholar. Now, in little more than a week, your department will be participating in an institutionally mandated Diversity Awareness Workshop, an activity about which Cossard has been skeptical in the past. You have been told by your dean that, because of a grievance that caused the institution some bad national publicity, everyone in your department must attend the workshop and only severe illness will be regarded as an excused absence. Klatschmaul tells you that Cossard has scheduled a job interview at another institution on the very day of the workshop. "I can't tell you how I know this," Klatschmaul says, "and you can't use me as a source. But this is definite: Cossard's going to call you the morning of the workshop and claim a sudden illness." You suspect that there may be some truth to Klatschmaul's allegations, but you also know that Klatschmaul resents Cossard for a negative promotion recommendation given several years ago and would like nothing better than for Cossard to get into trouble. What do you do?

- Do you suggest to Klatschmaul that supervising members of the department is your business and that this sort of tattling is inappropriate?

- Do you confront Cossard in order to learn if the allegation has any merit? If so, how do you respond if Cossard says to you, "You heard this from Klatschmaul, didn't you? Well, let me tell you Klatschmaul's no saint either because . . . " and lists reasons?

- Is your response any different if you find no corroborating evidence for any of Klatschmaul's earlier allegations?

- Is your response any different if Cossard really is an underperformer whom you would be happy to see leave the institution?

- Where do you draw the line between due diligence in being informed about what is going on in your department and mere gossiping that harms morale?

Case Study #5: Divide-and-Conquer or Bait-and-Switch

For a long time now, your department has had a high service load but relatively few majors. Because your institution generally allocates new faculty lines to departments graduating the highest number of majors each year, you are increasingly understaffed. While you conservatively estimate that you need at least two new full-time faculty members, the dean has finally agreed to allocate you one additional full-time line. You find yourself confronted with a dilemma. The easiest way to address the workload issue in your department would be to divert the funding for this new position into multiple adjunct hires. By doing so, however, you are afraid that you will merely be bandaging over the workload problems in your area and completely dooming your already slim chance ever to get a second additional line. Also troubling you is the possibility that the dean will feel that you have pulled a "bait-and-switch," requesting funding for one purpose but using it for another. Ordinarily, you would simply make an appointment with the dean to discuss this matter, but you need to act at once and the dean has just left for an extended research trip.

- Which takes precedence as you make your decision: the department's short-term needs or your longer-term strategy for addressing the staffing situation in your area?

- Even though you cannot consult with the dean, what steps do you need to take to make certain that your decision is fully understood at that level? Is this an appropriate instance in your institution to go over the dean's head and consult with the next highest level of administration?

- Is there an option that gives you the greatest amount of flexibility with the new position?

- What other information do you feel you need to know in order to make the best possible decision?

24

Departmental Ethics and Politics

The philosopher Aristotle viewed ethics and politics as intimately related. Ethics, he reasoned, involved the pursuit of happiness for individuals, and politics involved the pursuit of happiness for individuals *as members of societies*. Too often today, however, members of academic departments appear to be better versed in Machiavelli than in Aristotle. To them, departmental politics has nothing at all to do with ethics; it has everything to do with power. Power politics are, in fact, the great bane of academic life today. Many faculty members seem to spend a distressing amount of time forming alliances, grandstanding at public meetings, cutting secret deals, and undermining the initiatives of others, not for any fundamental principles in support of academic integrity or the welfare of students, but because they are convinced that "that's how the world works." Anyone who suggests that perhaps seeing everything in terms of political struggles is either not really how the world really works or how we in academic life have to work is likely to be dismissed as naïve, ineffective, or out of touch with the harsh realities of the professoriate today. Nevertheless, as a department chair, you are in an enviable position to depoliticize situations that can be handled in a far less adversarial manner, to move your department from being politically focused to being based in collegiality and consensus building, and most importantly to conduct the business of your discipline with high ethical standards.

Developing a Mission Statement or Code of Conduct for Your Department

If your department already has a mission statement or code of conduct, review it to see if it is appropriately phrased to support the ethical approaches to disputes and problem solving that will serve your program's best long-term interests. Mansfield University in northern Pennsylvania has adopted what it calls the "Mansfield Creed," establishing a code of behavior rooted in the institution's fundamental principles.

The Mansfield Creed

At Mansfield University, we develop leaders. We accomplish this by focusing on the four core values that have been our tradition since 1912: Character, Scholarship, Culture, and Service.

CHARACTER

We believe in integrity. We act with honesty and respect toward others. We take responsibility for our actions and reflect on their impact on ourselves and others.

SCHOLARSHIP

We believe in learning. We use rigorous, responsible, and critical inquiry to understand existing knowledge, acquire and share new knowledge, and apply what we learn. Each of us is both student and teacher.

CULTURE

We believe in celebrating humanity. We enrich ourselves and others by sharing and exploring our similarities and differences. We honor the past as we invent the future.

SERVICE

We believe in helping others. We work with others to improve the communities in which we now live and will touch in the future. Knowledge invests us with the power to improve our world and the responsibility to act.

Note. Developed by the Leadership Committee of the Focus on Student Learning Forum; last revised May 19, 2004.
See http://www.mansfield.edu/home/mansfieldcreed.pdf

Statements of principles like the Mansfield Creed provide a useful basis for an ethical approach to departmental governance (and a highly constructive approach to departmental politics) in several important ways:

- *They are based in the core principles of the body that developed them.* Although few faculty members would state explicitly that "the ends justify the means," the application of Realpolitik to the academic setting necessarily places an emphasis on power rather than ideals. Developing a statement of principles that reminds everyone of why you are there in the first place—to educate students, to acquire new insights, to serve the community, to create a community of scholars—can be an important way to break the cycle of viewing every choice or decision as merely part of a political game.

- *They are stated as positive affirmations of what people* will *do, not negative injunctions of what people are* forbidden *to do.* The Honor Codes and Codes of Conduct at many colleges and universities are largely negative documents. They include statements such as "I will not lie, cheat, steal, plagiarize the ideas or words of others, or act in a manner that will bring dishonor to" the institution. Rarely do such statements provide positive statements of what members of the institution *will* do and *why* that behavior is important to them. Creating an atmosphere for your department that moves beyond political maneuvering and deal making requires a positive focus on the direction your program wants to go, not a negative list of rules that causes individuals to begin searching for loopholes. Positive statements are also preferable to negative commands, since negative instructions only guide the individual in what *not* to do, not what he or she *should* do, often leaving the person wondering about a proper course of action.

- *They are inclusive and community building, not hierarchical or divisive.* Frequent use of the word "we" can be an important factor in setting a new, more constructive tone for your department. Too often honor codes and codes of conduct focus exclusively on the individual: They are statements of what "I" will not do. The Aristotelian approach to ethics and politics suggests, however, that social units need to be concerned with both the individual and the individual *as a member of a group.* Even principles stated in a bland third-person form ("The faculty member in this department is expected to . . . ") lose the advantage of creating a sense of community that is more effectively developed through the frequent use of the words "we," "us," and "our."

- *They move from general statements of principle to specific guidance that can be applied to day-to-day affairs.* Lofty declarations of belief in high moral standards are all well and good—as long as they are then crystallized into a form that helps your department members understand how these principles can be applied to what they actually do. In developing a statement of core beliefs for your department, ask yourself how such principles as open communication, respect for the ideas of others, commitment to scholarly integrity, and collegiality would be demonstrated in actual practice. How would meetings be different, memos and email exchanges improved, and conflicts resolved more equitably if those principles were applied in everyone's behavior?

- *They are concise, easy to remember, and are regularly incorporated into the life of the unit that created them.* A statement of principles that is simply laminated and hung on a wall ends up being yet one more political exercise. A brief set of values that everyone can remember and that provides a basis for training new faculty members, opening the first meeting of the year, and celebrating successes—not merely in teaching and scholarship but in working together as a successful academic community—has the potential for effectively improving the lives of those who study, teach, and work in your department.

Developing a Mission Statement or Code of Conduct for Yourself

Some department chairs will feel, of course, that a formal statement of principles simply does not fit their institutional culture. Perhaps there have been similar attempts to develop such a code in the past, and members of the department are now skeptical of such efforts. Perhaps the department is already so politicized that even the process of developing consensus about a code of shared beliefs would serve to exacerbate internal tensions. Perhaps such a notion simply does not suit the outlook and interests of most members of the department. All of these possibilities exist, and a sensible department chair will be aware of them before taking on a task that is likely to be counterproductive. Nevertheless, even if it is impossible for your department to agree on a statement of shared values and principles, it is perfectly possible for you as chair to develop your own set of administrative standards that can guide your program away from unproductive political infighting toward more constructive methods of operation.

No matter then whether you are drafting a document for public discussion and consensus or for embodying your personal philosophy of administration, there are certain basic factors to consider as you proceed.

Build Your Principles From the Mission and Identity of Your Institution, Discipline, and Departmental History

If, for instance, your institution has its primary mission in the area of teaching, then you should consider including such principles as student-centeredness, doing whatever is necessary to enhance the learning process, responsiveness to different styles of learning, maintaining rigorous academic standards, and promoting maximum student engagement. Departments with a strong research focus may find it important to stress the integrity of scholarship, collegial respect for the contributions of others, and advocacy for the principle of free inquiry. In disciplines such as sociology, social work, and health care, where service assumes an even greater significance than it has in other academic areas, the role that service plays in advancing the work of the department may need to be given a high profile. Whom does the department intend to serve, in what ways, and to what end?

Consider the Problems Your Department Has Experienced in the Past and, Even More Important, the Positive Directions It Can Take in the Future

Just as bad policies can result from attempts to prevent the recurrence of specific (and probably) rare problems in the past, so should statements of principles not be constructed simply in response to the difficulties the department has encountered. If collegiality has been a challenge in the past, then certainly it is appropriate to be aware of this in seeking ways for members of the department to work together in greater respect and harmony. Nevertheless, it is important also to include principles that move beyond solving this particular problem to taking your program where it needs to be as a community of scholars. Besides eliminating tension, what other benefits might accrue if greater collegiality existed? Would your program be more likely to offer a greater array of team-taught courses? Would student advisement be improved? Would you be more likely to be successful in obtaining grants? Would your department's retention rate for majors increase? By asking questions of this sort, you will begin to develop some clarity about the ultimate goals of your department—collaborative teaching, better advisement, higher levels of external funding, improved retention—for which uncollegiality and other immediate problems may serve as an obstacle.

Reflect on the Constituencies Served by Your Department and the Likely Audience for the Principles You Are Advocating

It is not uncommon for institutions and departments to have "codes of conduct" or policies outlining "what we expect from you" designed for students. It is far less common for either institutions or departments to reflect on the principles by which all constituencies are expected to live. As you consider the set of core values that will guide the activities of either your department as a whole or you as chair, pay attention not merely to "what we expect of you" but also to "what you can expect from us." And who is the "you" that is served by your department? Your constituents will almost certainly consist of students and other faculty members. But who else? What expectations might you have for your interactions with former students, parents of current and prospective students, college administrators, members of the surrounding community, donors and other supporters of your program, staff members at your institution, and the many others whom you serve in the broadest possible sense? What principles should they expect you to be following, and what do you consider to be your obligations to them as members of your larger community? In the case of current students, remember that the standards you are advocating should not merely seek to guide their behavior—there are plenty of other mechanisms at your institution for that—but also to model appropriate professional activity in your actions and in the actions of other members of your department.

Establishing appropriate and well-considered principles can be an important first step toward moving your department (and perhaps even your institution as a whole) away from viewing every situation as a political conflict and instead viewing every potential conflict as an ethical opportunity. As one of your institution's opinion leaders, you have the ability to change people's thinking from viewing curricular decisions as "non-aggression pacts" to constructive blueprints for achieving a compelling vision of the future. Ethical approaches to departmental decision-making are not achieved through individual documents or single proclamations by the chair. They can be achieved, however, through continual encouragement by the chair to focus every discussion that takes place in the discipline, not on how to "win," but on how to do what is right for the students, the unit's other constituents, and the institution as a whole.

Resources

Further perspectives on ethics and politics in an academic climate may be found in:

Bennett, J. B. (1997). *Collegial professionalism: The academy, individualism, and the common good.* Phoenix, AZ: American Council on Education/Oryx Press.

Bennett, J. B. (2003). *Academic life: Hospitality, ethics, and spirituality.* Bolton, MA: Anker.

Coffman, J. R. (2005). *Work and peace in academe: Leveraging time, money, and intellectual energy through managing conflict.* Bolton, MA: Anker.

Hamilton, N. W. (2002). *Academic ethics: Problems and materials on professional conduct and shared governance.* Westport, CT: American Council on Education/Praeger.

Lewis, M. (1997). *Poisoning the ivy: The seven deadly sins and other vices of higher education in America.* Armonk, NY: M. E. Sharpe.

Shils, E. (1997). *The calling of education: The academic ethic and other essays on higher education.* Chicago, IL: University of Chicago Press.

Starratt, R. J. (2004). *Ethical leadership.* San Francisco, CA: Jossey-Bass.

Wilcox, J. R., & Ebbs, S. L. (1992). *The leadership compass: Values and ethics in higher education.* San Francisco, CA: Jossey-Bass.

Four Case Studies in Departmental Ethics

Negotiating your way through the ethical challenges that will inevitably come your way as chair can be extremely difficult. One way to help you prepare for these situations is to reflect on various case studies that pose problems similar to those you may actually encounter. The four case studies in this chapter are fictitious, although they represent the sort of dilemmas that many chairs encounter. As in all case studies, the object of this exercise is not to find the "right" answer to each problem. These are situations that have no right answers (that's why they're so difficult to deal with) or that have multiple right answers, depending on the institution where they occur and the particular individuals involved. One of the best ways to benefit from the examples that follow, therefore, is to consider in each of them, not just what your course of action would be, but how you went about reaching that decision. Discuss the approach you would take with chairs of other departments. Consider what alternative strategies may exist for each situation. Decide what other information you feel you would need in order to make an informed decision: How would you go about obtaining that information? By the time you have given serious consideration to each of the four case studies, you will have learned valuable lessons about the strategies you will use when faced with ethical dilemmas and challenges. You may even learn a thing or two about your values that you had never fully realized.

Assume, in each of the following situations, that the institution you are working for has no specific policy for dealing with the matters in question. That assumption may or may not be true at your current college or university. The important thing, in the imaginary world of the following case studies, is for you to work your way through as though you have nothing to guide you except your own moral compass, common sense, and years of administrative experience.

Case Study #1: A Textbook Example

You are chair of a department in which one faculty member has recently published a major textbook in your field. The book has received excellent reviews, and the author has begun assigning the book as a required text in a course that all the majors in your program must take. One day, a student stops by your office and expresses a concern because this particular book is significantly more expensive than several other highly respected texts available in the subject that could easily have been adopted for the course. The student is on a very limited budget and worries about being able to continue in your program because of the expense. Somewhat reluctantly, the student also tells you that a number of others in the course regard it as a conflict of interest for this professor to require a textbook that results in the faculty member's own profit.

Later, a faculty member approaches you with a different issue concerning the same book. It turns out that this faculty member will be teaching a different section of the same course next semester and was just in the process of preparing a textbook order. This faculty member prefers the approach taken in another book, and your policy does not require that identical texts be used in multiple sections of the same course. The problem is that the author in your department has been pressuring the faculty member to adopt the text that that person has written. At first, these suggestions were fairly subtle, but they quickly escalated into hints that it would be taken as a personal affront if the new textbook is rejected by the other faculty member. Even worse, the faculty member who is in your office now is untenured and worries about defying the wishes of an influential senior faculty member who will be voting on a future tenure decision.

- What would you say to the student and faculty member who came to you on this issue?

- Which of the issues that they brought to your attention causes you the most concern?

- What would you say to the author of the textbook?

- What role do you think it would be appropriate to assume when you meet with the author? Would you see yourself more as a mentor who wishes to provide constructive advice or more as a supervisor who was going to issue an instruction to a faculty member who reports to you?

- Does the situation become simpler or more complicated if the following scenario also occurred?

You are just beginning to sort your way through these issues when another faculty member comes to see you. This faculty member has a concern about the textbook and its author that is different from either of those you've already heard. This faculty member's issue is that the textbook in question was written on university time, using university resources, and incorporating substantial amounts of information about and research conducted by the university's students and faculty members. According to the faculty member who is in your office now, your institution's intellectual property policy requires that any royalties resulting from the textbook must be given to the university, not kept by the author. This faculty member alleges that the author may be guilty of violating your institution's code of conduct by not signing the book's royalties over to the university from the very beginning. The faculty member states that you must take action immediately and that, if you don't, you'll be a party to a grievance that will be filed with the dean.

- Does this change from an ethical violation to a policy violation alter the way in which you will respond to this issue?

- Would your response be different if you knew that the author was not keeping the royalties but donating them to charity?

- Would your response be different if you knew that the author was not keeping the royalties but donating them to the department's annual fund?

- Would your response be different if *you* were the author of the textbook in question?

Case Study #2: Friends and Lovers

Your institution has fairly clear policies on amorous relations between supervisors and their direct reports and between faculty members and students. You do not, however, have a policy that provides you with any guidance about relationships between colleagues. This has never been a problem in the past, but two faculty members in your department are actively and publicly involved in a romantic relationship. Increasingly, individuals are raising concerns to you that the behavior of the two individuals, while not prohibited, is having a negative effect on your department's ability to function properly.

First, what began as a relationship between two individuals has now become something of a clique. The department has been split between those who support the burgeoning romance and those who feel that its public nature is distracting departmental attention from more important and pressing academic issues. You have had the impression that votes on departmental issues seem to be occurring on lines of these two "factions." You also suspect that several members of the department are voting, not on the basis of the issues, but on the basis of where they stand on the office romance. Your formerly congenial department has suddenly become politicized. You are concerned because you know a challenging promotion and tenure decision is coming up very soon, and you don't want any extraneous issues to distort that process.

To make matters worse, this is your last year in your term as chair, and one of the faculty members involved in the romance is seeking to be appointed as your successor. You seriously believe that, given your department's growing factionalism, such an appointment would divide your program further. You thought that you had found a way out of this difficulty when you reminded the person who wished to be named the next chair that the university had a firm policy against amorous relationships between supervisors and employees. The inflexibility of that policy, you had hoped, might either cause the relationship to cool or induce the faculty member to avoid pursuing the position. When discussing this with the faculty member, however, you learn this is not perceived as a problem since, should this faculty member become department chair, the other member of the relationship would immediately request a leave of absence. You reply that you're not certain anything short of a resignation would fit the policy. Besides, you suggest (still looking for an amicable solution) that since the department has submitted a major grant proposal naming the faculty member who would go on leave as principal investigator, a leave of absence might seriously jeopardize the program's ability to secure this important funding. Moreover, since chairs in your department serve for three years (or as long as six, if renewed), placing a tenured faculty member on leave for that entire period would not be in the best interests of the department as a whole or the continuing research agenda of the person on leave. Your observations are met with a cool and stony silence. Following that meeting, you find yourself being increasingly isolated by members of the clique. You are outvoted several times on issues that you had thought were fairly straightforward. Issues that you hoped to have resolved before stepping down as chair now seem likely to remain undone.

How do you go about solving this problem?

- Which are the ethical issues and which are simple management issues in this situation?

- Is it effective to discuss "the elephant in the room" (i.e., the amorous relationship that everyone knows about but so far has not addressed publicly) at a meeting of the department? Is the clique likely to resist this tactic, dismissing it as unprofessional and simply another political maneuver?

- Do you approach the dean about the possibility of staying on as chair for an extra year, during which time you believe the amorous relationship may unravel? Would you regard this suggestion as a good compromise or as unethical?

- Would your views in the matter be any different if both members of the romantic relationship were the same gender?

- Would your approach to the matter change if you had had a romantic relationship with another department member?

- Does the situation become more complicated or simpler if you find that you are receiving complaints from students, saying that the behavior of the two members of your department is making them uncomfortable and likely to leave your program?

- Would the situation become more complicated or simpler if the couple were to announce their impending marriage?

Case Study #3: Knowing Who Your Friends Are

The development office at your institution has long sent chairs a list of donors who had specified that their annual fund contribution be restricted to support that chair's department or program. You always regarded this as a good practice, since it allowed you to send hand-written notes to your donors, thanking them for their support. In fact, your notes were always well received, and contributions to your department have increased each year you've been chair. Last year, however, you learned of a problem that you were causing inadvertently through your practice of sending these notes. A few of your department members informed you that they felt pressured to make a contribution, since you know the names of all the donors and how much they've given. Junior faculty members said they were in a particularly uncomfortable position since you play such an important role in setting salaries and in deciding matters of contract renewal, promotion, and tenure.

You thought that you had solved this problem by asking the Development Office to send you a list only of external donors, omitting current employees from the list you received. Your solution, however, only led to a further problem. Those employees who had been contributors began to feel slighted because they had grown accustomed to receiving personal attention in the past, and "now it seems all you care about are the big money people outside the institution." As a result, it appears that, for the first time in years, your department's allocation of annual fund receipts may actually decline. You try to seek some compromise by asking the development office to send you only the names of contributors, not the amounts, but the staff tells you that they can't keep writing different types of reports for each department; in fact, they were about to tell you that you would have to receive the complete report again from now on. You assume that the issue is at least out of your hands, try to dismiss the concerns of your junior faculty as mere paranoia, and announce at a department meeting that you'll return to your practice of writing individual notes to all donors, including members of the department.

A few days later, the dean calls you in to talk about "this annual-fund business in your department." You assume you know what the issue is but, before you have a chance to explain your actions, you discover that the dean's interpretation of "this annual-fund business" is not at all what you had in mind. The dean is very concerned because all department chairs have been contributing to the *college's* annual fund at a level far higher than you have. Your contribution to the college has been relatively small, while you have made a larger contribution to your own department. "Now, I can't make you do anything," the dean continues. "Your contribution is your own choice. But I do have expectations, and I don't think it looks good for our college when I'm out raising external support and one of my own chairs doesn't seem to be with the program. Frankly, I think people get the impression you don't care about the college; you only care about your own discipline. I mean, donors want to know who their friends are, and so do I." As you leave the meeting, you start to think that maybe your junior faculty was not being quite so paranoid after all.

- Do you believe that the dean's behavior was unethical in speaking to you in this way? If so, how do you handle the situation?

- Can you find any solution to this situation that allows you to satisfy all the faculty members in your department, regardless of their desire to contribute to the annual fund?

- Since you already announced that you would reinstate your practice of sending notes to thank donors, do you reconsider this plan in light of what you've heard from the dean? If so, what reasons do you give for your actions?

- How might you use this situation to clarify to both the dean and your department your own standards of conduct as chair and your commitment to appropriate professional behavior?

Case Study #4: Bound by Past Practice

Your department is fortunate to have received, on an annual basis, a substantial faculty development fund that supports an extremely broad array of activities. Because of the generosity of a donor who makes this contribution, you have the luxury of allowing faculty members to participate in a large number of conferences, workshops, advanced coursework, certifications, research projects, and other activities that fall broadly into the category of "faculty development." While you have the nominal right to accept or reject each faculty development proposal that is submitted, the practice has been for the chair to approve whatever a faculty member desires. The generosity of the fund has not made a selection process necessary. One advantage to this approach has always been that it allows faculty members to be as innovative as they like. In fact, several new directions in your program began as a result of some rather unusual projects that the chair may not have approved if budgets had been tighter.

Increasingly, however, one member of your department has been causing difficulties related to this fund. This individual has been receiving monetary support for a number of years to develop an expertise in a field that you and many of your colleagues do not regard as particularly necessary for your program. Whenever you raise your concerns about this matter, the faculty member in question turns openly hostile. Many people in the past, you are repeatedly told, have used that fund to support project in areas that others didn't like at first, but those are now some of the discipline's most important initiatives. The faculty member tells you, "It's not appropriate for you to single out this project just because you don't support it. I have the same rights as anyone else." Nevertheless, the real problem, in your opinion, is that this particular faculty member was hired into the department because of his or her existing expertise, but has recently felt entitled to replace those courses with others in the area of the new subdiscipline. You are worried that if you continue to fund this faculty member's proposals, you would be viewed as endorsing a change of teaching assignment that the department has not accepted. It might also leave your program without courses it needs in that faculty member's original area. You try to discuss your concerns but are told, "You can't tell me not to complete this training now. If it were true that the department doesn't need me to teach courses in this new field, I should have been informed of that years ago. I wouldn't have wasted all my time with this new training. As you well know, I was given encouragement by previous chairs to do work in this area, and now you're just going to have to live with it." Privately, you suspect that previous chairs did not so much support the faculty member's retraining as avoid the issue in order to forestall conflicts like the one you've just had.

As an added concern, you suspect that the faculty member is using the excuse of ongoing faculty development work to shirk other duties in your department. Committee meetings have been missed. You are aware of several students who have complained that the faculty member is never around when needed. The faculty member has replaced refereed publications and presentations at major conferences with poster sessions at meetings that experts in your field regard as relatively insignificant. Because of repeated claims by the faculty member that your lack of support is just a personal vendetta, you decide to see if others share your views by discussing the matter openly at a department meeting. The result is a disaster. Several department members do echo your concerns, leading to a tirade by the faculty member who accuses them of misconduct with the fund: "You've been using this money for years for junkets and vacations and other nonacademic purposes. When you do fund retraining, you only do it so as to position yourself for paid consultancies. You're the ones who are unethical here. I'm the only one left in the department who has any standards!" The meeting is so uncomfortable that some of the junior faculty who will soon be up for tenure and promotion become cowed and recommend that the faculty member's funding be continued. Despite your best efforts, your department now seems more divided and the atmosphere more poisoned than ever.

- The angry faculty member was right about at least one thing: several other projects that did not originally have much departmental support did eventually prove to be important new directions for your department. How do you know that the faculty member is not correct in the current case?

- How do you deal with the faculty member's demands to teach in a sub-discipline that the department has not voted to pursue?

- Would it affect your approach if you suspected that the donor might discontinue the large annual contribution should allegations of impropriety become public? Could you live with the reputation of being "the one who cost us all that money?" Is such a large sacrifice proportionate to the problem you are trying to solve?

- If you were audited and had to explain the expenditures that occurred during your tenure as chair, would you feel comfortable doing so in light of how this situation has developed?

- Do you feel any obligation to previous chairs in your deparment whose past support of the faculty member's project created this situation? Does their precedent have any factor in your decision? Are you influenced by the fact that no previous chair had ever vetoed a faculty member's proposal for use of this fund?

- Do you now feel required to investigate the faculty member's sudden claims about the inappropriate behavior of other members of your department? Can you safely dismiss these claims as due to the anger of the moment?

- Was the open discussion a poor decision or were you right to discuss your concerns openly, even if the result was not what you had hoped?

- How do you deal with the faculty member's attempts to "hold the department hostage" through intimidation?

- Would your course of action be any different if:
  - You were stepping down as chair within a few months?
  - You were retiring within a few months?
  - The faculty member were someone with whom you personally had had a long personality conflict?
  - The faculty member were the spouse of your institution's president?
  - The faculty member were the child of someone on your institution's governing board?

25

Setting Annual Themes for the Department

In increasing numbers of colleges and universities, the idea of a campus-wide annual theme or special topic has met with a great deal of success. The individual theme selected by the college may be connected to its first-year experience program, it may be featured in a distinguished lecture series or visiting scholar program, or it may simply be an attempt to provide a feeling of greater unity or focus to the academic program as a whole. These institution-wide annual themes tend to be of great value because they can direct toward a single, significant goal much of the intellectual energy that is already present at the college or university but that would otherwise be dispersed in many different directions. In addition, college-wide annual themes can be used to generate grant proposals or sponsored programs that the institution may not have pursued without the impetus of the theme. Administrators tend to support annual themes because they invariably provide an opportunity for the institution to receive some positive recognition in the media. As a department chair, you may discover that all the reasons for adopting annual themes for your entire college or university can also make them extremely attractive for your individual program.

If your institution already has a procedure for selecting an annual theme in place, your department is probably best served by tying into this college-wide focus in some way. Doing so would be a clear indication of how your discipline functions as a citizen within the larger community and would bring you some positive attention. More tangibly, participation in a broader theme might allow your program to qualify for funding from the larger institutional sources. Nevertheless, if your institution does not yet have a mechanism for selecting an annual theme, this is all the more reason for your department to establish its own. You will be able to use your program's theme to make your department distinctive among its peers at your college, to build on this yearly focus in order to recruit desirable students and faculty members, and to take advantage of this annual activity to open new opportunities for departmental fundraising. If, as a department chair, you plan to seek some sort of higher administrative office, having established and successfully implemented a departmental theme program can be precisely the sort of project that allows you to demonstrate convincingly your creativity, entrepreneurial spirit, and strong institutional citizenship.

Choosing an Annual Theme

What sort of topics provide good annual themes for individual academic departments? The types of topics that your faculty members are likely to develop will be limited only by their collective imagination. Creating a discussion of this possibility, either in a face-to-face meeting or through an electronic forum, will produce more possibilities than any one department could implement. Nevertheless, as a way of priming the pump for this discussion, the following are a few major types of annual themes that you might suggest to your colleagues.

An Anniversary

What important development occurred in your discipline 10, 25, 50, 100, or 200 years ago? Will the coming year be the anniversary of a major figure's birth or death? (The figure that you choose could either be someone commonly studied in your department's courses or it could be a scholar who was responsible for a major achievement in your discipline. The anniversary of the birth or death of major authors, artists, composers, or performers frequently provides useful departmental themes.) It is not important that the anniversary you are commemorating be of a *person*. For instance, will next year be the anniversary of a landmark legal case of lasting importance to your field of study? Is there a major invention or discovery that has had particular significance in your field? Conceived along these lines, the anniversary theme can give your department a focus such as "The Impact of Ten Years Following Smith v. Jones: a Retrospective and Assessment," "The Life, Work, and Art of Rebecca Stowers Peabody: a Centennial Appreciation," or "The Development of Verbosity Theory: a 25 Year Legacy." Titles such as these remind the reader immediately both of the time period involved in your anniversary celebration and the important person, event, or discovery that is being examined.

A Publication

Is there a significant book or article that everyone is your discipline needs to read and discuss? If the work happens to be current, it may be possible to develop broad recognition for your discipline by bringing the author to campus and having that person discuss his or her work with a large number of faculty members and students who, because of your annual theme, have actually read the work and considered it thoughtfully. If your theme deals with an older work (a classic in your discipline, for instance), it may be possible to involve other departments in the events devoted to that year's focus, invite to campus a panel of scholars who will discuss the work from multiple perspectives, or encourage one or more members of your department to publish an update or reaction to this major work. This type of annual theme could lead your department to such titles as "From John Henry Newman's *The Idea of the University* to an idea for a *new* American University," "Plato's *Republic* and the Concept of 'Republic' in the Third Millennium," or "Hobbes and a *Leviathan* for a New Age."

A Commemoration

Is there a faculty member who is retiring during the coming year or has recently retired who could be the subject of your department's annual theme? Could you develop a year in which the students and faculty members of your department read and discuss this professor's publications, raise funds for an ongoing commemoration in honor of this faculty member's contributions, and invite back former students for a series of talks commemorating the lasting impact of this individual? Or, do you have a graduate of your program who has become distinguished through important achievements in your discipline who would be the appropriate subject of a yearlong study? Has a donor made a sufficiently large gift to your discipline that you could devote your department's monthly symposium or some other similar event to a discussion of topics and ideas of particular importance to this donor?

A Festival

Is it possible for your students to present their research in an annual festival that would both give them practice in summarizing their discoveries for their peers and bring desired attention to the achievements of your discipline? If so, is there any way in which you could connect their many diverse projects through the thread of a common theme? Making sure that faculty members and students alike have all read an agreed-upon collection of primary sources will improve the quality of the questions that everyone asks your student presenters, lead to an even stronger set of student research projects in the future, and provide a shared experience for the different members of your department. Alternatively, festivals can be organized around lecture series, faculty research presentations, or showcase performances or exhibits. The important factor in each case is that the festival offers your discipline a distinct focal point that can lead to classroom discussion in the weeks or months before the festival, include the external community in significant on-campus events, and provide encouragement for intentional learning through out-of-class readings, discussion groups, or panel presentations.

A Topical Focus

What current event can provide a theme worthy of discussion for every member of your department regardless of their individual specialties? For instance, national elections occur every four years: Is there a topic of concern in the election—or might even the election process itself be considered topical for your discipline—with the result that your department's annual theme could be tied to this significant activity once in every student's undergraduate career? Has there recently been an ethical scandal or congressional inquiry that has refocused attention on the way in which professionals in your field conduct their business? Has a new discovery or a revolutionary way of approaching information in your discipline been noticed by more than just a narrow range of professionals? Is there a proposed piece of legislation that has significance in your area? By using any of these approaches, you may be able to find an appropriate annual theme for your academic department. A topically focused theme can remind students, their parents, and your discipline's external constituents of the continued relevance of your field and its impact on their daily lives.

Implementing an Annual Theme

Once you and your departmental colleagues have selected the topic for your annual theme, the next question that may concern you is how you may wish to go about incorporating your new topic into what you do as a discipline. The exact way in which the annual theme will be used by the department depends a great deal on the nature of your institution and your individual discipline. Nevertheless, the following are some of the most common ways in which departments can use an annual theme in their activities.

Common Readings

Each member of the department, instructor and student alike, can share in a common experience related to your annual theme through reading assignments that go beyond the requirements of individual courses and provide the basis for discipline-wide discussions. Your department's common readings might range from brief articles that can be read in a single sitting to multiple books that are read one per month in an ongoing departmental "book club." Lists of upcoming common readings can be distributed at the end of the spring term to be completed over the summer or can be completed as needed throughout the regular academic year. The advantages of tying common readings to an annual theme are numerous. These experiences promote a sense of community in your department through a universally shared opportunity. They focus the attention of a large number of extremely diverse individuals onto a single topic, thus providing a greater degree of structure and meaning to their experience. And they encourage students to draw connections among discrete courses by introducing them to a single point of significant commonality.

Lecture and Discussion Series

Departmental themes can also form the basis for conferences devoted to your discipline's annual topic, high-profile lectures delivered by nationally recognized speakers, or a series of several lectures and discussions devoted to the topic that you have selected for that year. While a primary purpose of these events is to enrich the academic experience of your students and faculty members as a whole, a second important result of having several lectures and discussions devoted to your annual theme can be to bring the larger community to your campus, thereby reinforcing the long-term significance of work in your discipline. Series of lectures and discussions can provide a valuable synergy among what the students are learning in their courses, contributions your faculty members are making in their scholarship, and public awareness of the issues raised by your annual theme.

Grant Applications

One of the most attractive features about annual themes to department chairs is that they provide built-in opportunities for seeking external funding support. Funding agencies are much more likely to provide support to a program that is fully integrated (as a properly selected annual theme would be) with a department's individual mission, strengths, and areas of distinction than they are to any number of seemingly random topics. After establishing a successful track record with your department's annual theme, your institution may even be willing to pursue challenge grant opportunities to provide an ongoing endowment for the events associated with your program's annual theme. External support acquired in this way allows your department to be creative in planning activities in support of your annual theme without unduly drawing on your institution's internal resources. Moreover, an event that is funded through a grant or gift always seems to attract more attention and provides a department with opportunities for seeking positive exposure in the media.

Awards

One additional way to obtain positive media recognition is to present a highly publicized award in conjunction with the annual theme. If your department recognizes an individual for distinguished service in your field or a lifetime of contributions to whatever topic you have selected, you will develop an automatic opportunity for positive publicity surrounding your program, create stronger ties to the individual whom you are honoring, and create an occasion in which members of your community outside of your department and institution will certainly wish to participate. Other types of awards that can be offered in conjunction with your department's annual theme are scholarships for outstanding student research in this area, commendations for the best graduate-student presentation on your department's topic, and recognitions of outstanding achievements by other academic programs in this area.

First-Year Experiences

Nearly every college or university has some sort of first-year experience program designed for new students, ranging from extended orientations to comprehensive programs of courses, cocurricular experiences, and extracurricular activities that fully integrate each new student into the academic community. But what about a "First-Year-*In-Our-Department*" experience for new majors? Offered in conjunction with a semester-long or year-long course for new majors, cocurricular sessions devoted to your annual theme can help students understand from their very first contact with your department why your discipline is unique, exciting, and relevant. More advanced students could mentor entering students, leading discussions related to that year's topic and providing the sort of guidance that will help the students succeed.

Course Clusters

One of the ways in which institutions are attempting to break down the barriers between discrete courses and help students see how the experience of one discipline is related to another is through the creation of carefully designed course clusters. In this system, each cluster takes a particular theme—perhaps an historical period, a social problem, or an interdisciplinary focus—and explores that topic in two, three, or four courses that a group of students takes simultaneously. Designing one or more course clusters in which your department's annual theme is featured prominently can be an effective way to relate your discipline to others at your institution (or to relate different sub-disciplines within your own department) and keep your department's contributions fresh and topical.

Advantages of Annual Themes

Once you have begun experimenting with annual departmental themes along the lines outlined above, you are likely to notice several advantages that will begin accruing to your department and to you as chair. A few of the advantages of having a departmental annual theme follow.

Leveraging

By uniting what would otherwise be unrelated courses, lectures, or campus events through your annual theme, you can make each of these individual activities more significant as part of a larger, noteworthy project.

Publicity

Individuals and agencies (including those who provide sources of external funding) are unlikely to pay much attention to an occasional lecture or guest speaker; however, they are much more likely to notice an event in what you have developed as an extended series. It is easier for local newspapers and television or radio stations to cover "Tonight's Discussion in This Year's Ongoing Series Devoted to . . . " than to devote scarce resources to covering a speech or panel discussion in your department that seems unrelated to a larger purpose.

Interaction

The annual theme will also prompt numerous opportunities for you to interact with other departments on your campus, other colleagues at different campuses, and interested members of the community. Your annual theme is one important way that you can help your department serve external constituents more effectively and attract their interest in how they may better serve the ongoing needs of your department.

In this way, a well-selected annual theme can simultaneously provide your department with a new focus for its discussions and curriculum, an expanded set of possibilities for obtaining external funding, enhanced visibility, and renewed opportunities for engagement with other departments at your institution. By promoting an annual theme in your department, you will be taking another step from merely managing what currently exists to leading your discipline toward where it may go in the future.

26

Setting Course Rotations and Schedules

For many chairs, preparing each term's course schedule may seem the most mundane of their responsibilities. Course schedules and rotations may seem overly fixed at some institutions owing to history and inertia. At others, faculty members may begin to view offering certain courses at certain times almost as an entitlement. Even more often, chairs set course schedules with relatively little thought given to the overall picture of the discipline's needs and maximum benefits. As a result, certain sections end up getting canceled—or allowed to run, grudgingly, by the dean—since their enrollments are so low. Students approach graduation only to discover that they are missing essential courses that are not on the course rotation for another several semesters. Facilities are used inefficiently because little thought was given to their optimal usage when course schedules were made.

The following are a few commonplace rules that every chair should keep in mind, both in creating the department's course schedule for an individual term and in developing a long-term course rotation for the program.

Don't Compete With Yourself

One of the scheduling problems that departments inadvertently create for themselves is competing for the same students in multiple sections. This problem can arise in a number of different ways. First, it can occur when two or more courses likely to be taken by the same pool of students are either offered at the same time, overlapping course periods, or one after the other in buildings that are very far apart. Second, it can occur when too many options exist for the same limited pool of students during the same term, with the result that each option ends up enrolling too few students. The solution to this problem has partly to do with course scheduling and rotations, partly to do with curriculum development. In other words, it may be fairly easy to begin reviewing the schedule for each term or each academic year with an eye toward avoiding the most obvious scheduling conflicts, but it is far more difficult to deal with problems that arise from poorly considered program requirements. Curricula that require too many specific courses, as opposed to offering several options from a list—particularly if those specific courses must be taken in a specific sequence—can end up creating course gridlock for students. Therefore, you should devote one department meeting each year to consideration of the schedules planned for the next several terms, the long-term course rotation, and the general curricular requirements to determine where you may be creating problems by competing with your own courses. Indeed, if such an analysis is not a required part of your institutional program-review procedure, you should adopt it as part of your own departmental operating procedures.

Schedule in "Contingency Plans" When Offering Multiple Sections of the Same Course

Your department may offer several different sections of the same course because student demand for it is so great that these sections always "make." But sooner or later, whether due to a temporary enrollment decline or shifting patterns of student needs or desires, your department may be in a situation where one or more of these sections may not be needed in a given term. In these cases, it is highly desirable to have a contingency plan developed well in advance that will guide you in how sections may be collapsed and other duties assigned to the faculty member(s) involved. One solution is to schedule multiple sections of courses in pairs. In other words, instead of scheduling four sections of the same course at 9:00, 11:00, 1:00, and 3:00, you may consider scheduling two sections at 9:00 and two sections at 3:00. (This solution presumes, of course, that all sections are not taught by the same faculty member.) The advantage of this approach is that, if enrollments in any one of these sections is very small, it can easily be merged with another section at the same time. Students' schedules will not have to be rewritten since they obviously have that course period free already. Nor are you competing with yourself in this way, since these are multiple sections of the same course, not similar courses taken by the same students. If you do not wait until the very end of registration to collapse the sections, you may be able to open up a section of a different course for which there is sufficient student demand and reassign one of the faculty members to that course.

Spread the Day

Departments also create problems for themselves in scheduling by failing to take full advantage of every course period in the day. The popular course times with students and faculty members may be at 10:00, 11:00, and 1:00, but it does a disservice to both groups to over-schedule these periods. Students find it more difficult to make schedules if many of the courses that they want to take are all offered at the same time. Faculty members may have their courses canceled for low enrollments since students are not free at that time of day to take them. Taking full advantage of the day makes better use of your facilities and avoids the waste that results from classrooms and laboratories that are heavily used for only three or four hours a day, while they sit largely unoccupied for eight or more hours.

Review Rotations With an Eye Toward When Students May Declare Majors

Different programs and different institutions have students who declare majors at different times. At some institutions, it is required for students to declare their majors in the second semester of their second year. In certain programs, including music and nursing, students are expected to declare a major or intention to major almost immediately upon beginning their first year. Regardless of the situation that exists for your program and institution, it can be an extremely valuable exercise for you to walk through your course rotation with the view in mind of making a tentative schedule for a student who enters your program at each possible moment. For instance, if students declare majors only at a particular time in the year, do this exercise for each year beginning at that point. If students can declare majors each term, do it for each term. What courses required for the major are students likely or required to bring with them at the time when they enter your program officially? What courses will they still need before they graduate? Will they be able to get those courses, in the correct order and in a timely manner, within a standard 4- or 5-year undergraduate program? Where in your course rotation do you see bottlenecks forming or unmet student needs likely to occur? Can you begin planning for other alternatives that you may be able to offer students such as waiving certain requirements that you are authorized to waive or recommending alternative courses from other programs at your institution?

Develop Alliances With Other Key Departments

Nearly every department knows of other departments with which they are in some sort of symbiotic relationship. Either that department offers service courses that are required or highly desirable for your majors or your program does that for the other department. Perhaps one of the departments offers a general education course that is particularly appropriate for students in the other program. Perhaps you share (or *could* share) facilities, equipment, or clerical support with the other program. For these and any number of other reasons, it may be highly desirable for you to go over course rotations with one another well before you need to submit them to the registrar. There may be relatively small adjustments you can make to the times, days, or terms when certain courses are offered that can help you maximize enrollment in both departments. Reviewing schedules in common is also a good way for both programs to take the greatest advantage of shared facilities and equipment, avoid conflicts in making assignments to shared clerical staff, and foster good institutional citizenship.

Consider Revising the Curriculum to Incorporate Pedagogical Needs and Likely Enrollment Patterns

One of the common failings we share in academic life is the tendency to throw a course at every perceived student need. If students are having difficulty adjusting to the institution upon their first arrival there, we create new "Introduction to College" courses. If students are perceived to be poor writers or lacking in quantitative skills, we develop new required composition courses and statistical sequences. If we feel that students need exposure to other societies or ethnic groups, we fill our curricula with international studies or multicultural studies courses. This tendency frequently carries over into departmental programs. Sometimes prompted by discipline-specific accreditation or certification bodies, sometimes prompted by our own desires to improve our programs, we create a host of individual courses to achieve individual pedagogical goals—even when individual courses are not specifically necessary. It is perfectly possible, for instance, for a student to receive an orientation to the university, improve his or her writing skills, and become exposed to other cultures all in the same course. In much the same way, it is desirable to pull back periodically from your curriculum and ask:

- What are the specific pedagogical aims we are trying to achieve in our program?

- How might those aims be achieved, not necessarily through individual courses, but through well-planned learning objectives developed for all of our courses?

- Are there any pedagogical aims that are better achieved through cocur-ricular requirements (such as non-credit-bearing portfolios, lecture series, or pre-professional organizations) than through discrete courses?

- Are there other pedagogical aims that are better achieved, not through any one course, but across a course cluster?

- Are there any pedagogical aims that, while desirable, are simply not such a high priority that they should be required parts of the curriculum?

By using this type of review, you may be able to reorganize and simplify your curriculum so that it achieves your essential aims better than your current approach does and gives you and your students greater flexibility in course planning and selection. Approached creatively and with a strong desire to develop a program that is in your students' best interest, many impassable scheduling problems may prove to have been mere artifacts resulting from the way in which your curriculum had been structured.

27

Building Strong Connections Beyond Your Department

While most of the work of department chairs tends to focus on the faculty who actually hold membership in the department, chairs have many other constituents as well. There are students, parents of students, other department chairs, professional colleagues at other institutions, senior administrators, and at times even the media to contend with. In order to be successful as a chair, you will need to know how you can best serve these external constituents, where to draw the line with them, under which circumstances to turn to them as allies, and when it is desirable to maintain a distance. Mastering these skills can be challenging, and your progress will be determined, in part, by your own personality and the needs of your department. But no chair can afford to be focused so inwardly on the department itself that these essential ties are not maintained.

Students

Unless your department is almost exclusively focused on research, students are likely to be your raison d'être. Maintaining good ties with students can help build your major, preserve solid enrollments in departmental courses, and enhance the reputation of your discipline across campus. Unhappy students can ruin a program and, in the most extreme cases, bring an early and unfortunate end to a chair's career. But how do you *as chair* maintain the proper relationship with students? You're probably already familiar with how to interact with them and where to draw the lines *as a faculty member*. The difficulty comes in that, as a department chair, you now have responsibility for the interactions of many of your colleagues with their students. You may be tempted to adopt an approach in which "the faculty member is always right" or "the student is always right," but as you will soon discover, actual situations are rarely that simple.

One appropriate place to begin maintaining strong ties with students is to understand precisely what the faculty/student and chair/student relationship should be. There is a great deal of talk in academic circles of the student as customer, and this type of description tends to rankle faculty members just as much as it appears to make sense to admission counselors and certain senior administrators. The fact of the matter is that a student's relationship with a college or university is complex. There are aspects of your students' relationship with your institution in which they are customers: The way in which they are treated by the business office, when they make a purchase in the bookstore, order lunch in the dining hall, or lease a room in a residence hall are all situations that deserve to be governed by a customer-service model at your institution. But the relationship a student has with a faculty member and with you as chair should not be the same as that which a customer has with a business; it should, to the contrary, be far more similar to that which a client or patient has with a licensed professional.

Here's the difference. Imagine a customer going into any business, for instance a restaurant. As long as the customer adheres to certain general rules of conduct—not smoking where that is not allowed, dressing appropriately, not bothering the other customers, and so on—that customer is entitled to order and receive anything that he or she can pay for. This is true even if the request is illogical, unhealthy, or unwise. If a customer in a restaurant wants four entrees or only items containing the letter "q," that person is perfectly within his or her right to be served them, as long as they are paid for. But now imagine a customer going to see a licensed professional, for instance a physician. That same person is not entitled to be "served" any prescription that he or she can pay for, nor can the person even demand any service or procedure that they wish. The professional is always expected to consider the client's or patient's *needs*, not merely the person's *desires*.

So it is with the student's relationship with the faculty member and the chair. Students may demand that certain rules be waived for them, that the decisions of a professor be overturned, or that they be allowed to enroll in a certain course. Your responsibility as chair of the department is, however, always to determine whether that is what a student needs and whether that decision is in the student's best interest. Your position as a professional, in other words, requires you to exert your best professional judgment. You must be the arbiter of when exceptions are to be made and when decisions are to be overturned. If that were not the case, many departments could suffice with rulebooks or policy manuals rather than living, breathing heads of the department.

In so doing, there will inevitably be instances in which you conclude that the student is right, and you may need to take up that student's case in opposition to one or more members of your department. You should do so clearly, uninfluenced by favor, and politely, explaining your reasons calmly to the faculty member(s) in private whenever possible to avoid unnecessary humiliation. Your goal throughout should be to act within a consistent set of general principles, and as justly as possible, always guided by what will ultimately best serve the students, not by their emotions, threats, or immediate desires.

Parents

Active and intense parental involvement in higher education seems to be the result of an overall shift in how many people view education and their role in it. At one time, it was not at all uncommon for a department chair or faculty member to go through an entire academic year with absolutely no parental contact except perhaps at officially scheduled events like family weekends. Today, however, it is not at all unheard of for parents—even of graduate students—to contact faculty members, chairs, and senior administrators to appeal decisions that have been made regarding their children, ask for information about grades and course attendance, challenge grades once they have been assigned, and generally serve as advocates for their children on a wide range of issues. The term "helicopter parents"—coined by Cline and Fay (1990)—has become widely used by administrators to describe parents who always seem to be "hovering over" their children, never completely letting them try out their independence, even in college. Parents tend to visit campus more readily, and students are much more likely to return home most weekends than were students of the 1960s, 1970s, or 1980s.

Parental involvement in college can be a double-edged sword. On the one hand, many parents can be confrontational and end up interfering with the very educational process that they claim to be so important for their children. On the other hand, they can exert an influence on students that goes far beyond what faculty members can sometimes do, compelling slothful students to be more responsible and changing the behavior (if not always the attitudes) of those who are disrespectful, aggravating, or belligerent. As a result, it serves the chair well to maintain as positive a relationship as possible with the parents of students taking courses in the department.

Often conversations with parents may begin on the basis of incorrect information. The parent may, for example, contact the chair seeking information about grades that is protected under the Family Educational Rights and Privacy Act (FERPA). Since the vast majority of college students are over the age of 18, the amount of information about a student's grades that you are legally permitted to share with a parent is severely limited. You may wish to consult the U.S. Department of Education's web site on FERPA (see http://www.ed.gov/policy/gen/guid/fpco/ferpa/index.html), always bearing in mind that the repeated phrase "parents or eligible students have the right" refers only to parents of students who have not yet reached 18 years of age. Once students come of age, they have the right to determine whether their grades will be shared with their parents even if the parents are paying tuition. You might wish to investigate what procedure your institution has in place that allows students to waive their FERPA rights. Then you can assure the parent that, once such a waiver has been filed, you will be happy to discuss the matter further. Another alternative may be to suggest a face-to-face meeting with the parent, the student, and any faculty members from your department whose courses the student may be taking. In such cases, you may ask the student openly whether his or her grades may be discussed with the parent. (Your institution may also demand that this permission be given in writing; even if it is not required, it is always desirable to have a written waiver on hand, and you may wish to come to the meeting with such a form ready to be signed.) Face-to-face meetings can be far more productive than lengthy telephone calls or email exchanges, since they allow faculty members to explain directly to the parent certain grading policies or behaviors of the student that may have been inaccurately represented to the parent in the past. They also gather all of the principals together into a room at the same time, making it much less likely for alternative claims of truth to go unchallenged.

Parents also sometimes incorrectly assume that, as your faculty members' "boss," you are free to dictate every aspect of how they conduct their courses, evaluate students, or decide priorities. It may be helpful to explain that, just as a faculty member's relationship to a student is much closer to that of a physician to a patient than a clerk to a customer, so is your relationship to your faculty much closer to that of a hospital administrator to the resident staff than to that of a foreman to a factory worker. In other words, hospital administrators do evaluate members of their resident staff, work to keep the institution functioning smoothly, and help plan for desirable future developments. Hospital administrators *don't* overrule the diagnoses of the resident staff or prescribe alternative therapies. While you may consider any information the parent shares about a faculty member's professional conduct (subject, of course, to your ability to find corroborating evidence), you will not be overturning any specific decision that you have authorized your faculty to make. To do so would be contrary to professional standards of academic freedom and collegiality.

Although they are focused on the pre-college environment, Whitaker and Fiore's (2001) *Dealing With Difficult Parents: And With Parents in Difficult Situations* and McEwan's (2004) *How to Deal With Parents Who Are Angry, Troubled, Afraid, or Just Plain Crazy* contain a great deal of advice on how to respond to overly aggressive or angry parents, accusations that you or members of your faculty are being unfair, and ways to use tone and body language to reduce tension in extremely emotional situations.

Other Chairs

Your relationship with chairs of other departments is likely to be complex as well. At times, other chairs are your colleagues, the people with whom you need to work effectively for the good of your institution. At other times, these same chairs are your competitors, the people who are often seeking the same resources that you are seeking, including students, staff support, and institutional dollars. That balance can be challenging to maintain, but succeeding at it is a primary factor in determining your success (or at least your happiness and peace of mind) as a chair. Your general rule of thumb should be to see yourself as a collaborator with your fellow chairs for *at least* 90% of the time, and as competitors for *no more than* 10% of the time. This is definitely one situation in which the motto "There is no I in TEAM" takes precedence over "Nice guys finish last."

The reason cooperation among academic chairs is so important is that departments are symbiotic entities. It is the rare academic program that enrolls students who do not take courses from any other department. In other words, your department needs good rapport with other departments, and they need you. For this reason, seek as many opportunities as possible for interdepartmental cooperation. Requests for large budget items tend to be funded much more quickly if they are submitted with the support of several departments that have demonstrated that they can think strategically, share resources, and work together to set priorities for the good of the institution. If you are offering faculty development training in some area that would be useful to faculty members in other departments, offer this opportunity to other chairs. (At the very least, you will be advertising your efforts. Even better, you may prompt other chairs to reciprocate by offering help with some project that you need done.) If you are a seasoned chair, demonstrate a willingness to mentor your junior colleagues. If you are aware of a significant achievement made by faculty members in another department, be open, sincere, and generous with your praise. These efforts will do far more to strengthen your department in the long run than will constant (and ultimately futile) interdepartmental competition.

Colleagues

The tenor of your relationship with chairs of other departments at your institution should also guide your behavior toward chairs in your discipline at other institutions. Admittedly, you will at times be competing with them for students and other resources. Nevertheless, you will profit more by making the first move toward establishing a cordial, reciprocal relationship than you will if you simply regard your colleagues at other institutions as competitors. These colleagues can be resources for you in ways that no one else can. They may have experience working with a discipline-specific accreditation body, government agency, or professional organization that your own institution's department chairs will not. They may have faced certain problems or opportunities that are different from those experienced by your local peers. You might wish to explore with these colleagues opportunities that can strengthen both of your programs. Is there, for instance, a speaker that neither of you can afford individually but that can be brought to at least one of your campuses if you pool resources and open the event to students in both programs? Can you provide one another with external reviews of each other's curriculum, facilities, and resources in ways that provide significant cost savings to both institutions? Is it possible to suggest an informal faculty exchange for a course or a semester as a way of enriching your discipline and providing additional stimulation for a member of your department? Are there types of training that you can offer at the other institution because of special expertise among your faculty? Any of these possibilities can be extremely valuable in opening lines of communication with colleagues who can more than reciprocate your generosity by bringing new ideas and possibly even supplementary resources to help improve your program.

Senior Administrators

The level of academic administration regarded as middle managers varies from institution to institution. This designation is sometimes extended to chairs; sometimes only deans or vice presidents are thought of as providing an institution's middle management. However the term may be applied at your institution, there will be times in which you feel very "middle" indeed—pressed between the competing demands of your students and faculty on one side and your institution's board, president, and vice president(s) on the other. Chairs can often feel like little more than a conduit, trying to explain their faculty's needs and positions upward, striving to justify their senior administrators' decisions downward. It can be an uncomfortable position to occupy.

How you relate to your senior administrators has a lot to do with your institutional structure and, frankly, with their respective personalities. Some senior administrators treat you as a colleague, confiding in you, seeking your advice, and carefully weighing your perspectives. Other senior administrators expect you to implement their policies unquestioningly, praising you when they find you to be compliant and efficient, less satisfied when they feel you are not on board with a significant policy decision. Although no single approach will help you maintain strong ties with all senior administrators, in the vast majority of cases the qualities that will benefit you the most are *candor, cordiality,* and *confidentiality.*

No one likes to be blindsided. The most uncomfortable moments one can have are when, in public meetings, information or opinions that could and should have been shared privately are suddenly and unexpectedly announced. Some chairs may feel that this sort of grandstanding "is popular with the troops" and serves them well with their own faculty. Nothing could be further from the truth. Most faculty members are embarrassed when they feel that their chair is trying to "one up" even an unpopular senior administrator or to make that person feel uncomfortable. Moreover, these tactics are extremely ineffective in positioning the department favorably for any type of decision in which that administrator plays a role. Most senior administrators prefer chairs to speak to them bluntly (and in a timely manner) behind closed doors about disagreements they may have with priorities or policies of that administrator. Once disagreements are aired and discussed privately, however, most senior administrators will want those reporting to them to speak with a single voice once a decision has been made. To do otherwise is to undermine an institution's ability to make any progress. It invites constant reconsideration of decisions that have already been made, promotes passive-aggressive responses to policies that one does not like, and is conducive to extremely poor morale throughout the institution.

Speaking bluntly to a senior administrator is not the same thing, however, as speaking rudely. With candor must come cordiality. There are, admittedly, senior administrators who are less than fully effective in their positions. There are even some who should probably be removed from office. But there are few, if any, administrators who act out of malice or a desire to harm their institution or any part of it. In other words, senior administrators can be wrong. They may be ill advised or ill informed. But they are rarely evil, despite common stereotypes. As a result, they deserve the type of cordiality that one would extend to any faculty colleague. They deserve to hear differences of opinion presented calmly and from a factual basis, not emotionally and in an accusatorial manner. Moreover, they deserve to have their confidences kept. Few violations of trust can destroy a department chair's credibility as quickly as revealing information provided by a senior administrator without that person's permission. Colleges and universities tend to thrive on the free flow of information. Nevertheless, there are times at which certain information cannot yet be revealed—because other individuals deserve the courtesy of being brought into the loop first or because certain aspects of the decision are still pending—and chairs who value their careers will honor this need for confidentiality.

The Media

Another situation in which confidentiality can be extremely important is when a chair has been contacted by the media. Each institution needs to have a clear policy for speaking with the media. In most cases, chairs will either be required or expected to consult first with their direct supervisors and with the institution's office of public affairs or college relations. Some institutions even forbid contact with the media aside from designated campus spokespersons. For this reason, your individual policy for handling the media should be never to take cold calls. If contacts to your department must be routed through a secretary, receptionist, or administrative assistant, leave instructions that calls and visits from representatives of the media are *never* to be put through to you immediately. Instead, they should indicate that you are unable to take the call, ascertain the reason for the call, and obtain a way to contact the media representative at a later time. Once you have this information, you can consult with the appropriate individuals on your campus and determine the best way for this contact to be returned. It is quite possible that it will be preferable for someone other than you to return the call or visit.

If you are the one designated to reinitiate the contact with the media, be gracious but keep your remarks within limits. If the topic being discussed is at all a sensitive issue (and even, in most cases, when the topic appears completely innocuous), decide in advance what you will say and then go no further. Remarks may be misconstrued or taken out of context. If you prepare carefully, you are less likely to say something that you will regret later. Do not answer questions that are not asked, but if you are asked a question that will take you into an area that seems inadvisable, turn the question toward an area that you can answer. Try (very politely) to take command of the situation by using the opportunity to get out the message that you wish to convey. In instances where the questions are about sensitive issues, try to have a third party present who can provide assistance to you when necessary and who can serve as a witness to what you actually said. If it is not possible to have a third party present, ask if you might tape the interview. (If it serves no other purpose, you can always use this tape to critique your own performance and consider how you might improve it the next time.) Try not to appear nervous, although it is quite natural that you will be; most department chairs do not have much practice dealing with the media, and when they do these experiences often occur in tense or difficult circumstances.

RESOURCES

Several resources are also available to help you work more effectively with the media. Among the best of these resources are:

Cohn, R. (2000). *The PR crisis bible: How to take charge of the media when all hell breaks loose.* New York, NY: St. Martin's Press.

Hoffman, J. C. (2001). *Keeping cool on the hot seat: Dealing effectively with the media in times of crisis.* Highland Mills, NY: 4 C's Publishing.

Stewart, S. (2003). *Media Training 101: A Guide to Meeting the Press.* Hoboken, NJ: John Wiley & Sons.

REFERENCES

Cline, F., & Fay, J. (1990). *Parenting with love and logic: Teaching children responsibility.* Colorado Springs, CO: Piñon Press.

McEwan, E. K. (2004). *How to deal with parents who are angry, troubled, afraid, or just plain crazy* (2nd ed.). Thousand Oaks, CA: Corwin Press.

Whitaker, T., & Fiore, D. J. (2001). *Dealing with difficult parents: And with parents in difficult situations.* Larchmont, NY: Eye on Education.

28

A Departmental Center for Excellence in Teaching and Learning

Centers dedicated to the improvement of teaching and learning have now become common features on most college campuses. These centers—frequently bearing such titles as Center for Excellence in Teaching and Learning or Center for Innovations in Teaching and Learning—play a significant role in improving student learning, exposing faculty members to alternative forms of pedagogy, and exploring the role that technology can play in the learning process. Yet precisely because these centers have become so common, chairs may be tempted to ask: Why would I need a *departmental* center for excellence in teaching and learning? Hasn't that function been superseded by offices that serve the entire institution? Isn't there an economy of scale achieved by a university-wide center for pedagogy that cannot be matched even by fairly large departments?

- If your institution does not yet have its own center for teaching and learning, then your department *needs* to have one. By establishing such a center you will be doing a favor for your faculty and students by enhancing the learning process in your discipline and for your institution as a whole by providing a model for the advantages that could be obtained if this approach were adopted campus-wide.

- If your institution already has such a center, you may still want your own departmental "branch office" to explore pedagogies that are more appropriate for your discipline, to examine software packages that may be more useful for teaching and learning in your area than in others, and to inculcate the methods of scholarship suitable to your field that may not be as transferable to other fields across the institution. When you are establishing a departmental center that will exist in addition to a center serving the entire institution, you should partner closely with your campus-wide center in order to avoid unnecessary duplication of efforts, obtain information about additional resources, and avoid appearing as if you are attempting to infringe on another office's territory. You may even wish to use the term "branch office" or "departmental outlet" for the larger center in order to clarify that your desire is to enhance the campus center, not to replace it.

Unlike campus-wide centers dedicated to improving the quality of teaching, your departmental center need not occupy a great deal of geography. It may be little more than a notice board, bookshelf, or workstation in a departmental office. In some cases, it may not be a physical entity at all, but rather a "moveable feast" that occurs whenever and wherever there is an activity that it sponsors. For instance, your departmental center might consist entirely of a workshop series, monthly discussion group, and electronic bulletin board. By means of your department's web site or course-management system, your department's entire center can be a virtual center—an idea of commitment to the importance of excellence in teaching rather than a specific location.

However you configure your departmental center, you should begin by developing a clear notion of the sort of activities your center might sponsor and the goals that you wish it to achieve. While many of these objectives depend on your discipline and institution, the following are suggestions that many department chairs will find applicable to their areas.

Methods

While there are many pedagogical methods that work across any number of disciplines, each academic area has methods of instructing and engaging students in intellectual inquiry that are unique to its particular fields. These methods are unlikely to be addressed in campus-wide centers for teaching and learning and lend themselves perfectly to departmental centers. For instance, in the fine arts, the critique is frequently used as a teaching tool in ways that are very different from the methods of other academic disciplines. But few opportunities exist on many campuses for art teachers to improve their skills at supervising truly outstanding critiques. Similarly, law schools tend to rely heavily on the case study. Nevertheless, few teachers in law programs receive formal training in how to *lead* case-study sessions as opposed to merely participating in them. A discipline-specific center devoted to teaching excellence can assist faculty members in developing their skills at conducting such vital instructional activities.

You might find that your faculty needs teaching methods that are not unique to your discipline, but that are not specifically addressed by the campus-wide center for teaching and learning. Moreover, departmental centers might serve other purposes not currently addressed campus wide, such as inculcating good teaching methods in the program's graduate students or even upper-level undergraduate students. Adjunct faculty members with little teaching experience might also be encouraged, or even required, to participate in some of the department's programs on instruction shortly after they begin work at the institution.

Some of the more general instructional methods explored by your departmental center might include techniques for making students more active learners in the classroom, even in courses where there is no research component or similar contact with primary sources of information. The following are examples of teaching strategies that are designed to promote students' active involvement with course material.

Inside/Outside Circles

Organize the students of the course into two concentric rings, each containing the same number of students. (In very large courses, it may be helpful to use several pairs of concentric rings so that each group contains no more than 20 students.) Assign the students a problem or topic to discuss in pairs consisting of one student from the outer circle, one from the inner circle. After a set period of time (usually only one to five minutes), have one of the circles rotate so that each pair changes. Repeat this exercise three or four times until each student receives a variety of perspectives on the topic, different ways to solve the problem, or opportunities to explain how a task is best accomplished.

Send a Problem

Divide the students of the class into groups of approximately six to ten. Have each group develop a problem or discussion question based on the material covered in that unit. They should also come up with their own solution to the problem or set of key points to be discussed on that issue. Each group then sends its problem to another group, receiving a problem in return. After each group has worked on each of the available problems, the entire class is then reconstituted and the various solutions and discussions are compared.

Top-Ten List

Working in groups, students are assigned the task of creating lists—in reverse priority order—of the top ten facts or observations about a particular unit.

The goal is not merely to identify what students believe are the most significant observations about the material, but to weigh them in significance. Making the answers humorous is a desirable, though not required, component of the assignment.

Game Show

Almost every season introduces some new and highly popular television game show. Choose whichever game format is currently popular, adapt its format to your discipline, and use this structure for a unit review or to prepare for an examination. In larger courses, break the students into separate teams, have each team prepare questions in the appropriate format, and use the questions to help the students master the material or approaches covered in the course.

The Muddiest Point

This technique [developed by Thomas Angelo and Patricia Cross in *Classroom Assessment Techniques* (Jossey-Bass, 1993), p. 154] can promote active learning and provide the instructor with mid-course feedback on where students are still having the greatest difficulty. Students simply complete a small form stating, "The point that is still the most unclear for me about this unit is . . . " and give it to the instructor. Students may also be broken into groups to help explain to one another the points about which one or more of their members still find confusing.

Faculty members sometimes claim that such classroom techniques are merely gimmicks and are thus inappropriate for use in college-level courses, or that they are even demeaning to good students who would benefit more from traditional lecture and discussion. In fact, however, students at all levels of academic ability tend to become more engaged with course material and perform better on classroom assignments and exams when faculty members adopt a broader array of innovative teaching methods. The key is not necessarily to adopt the specific teaching methods outlined above, but to find some approach that fits each professor's individual teaching style and encourages students to engage actively with the material. The advantages of the methods explored here are that they get students out of their seats, compel them to interact with one another, and engage them in teaching the material—not just listen passively. As a department chair, you should encourage your faculty to be creative in developing interactive teaching techniques that are most appropriate to your discipline and to the students who tend to enroll at your institution.

Technology

Every discipline is aware of certain software applications or technology that are perfect for its instructional mission, even if they may not be of any importance to other programs. Campus-wide centers for teaching and learning generally conduct training sessions on items of hardware or software programs that are used throughout academic disciplines, but how do faculty members learn about individual items of technology that are unique to your field? Departmental instructional resource centers are perfect for this more specialized approach to instruction. Through your departmental center, you can pilot new applications as they become available, provide training that is adapted to your discipline's unique methodology, and test these approaches with small groups of students or select course sections.

Because your departmental center for teaching and learning is smaller and more nimble than your campus-wide center—and because it has a more focused mission—it will be able to incorporate new advances in technology much more rapidly than can your larger institutional structure. For instance, when iPods and other mp3 players first became widely used by college students, departmental centers for teaching were among the early adopters of this new technology for pedagogical purposes, locating (and sometimes creating) instructional Podcasts in their disciplines, providing students with access to royalty-free musical examples in their music history courses, and disseminating information to majors in a format that reached students in an accessible and timely manner. As other new technologies appear on the market, your departmental center can serve as a leader at your institution in exploring their academic uses, incorporating them into pilot sections of courses, and using them to improve student learning.

Discussion Groups

Even a virtual departmental center for teaching and learning can serve as a magnet for various types of discussion groups dedicated to the consideration of student learning. Discussion groups sponsored by your departmental center might focus on a particular book, topic, or method of instruction. You might consider forming a book discussion group that deals with some aspect of teaching or learning unique to your discipline. For instance:

- *Practicing Science* (National Science Teachers Association, 2001) might be particularly useful if your department addresses one of the natural sciences.

- The *Handbook for Teaching Introductory Psychology* (Hebl, Brewer, & Benjamin, 2000), *Teaching Introductory Psychology* (Steinberg, 1997), or *The Professor's Guide to Teaching* (Forsyth, 2002) might be used in a psychology department.

- *Teaching Mathematics in Colleges and Universities* (Friedberg, 2001) could be used in a math department.

- *The Letter Book* (Dinitz & Fulwiler, 2000) might be employed in an English department.

- *Teaching Theatre Today* (Fliotsos & Medford, 2004) would be good for a theatre department.

Nearly every discipline has at least one major textbook exploring pedagogical approaches that are suitable at the college level. Even in cases where your faculty members vehemently disagree with the perspectives introduced in such a text, establishing a discussion group that deals with one of these books can prompt invaluable reconsideration of how material is taught in your department, why it is taught in the manner it is, and how instructional techniques may be improved.

Moreover, if your campus-wide center for teaching and learning isn't even sponsoring discussion groups about *non*-pedagogical books that may help your department in your teaching mission, you might want to consider having your departmental center assume this task. For instance, a Great Books Discussion Group, in which faculty members meet once a month to discuss a work by Sophocles, Machiavelli, Jane Austen, or Zora Neale Hurston can help your faculty members recall what it is like to feel like a student again, provide sources of enrichment for their courses, and offer an opportunity for the department to get together to discuss matters other than current courses and institutional challenges. Similarly, taking a semester as a faculty to grapple with particularly challenging texts—Thomas Pynchon's *Gravity's Rainbow*, Oswald Spengler's *The Decline of the West*, Ludwig Wittgenstein's *Philosophical Investigations*, Martha Nussbaum's *Upheavals of Thought*, or Michel Foucault's *The Archaeology of Knowledge*—can benefit teaching in your department in a number of ways. It can help promote new scholarly agendas, foster interdisciplinary approaches, and help even the most senior faculty member recall that sometimes merely comprehending several pages of text can be a challenging academic pursuit.

Other ongoing discussion groups might not deal with particular books but with key theories, methods, or topics that are significant in your discipline. For instance, a discussion group might be devoted to the uses of simulations or the case study technique in your discipline. Perhaps a discussion group can be formed to discuss the impact of a new perspective that emerged from a national conference in your discipline on the curriculum of your program. Remember, too, that not all of these discussions need to be face-to-face. Listservs, intranets, course management systems, and threaded discussion pages make it possible for your department to discuss these topics asynchronously and electronically.

Mentoring

Another extremely valuable function of a departmental center for teaching and learning, particularly for a department with several junior faculty members, is a formal mentoring program. Departmental teaching mentors should be given clear guidance that their focus as a mentor must be formative, not summative. That is to say, the purpose of the formal mentoring program in your department must be to help teachers improve their skill as instructors, not to evaluate them for the purposes of contract renewal, promotion, or tenure. Departmental mentors should also be reminded that simply because a faculty member does not teach in the same way that they teach, this does not mean that the mentee is not teaching effectively; the important consideration must always be whether students in the course are engaging effectively with the material, learning information and skills at an appropriate level, and progressing through the material of the course in an effective and timely manner. Mentors can be encouraged to sit in on courses, review tapes of class sections, go over exams and course materials, open their own classes for faculty observation, and provide other constructive services that will improve the teaching of their colleagues in the department.

Clinics

Clinics are a particular type of discussion group aimed at problem solving, brainstorming, and coping with the inevitable challenges that arise in college-level teaching. Each participant in a clinic brings one or two particularly challenging situations that have arisen recently in their teaching for other faculty members to reflect on, discuss how they might have been handled differently, and develop strategies for addressing similar issues in the future. Clinics are particularly useful departmental devices for improving teaching since they focus on a current problem, provide additional insights on how it might be handled, and help develop the problem-solving skills of the faculty as a whole.

Conducted on a regular basis, clinics serve to foster creativity in teaching strategies among the faculty and an esprit de corps. In some departments, "virtual clinics" can be created online. Blackboard™ and certain other course management systems allow messages to be posted anonymously to threaded discussions. In this way, faculty members could submit problems for discussion and receive advice while protecting their identity. Even in situations where teaching clinics are held face-to-face, it is often desirable to provide a mechanism whereby faculty members can submit anonymous "case studies" to be critiqued and discussed by the department as a whole. This helps junior faculty members to feel free to participate, since they may be reluctant to present problems they encounter to the very colleagues who vote on their promotions and tenure decisions.

RESOURCES

As you continue to develop your plan to create your departmental center for excellence in teaching and learning, there are additional resources that you might want to consult. Among the best of these resources are:

Barkley, E., Cross, K. P., & Major, C. H. (2004). *Collaborative learning techniques: A handbook for college faculty.* San Francisco, CA: Jossey-Bass.

Fink, L. D. (2003). *Creating significant learning experiences: An integrated approach to designing college courses.* San Francisco, CA: Jossey-Bass.

Johnson, G. R. (1995). *First steps to excellence in college teaching.* Madison, WI: Atwood.

Leamnson, R. (1999). *Thinking about teaching and learning: Developing habits of learning with first year college and university students.* Sterling, VA: Stylus.

Seldin, P., & Associates. (1995). *Improving college teaching.* Bolton, MA: Anker.

Weimer, M. E. (2002). *Learner-centered teaching: Five key changes to practice.* San Francisco, CA: Jossey-Bass.

Wulff, D. H., Jacobson, W. H., Freisem, K., Hatch, D. H., Lawrence, M., & Lenz, L. R. (Eds.). (2005). *Aligning for learning: Strategies for teaching effectiveness.* Bolton, MA: Anker.

REFERENCES

Angelo, T. A., & Cross, K. P. (1993). *Classroom assessment techniques: A handbook for college teachers* (2nd ed.). San Francisco, CA: Jossey-Bass.

Dinitz, S., & Fulwiler, T. (2000). *The letter book: Ideas for teaching college English.* Portsmouth, NH: Boynton/Cook.

Fliotsos, A. L., & Medford, G. S. (2004). *Teaching theatre today: Pedagogical views of theatre in higher education.* New York, NY: Palgrave Macmillan.

Forsyth, D. R. (2002). *The professor's guide to teaching: Psychological principles and practices.* Washington, DC: American Psychological Association.

Friedberg, S. (2001). *Teaching mathematics in colleges and universities: Case studies for today's classroom.* Providence, RI: American Mathematical Society.

Hebl, M. R., Brewer, C. L., & Benjamin, Jr., L. T. (2000). *Handbook for teaching introductory psychology: Vol. 2.* Mahwah, NJ: Lawrence Erlbaum Associates.

National Science Teachers Association. (2001). *Practicing science: The investigative approach in college science teaching.* Arlington, VA: NSTA Press.

Steinberg, R. J. (Ed.). (1997). *Teaching introductory psychology: Survival tips from the experts.* Washington, DC: American Psychological Association.

29

Developing Colleague-Based Support for Teaching, Scholarship, and Service

Every department chair wants his or her discipline to be known for the excellence of its instruction, research, and service. As a result, chairs expend a great deal of effort nurturing these activities by mentoring individual faculty members, sponsoring faculty development workshops, purchasing books and software designed to assist scholars in their work, and tailoring their evaluations of faculty members to foster continual improvement in these areas. One opportunity that chairs may overlook, however, is the significant role that each faculty member's colleagues can play in setting high departmental standards for teaching, scholarship, and service and in developing strategies to ensure that those standards are met. Three similar and interrelated approaches to colleague-based support in essential faculty activities—teaching circles, scholarship networks, and service alliances—can set a desirable tone of mutual support in a department, foster esprit de corps, and produce results far more rapidly than can many top-down methods. Although campus-wide centers for teaching and learning sometimes sponsor such groups, they tend to focus on instruction, whereas departmental groups can extend to scholarship and service. Moreover, colleague-based groups provide opportunities to explore pedagogy, research, and service in the discipline, making them singularly appropriate to serve as key parts of your department-level faculty development program.

Teaching Circles

Teaching circles were first developed by Daniel J. Bernstein at the University of Nebraska in the early 1990s as a means of applying strategies learned from the Quality Circles used by many Japanese corporations to the academic environment. What is not widely remembered, however, is that Bernstein (1996) began his effort as a *departmental* initiative. There are many reasons for establishing a departmental teaching circle. You may be chairing a department that is large enough to have its own critical mass for a discipline-specific teaching circle. You may be working in a discipline in which the pedagogical methods—lab work, archaeological digs, management internships—are so unique that they are not being adequately addressed by other teaching circles on your campus. Or you simply may wish to establish a teaching circle as a team-building exercise in a department that has become fractious or that is too new to have developed a group identity.

What is a teaching circle? Hutchings (1996) perhaps provided the best short description of teaching circles, defining them as

> a variety of arrangements through which (1) a small group of faculty members (typically four to ten ...) (2) makes a commitment to work together over a period of at least a semester (3) to address questions and concerns about the particulars of their teaching and their students' learning. (p. 7)

Teaching circles may simply be organized around a shared desire to improve instruction. They may also focus on applying a particular text or technique to each faculty member's method of instruction, addressing certain problems or challenges of common concern, teaching specific courses or types of courses, or providing instruction in a particular discipline.

Teaching circles that are based on shared consideration of particular books are perhaps the easiest to organize and may well be the quickest way for you to initiate this type of colleague-based support of instruction in your department. Suitable books on which to base a teaching circle include:

- *Effective Grading* (Walvoord & Anderson, 1998)

- *Engaging Ideas* (Bean, 2001)

- *Leaving the Lectern* (McManus, 2005)

- *The Courage to Teach* (Palmer, 1998)

- *Teaching at Its Best* (Nilson, 2003)

- *What the Best College Teachers Do* (Bain, 2004)

- *Making Their Own Way* (Baxter Magolda, 2001)

Each of these works may conveniently be divided into three or four parts to be discussed at gatherings two to four weeks apart. Discussions may begin with a general reflection on the argument presented in the portion of the book read for that meeting, its strengths and weaknesses, and incidents that have occurred in each participant's teaching that relate to the material being discussed. It is in the last of these areas that the real value of the teaching circle lies. Each participant should be encouraged to introduce specific situations, difficulties, and challenges that have arisen recently in his or her classes, using the circle as a sounding board for discussing ways to approach them. The book provides an "excuse" for the teaching circle to take place, while the real benefit of the activity comes in the mutual support and advice that the participants offer each other. The situations described in the book you are reading act as a springboard to launch the group into more reflective and intentional approaches to their teaching. The members of the teaching circle become coaches to one another as they each make progress in their own teaching. While the insights gained from the book discussed are frequently useful, many participants in a teaching circle will tell you that it's the support and advice they've received from the other members that is invaluable.

You could also construct a teaching circle around particular methods of teaching such as engaging students in large courses, developing projects that help improve critical thinking skills, teaching online courses, working effectively with students who are located at multiple remote sites, supervising theses, leading discussions, incorporating simulations and case studies into coursework, teaching statistical methods to students who lack a solid background in mathematics, increasing creativity, using community service-learning as an instructional method, or taking full advantage of the pedagogical value of a new form of technology. Alternatively, your department may create a teaching circle that addresses your discipline's introductory course, internship, or senior seminar. No matter how the focus of your teaching circle is chosen, it is the repeated gathering of the same relatively small group of faculty members—who will begin to understand one another better and to see their own pedagogical approaches in a new light—that will be of the greatest importance to your discipline. Teaching circles that are originally formed for some particular purpose frequently continue semester after semester, even when the original purpose has been fulfilled. Participants find that having a built-in support group and understanding and encouraging colleagues is the real significance of the teaching circle.

Scholarship Networks

Scholarship networks formally began in the College of Liberal Arts and Social Sciences at Georgia Southern University in the mid- to late-1990s as a means of building on the recognized value of teaching circles, expanding this philosophy into other areas of faculty performance. The goal was essentially the same as that of the teaching circle—to establish colleague-based support of one's work as a faculty member through a small gathering of individuals who would meet on a set schedule to report progress, discuss concerns, and critique one another's work—but in the area of research, scholarship, creative activity, and professional development, rather than in instruction. Three factors led to the development of scholarship networks. First, many junior faculty members were being faced with expectations for publications, conference presentations, juried exhibits, and other forms of scholarly and creative activity. They had strong institutional support, but relatively little training in what they needed to do to be successful in this area. Second, a number of senior faculty were facing stalled or at least somewhat slowed scholarly agendas. They had already established their careers, having earned promotions and tenure, but their initial scholarly projects were completed or no longer seemed as interesting, and they were left in the dark as to where their scholarship needed to progress. Third, between these two poles were mid-career faculty who had expended a great deal of energy in becoming superb teachers but needed guidance in advancing their scholarship to be promoted to the rank of full professor and to undergo positive post-tenure reviews.

Scholarship networks proved to be a highly useful means of addressing all of these challenges. Some of the first networks were developed around specific approaches to scholarship and, almost immediately, resulted in a sudden increase in scholarly activity. Because the groups met on a regular basis, and colleagues came to expect progress reports on what had been accomplished since the last meeting, faculty members self-imposed deadlines and actually produced articles and presentations, rather than mulling them over month after month. Moreover, the scholarly works that were produced were stronger as a result. Younger faculty members had a supportive group of colleagues with whom they could practice their presentations before going to conferences, improving any sections that did not work effectively. Articles were critiqued to make them tighter, less prone to jargon, and more persuasive. Because the audience for these scholarly works was perceptive and intelligent but perhaps not completely familiar with each specific area of research, participants quickly realized where their arguments were clear and where the evidence was muddier than they initially realized. An additional benefit was an increase in the number of collaborative and interdisciplinary projects that resulted as each scholarship network progressed from a collection of independent researchers to a team of scholars working on shared projects.

One of the great values of scholarship networks is that they can help bring appropriate recognition to nontraditional areas of scholarship. Many forms of creative activity, for example, do not lend themselves to the type of pre-release peer review and publication found in other scholarly disciplines. New outlets for scholarly activity resulting from new technology, interdisciplinary approaches that do not fit conveniently into academic pigeonholes, and other types of contributions that scholars make outside of their disciplines are often dismissed as "insufficiently rigorous." Scholarship networks are useful in addressing this challenge in two ways. First, they serve to educate their own members—and, by extension, others with whom their members have influence—on the full spectrum of scholarly activities occurring at colleges and universities. Second, they provide an early alert to faculty members who are engaged in nontraditional forms of scholarship on how to describe their scholarly contributions to promotion review committees that may not immediately understand their significance or importance.

The potential for scholarship networks within individual academic departments is great. In larger departments, they can be natural outgrowths of a formal mentorship program. Senior faculty members can provide their junior colleagues with much-needed guidance, contacts, and support. In return, junior colleagues can provide a potentially greater contribution to senior members of the discipline by exposing them to new perspectives on established projects, fresh applications for work that is already well under way, and additional ideas for those whose research has gone stale. Faculty members tend to like scholarship networks because they demonstrate a sincere commitment to continued progress in the discipline. Senior administrators tend to like scholarship networks because they are a low-cost way to improve the institution's reputation and research productivity. Unlike more top-down approaches to improving scholarly activity, these groups reinforce the collegial, consensus-building approach that department chairs want to encourage in their departments. They are one of the relatively few administrative innovations that almost everyone appears to support from their introduction, and their value only continues to grow over time.

Service Alliances

Service alliances are the logical extension of the colleague-based support for professional activity found in teaching circles and scholarship networks to the last part of the professorial triad: contributions to service. All too often in faculty development and evaluation systems, service appears to be the underappreciated stepsibling of its more glamorous counterparts, teaching and scholarship. In systems where each aspect of professional activity is assigned a weight for the purposes of evaluation, service almost always receives far less consideration than do contributions to instruction or research. At some institutions, contributions to service are, either explicitly or implicitly, treated as pass/fail while achievements in instruction and scholarship carry letter grades. In other words, teaching and research are deemed important; service is something that one merely does enough of in order to get by.

Compounding this difficulty is the fact that many people don't understand what service really is or can be. They associate service with merely being a member of the right number of committees or holding office in professional organizations. But just as we have realized how much more teaching is than simply classroom instruction and how much more scholarship is than refereed publications, it seems an appropriate moment for a new *Service Reconsidered* to take its place alongside *Scholarship Reconsidered* (Boyer, 1990) and the more recent *Learning Reconsidered* (Keeling, 2004). Simply put, service is the category of contribution that subsumes everything else one does as a faculty member. Teaching is a form of service performed for one's students. Scholarship is a form of service performed for one's profession. The traditional view of what constitutes service is far narrower than it needs to be.

On campuses today, service is recognized and supported through such efforts as community service-learning; service-based internships; collaborative efforts between faculty members and the offices of student life, residential life, and alumni affairs; targeted recruitment weekends sponsored by individual programs in collaboration with the admissions office; lecture or concert series designed to bring the community onto campus or to raise funds for a particular project; and community outreach efforts. Professors of accountancy complete tax returns for the elderly and indigent. Professors of political science hold workshops on how to register to vote, issues arising in upcoming elections, and post-election analysis of trends. Professors of foreign languages sponsor folk festivals, international cuisine demonstrations, and presentations on events abroad to members of the community. Many of these service activities require some degree of organization in order to be effective. They are not the contributions of individuals who simply volunteer for committees or run for office. It is in this more complex approach to service that service alliances can be extremely important.

A departmental service alliance might begin by asking the question: What particular talent or resource do we possess as a discipline that can somehow be directed toward the greater good? Then, just as teaching circles and scholarship networks meet on a regular basis to discuss progress and challenges relating to their areas of focus, the service alliance works toward making one or more specific service projects a reality. In the course of these discussions, the service alliance can also function as a support group to address the other service contributions of its members. If there is a challenge facing a particular committee on which one of the members serves or there is a problem that has arisen for an organization on which a member serves as an officer, the service alliance can provide advice, counsel, and a sympathetic ear. As with the other types of colleague-based support, service alliances may owe their existence to a particular project they are designed to undertake, but their continued value will be found in the way in which each member assists the others in improving their contributions to an important aspect of their professional lives.

Inevitably, teaching circles, scholarship networks, and service alliances will change their focus as these groups develop their own style of working over time. In fact, teaching circles have been known to transform themselves into scholarship networks (and vice versa). Whatever form they may take, their key benefit always comes from their ability to improve communication within the department, promote collegiality, and offer opportunities for peers to help one another as they work together for improvement.

REFERENCES

Bain, K. (2004). *What the best college teachers do.* Cambridge, MA: Harvard University Press.

Baxter Magolda, M. B. (2001). *Making their own way: Narratives for transforming higher education to promote self-development.* Sterling, VA: Stylus.

Bean, J. C. (1996). *Engaging ideas: The professor's guide to integrating writing, critical thinking, and active learning in the classroom.* San Francisco, CA: Jossey-Bass.

Bernstein, D. J. (1996). A departmental system for balancing the development and evaluation of college teaching: A commentary on Cavanaugh. *Innovative Higher Education, 20*(4), pp. 241–248.

Boyer, E. L. (1990). *Scholarship reconsidered: Priorities of the professoriate.* Princeton, NJ: The Carnegie Foundation for the Advancement of Teaching.

Hutchings, P. (1996). *Making teaching community property: A menu for peer collaboration and peer review.* Washington, DC: American Association of Higher Education.

Keeling, R. P. (Ed.). (2004). *Learning reconsidered: A campus-wide focus on the student experience.* Washington, DC: National Association of Student Personnel Administrators and American College Personnel Association.

McManus, D. A. (2005). *Leaving the lectern: Cooperative learning and the critical first days of students working in groups.* Bolton, MA: Anker.

Palmer, P. (1998). *The courage to teach: Exploring the inner landscape of a teacher's life.* San Francisco, CA: Jossey-Bass.

Nilson, L. B. (2003). *Teaching at its best: A research-based resource for college instructors* (2nd ed.). Bolton, MA: Anker.

Walvoord, B. E., & Anderson, V. J. (1998). *Effective grading: A tool for learning and assessment.* San Francisco, CA: Jossey-Bass.

30

Designing and Implementing a Successful First-Year Faculty Experience Program

The value that first-year experience programs play in the academic success of students has been established by numerous studies (e.g., Tobolowsky, Cox, & Wagner, 2005). As a result, campuses all across the country are establishing programs designed to integrate students more fully into the campus community, expose them to the institution's cherished traditions, and provide them with the resources they will need in order to succeed at work that is new to them. But what about faculty members? Frequently, new faculty members arrive at a college or university with only a tentative idea of the institution's fundamental values, the role that they will be expected to play on campus, how they will find the information needed for them to succeed, and the expectations by which they will be judged throughout their professional careers.

Too frequently institutions try to address these needs and concerns through a short orientation program in which everything that newcomers to the college or university could possibly want to know is covered in one or two days, or even in a half-day session. The question that is rarely asked is: *If short, intense orientation programs don't work for students, why do we expect them to work for faculty members?* Instructors often make transitions that are at least as dramatic as those made by first-year students. They may be emerging from a graduate program at a research university to begin a position in which they will be teaching mostly undergraduates at a liberal arts college. They may be arriving from situations in which they were surrounded by advanced majors and graduate students with an inherent love for their discipline only to find themselves teaching required courses to students who want only to get that particular class out of the way. New faculty will arrive on your campus from a place where they knew the basic values and rules for success, had a well-developed core of colleagues, and were highly proficient at what they did (otherwise, you would not have hired them in the first place). In their new role as faculty members, they won't know the ground rules, will have few if any friends, and will need to prove themselves all over again. To help new faculty members adapt to such an environment, you don't need an orientation; you need a *faculty first-year experience program.*

Faculty first-year experience programs are structured to offer information to new faculty members in a timely manner and at a pace at which it can be absorbed. The people organizing these programs recognize the anxieties inherent in operating in a new environment. They provide advice, access to information, and support. And then, as in any good first-year experience program, they wean the individual away from the program itself, allowing the new faculty member to succeed on his or her own. Faculty first-year experience programs are frequently run out of faculty development offices or centers for teaching and learning. But what can department chairs do if their institution does not offer such opportunities? One solution is to create a departmentally based program. In fact, in situations where no institution-wide faculty first-year experience program exists, it is *incumbent* upon department chairs to help fill that gap.

If you are thinking about designing and implementing your own faculty first-year experience program, here are a few best practices that you will want to keep in mind to make sure that what you design is as useful as possible.

Be Certain to Distinguish the Formative Aspects of Your Faculty Development Efforts From Any Summative Decisions You May Need to Make

You should conduct several different types of meetings or sessions with your new faculty members. Some of these sessions should be *formative*: Work through issues with each faculty member to improve the quality of his or her instruction, bring the faculty member into a more constructive relationship with his or her peers, and nurture the quality of your new hire's scholarship or creative activity. You should also meet with each new faculty member for *summative* purposes: You need to make or announce decisions on such matters as contract renewal and salary. If you do not, specifically and clearly, distinguish between these two very different kinds of activities, new faculty members are likely to confuse them. They are less likely to confide in you about their challenges with teaching if they think that you are collecting information to "use against them" when it comes to allocating a raise or offering another year's contract. (As a department chair, you need to be sensitive to the very real vulnerability that new faculty, untenured and unproven, may be feeling.) For this reason, make an effort to go *out of your way* to clarify the purpose of a meeting from the start. Begin meetings by saying something like the following:

> Today I'd like each of us to talk about a challenge that we're having in the classroom. Then we can all offer specific suggestions or insights into how we might try meeting that challenge. No matter how good any of us is as a teacher, we can all do better, and there are always some new difficulties that we'll be facing in teaching a class. So, the point is not to judge here, but rather to work together to get better. I'll go first. Here's a challenge that came up in one of my classes the other day, and I'm still working my way through what I could have done better. What happened was . . .

An introduction like this makes it absolutely clear to the new faculty members what the purpose of the session is: You are there to help them, not to evaluate them. By candidly offering examples of how even you are still making progress toward improving your instruction, you will help your faculty members open up to one another, view the faculty first-year experience program as a useful opportunity for professional growth, and begin making real progress.

Alternatively, in a session where you really are evaluating the faculty member, you can begin by saying:

> Today we're going to switch roles a bit, and I'm going to shift somewhat from being your mentor to taking on my supervisory role. It's kind of like when you change roles from offering students advice on drafts of their papers to actually assigning them grades. So, you can think of today as rather like the day that a grade on an assignment comes in. Here's where I think that your strengths and weaknesses have been this year . . .

Organize Your Sessions With New Faculty Members Along the Lines of "What Do They Need to Know Now?" Rather Than "What Seems to Make the Best Self-Contained Topic?"

As academics, we tend to organize the information that we present in ways that seem to make the best sense to us, forgetting that individuals who are learning this information for the first time may actually have entirely different needs or abilities to absorb what we are presenting. In other words, it may initially seem to make sense to organize a group of faculty development sessions topically around Campus Traditions, Employee Benefits, Institutional Exam Policies, and Teaching Introductory Courses. But these thematic groupings are unlikely to reflect the actual needs of first-year faculty members. For example, if people who are new to your campus hear all of the college traditions at once, they are almost certainly not going to remember the many nuanced distinctions among Fall Homecoming, Spring Fling, and Summer Alumni Weekend. In much the same way, a general overview of everything one needs to know about how to teach introductory courses is likely to cause new faculty members to become frustrated (because they are now learning how they should have constructed that syllabus which has now been in place for the last six weeks) or to experience sensory overload (because they are hearing about the best ways to construct final exams when what they really need is the *time* to write their midterm exams). Rather, you will develop a much more useful session by looking only a short distance into the future and asking yourself, "If I were a newcomer, what would I need to know now?" Perhaps one of your special campus traditions will be taking place within the next two to three weeks; that is the time to talk about the meaning of Founder's Day or Family Weekend or Community Appreciation Week. Spending five or ten minutes talking about this activity in a session that also includes other time-sensitive information—how to submit campus book orders that are due within a month, the best way to bring budget requests to your attention in time to incorporate it into your annual request, your institution's expectations about reporting students whose mid-course progress is unsatisfactory or who have excessive absences, and so on—will acclimate your new faculty members much more quickly than will a set of workshops tailored to your needs and schedule instead of theirs.

Remember That a Well-Organized Faculty First-Year Experience Program Includes Group *and* Individual Activities

Newer faculty members tend to have two not-wholly-compatible needs. On one hand, they need peers; they need to know that they are not alone, that others are experiencing similar challenges and frustrations, and that there is a social environment in which they can fit and play a part. On the other hand, they need guidance; they need to vent, ask questions that they may be embarrassed to ask in front of others, and feel comfortable letting their guard down. These different needs can best be addressed by constructing your program so that your new faculty members have an opportunity to meet with a mentor (you or some other experienced faculty member, either within or outside of your department) and in a group of others who are like them.

Depending on the size of your department, you should organize these activities differently. Your department may be small enough that a critical mass can only be obtained by offering your faculty first-year experience program to everyone in their first three or four years at the institution or even everyone who has not yet been reviewed for tenure. Other departments may be large enough to include only teachers who are actually in their first year on the faculty. More important than how long faculty members have served is to create a program with enough participants to have meaningful exchanges, serve as a support group, and provide a diversity of opinions. Similarly, there is no perfect frequency for first-year faculty members to meet one-on-one with you, even if for nothing more than an attitude check. At some institutions, regularly scheduling meetings once a week is too often; at others, setting time for formal meetings only once a month is too rare. You will need to use your best judgment to determine a proper rhythm for these meetings based on your own administrative style, the amount of support required by your new faculty, and the "personality" of your college or university.

Use a Connected Topic as a Theme to Guide Your Program

Building a Faculty First-Year Experience Program around a specific topic or book helps connect your different sessions, even if the topic itself occupies no more than five or ten minutes of each session. Useful books around which to build an effective semester-long or year-long series include:

- *What the Best College Teachers Do* (Bain, 2004)

- *The Professor's Guide to Teaching* (Forsyth, 2002)

- *Effective Grading* (Walvoord & Anderson, 1998)

- *Engaging Ideas* (Bean, 1996)

- *Successful College Teaching* (Baiocco & DeWaters, 1998)

A more topic-oriented approach might be built around ideas like Student Learning Styles; Tying Scholarship to Teaching; Active Learning and Maximum Student Engagement; Addressing the Needs of the Whole Student; Service, Learning, and Service-Learning; or other subjects suited to your institutional culture. In some ways, the book or topic of the program provides the *excuse* for the meeting, session, or workshop; the real progress results when faculty members build outward from the expressed purpose of the program to deal with their own needs as new faculty members and the actual situations that they encounter in their classes.

Including Information From Other Offices Divides Your Burden and Begins Building a Network for Your Faculty Members

There are important contacts that your faculty members will need to have in the business office, the registrar's office, student life, the computer and information resource center, and other departments. By including individuals from these other offices in your program, you relieve yourself of the necessity of answering every question and leading every discussion. This will also help you make your new faculty members true citizens of your college or university. Teach newcomers not only about available resources but also whom to call in offices on campus relevant to their needs. By introducing new hires to a broader range of people than they are likely to encounter in your department or building, you are playing an important role in their overall socialization to the campus.

Experienced department chairs understand the very real possibility of losing a valued new faculty member because he or she never quite feels at home or is unsuccessful in finding an appropriate circle of friends. By helping your newcomers make contacts within the larger academic community, you are taking a positive step toward making them happier, more productive, and less likely to leave the institution too soon.

Keep in Mind the Needs of Different Types of First-Year Faculty Members

New faculty hires may include people who have just completed a doctoral program and have never held a full-time teaching position. They may include individuals with some experience, possibly at the adjunct level, at another institution. And they may include extremely experienced faculty members who, while they are new to your institution, are certainly not new to the profession. All of these individuals will have different needs, and your program needs to recognize this diversity of experience. Some will need to be guided in how to design a course while others will merely need to know about local customs, procedures, and traditions. More seasoned faculty members will become disengaged if the assumption at every session is that those in attendance are teaching their very first course. Inexperienced faculty members are likely to become frustrated if they feel that you have made assumptions about what they know that are simply not accurate for them. Allow enough flexibility in your program so that these differing needs will be met. Avoid, however, providing too much choice on whether one *wishes* to attend; the faculty members who most need a program of this sort are those who already have significant exposure to teaching at another institution. By making your program optional, the very people who most need it will be those who will elect not to participate in it. Instead, schedule a variety of activities and types of information in each session so that everyone will gain something from the time devoted to your program and will find the experience interesting enough to continue.

Whenever Possible, Try to Make Your Program Highly Participatory by Providing an Opportunity That Results in the Creation of a Useful Product

It sends the wrong message to conduct sections on the importance of active learning by doing nothing more than lecturing to those in attendance. It sends an equally wrong message to take up the time of extremely busy junior faculty members with a series of discussions that, while perhaps presenting useful theories and general concepts, seem to have little practical bearing on their immediate needs. As a result, it is valuable to focus at least part of your faculty first-year experience program on the creation of some tangible product that the faculty members will need in the very near future. At some institutions, the most appropriate product to create is the annual report or portfolio of teaching, scholarship, and service that each faculty member is expected to compile. At others, faculty members may spend part of their second semesters critiquing each others' first-semester syllabi, examinations, and course materials to discover how these items may be improved, how courses may be better structured to achieve the department's learning goals, and how better to evaluate student achievement. In still other cases, each faculty member may be asked to develop a conference presentation that will be practiced before the other new faculty members, assessed critically for ways in which it may be improved, and rehearsed until it reaches the level that the faculty member and the chair are satisfied with. By using workshop time to create any of these products, faculty members are less likely to view the faculty first-year experience program as yet another requirement to be endured and more likely to appreciate its positive value from the very beginning.

However you organize your department's development program for new faculty members, remember that it will be most successful when you try to anticipate the needs of the faculty members, pay due attention to your institution's culture and expectations, and provide the same sort of varied opportunities that we, as instructors, try to provide in the courses where the greatest amount of learning occurs.

REFERENCES

Bain, K. (2004). *What the best college teachers do.* Cambridge, MA: Harvard University Press.

Baiocco, S. A., & DeWaters, J. N. (1998). *Successful college teaching: Problem-solving strategies of distinguished professors.* Boston, MA: Allyn & Bacon.

Bean, J. C. (1996). *Engaging ideas: The professor's guide to integrating writing, critical thinking, and active learning in the classroom.* San Francisco, CA: Jossey-Bass.

Forsyth, D. R. (2002). *The professor's guide to teaching: Psychological principles and practices.* Washington, DC: American Psychological Association.

Tobolowsky, B. F., Cox, B. E., & Wagner, M. T. (Eds.). (2005). *Exploring the evidence: Vol. III. Reporting research on first-year seminars* (Monograph No. 42). Columbia, SC: University of South Carolina, National Resource Center for The First-Year Experience and Students in Transition.

Walvoord, B. E., & Anderson, V. J. (1998). *Effective grading: A tool for learning and assessment.* San Francisco, CA: Jossey-Bass.

31

Helping Faculty Members Create Successful Résumés

Department chairs are often asked to review someone's résumé. Either there is a new hire to be made or the chair must submit a recommendation about some other major personnel decision, such as promotion, tenure, merit increase, performance appraisal, and the like. Or the chair may be asked to assist a member of the department with improving the format of a résumé that will be submitted with a grant proposal, award application, or request for a publication contract. What is the most useful advice that department chairs can give a faculty member, particularly one who simply needs a few well-chosen hints that will restructure a perfectly good curriculum vitae and make it truly spectacular? The following suggestions—some of them all too frequently overlooked—can really make a difference to your faculty.

Don't Assume That Your Curriculum Vitae Can Take Only One Form

Computers make it extremely easy to maintain a résumé file that contains your pertinent professional and biographical information so that you can pull it together for a specific purpose very quickly. While your curriculum vitae is a factual document (i.e., absolutely everything in it must be accurate, clear, and verifiable), it is also a rhetorical document (i.e., you are submitting it because you are trying to persuade someone of something.) For this reason, every time you are about to create a version of your curriculum vitae, ask yourself . . .

- "What will someone who examines this document need to know and to conclude in order to say 'yes' to me?" Once you have a clear answer to that question, you will know immediately how to structure your résumé. In other words, depending on the purpose you are trying to achieve, certain aspects of your achievement will need to be highlighted and certain things minimized or omitted. In applications for promotion and tenure, for instance, most institutions require documentation in three essential categories of performance—teaching, scholarship, and service (although the exact terminology used may differ from institution to institution)—and rely on a résumé, in addition to certain supporting materials, in order to evaluate applicants. But faculty members frequently do not structure their résumés in such a way as to make evaluation of all three areas easy for reviewers to conduct. In this case, it may be useful to have three clearly labeled sections (TEACHING, SCHOLARSHIP, and SERVICE) with roughly similar subsections under each heading. If, for example, it seems appropriate to include a brief "Philosophy of Teaching," include "Philosophy of Scholarship" and "Philosophy of Service" sections, too. Reviewers are likely to care about more than just the number of courses you've taught, articles you've published, and committees you've served on, so include some information on the quality of these achievements as well. Do you have median scores for student evaluations that can be compared to others in your unit? Do you have information on the number of your students who have gone on to graduate school or, at least, to success in their upper-level courses? Can you discover the acceptance rates of the journals in which you publish or the general qualifications of the referees? Did your service contribution result in any particular new course of action, award, or lasting product? In a different situation, if you are applying for an administrative appointment, you will want to restructure your curriculum vitae so that it highlights the opportunities you have had for managerial or leadership roles. Too frequently applicants for administrative roles submit résumés that make a clear case for numerous scholarly and instructional accomplishments, while leaving their administrative success in the background. It is always important to structure a curriculum vitae so that it clearly and convincingly states the case you wish to make.

- "Who will be reviewing this résumé? What can I be certain that they will know? What are they not likely to understand?" If you use abbreviations, for instance, for the journals in which your publications appear, will everyone who reviews your material know what those abbreviations mean? Will they know whether a journal is highly competitive and thus evaluate your accomplishment appropriately? If reviewers are unlikely to be aware of this information, you may need to assist them. Write out the names of journals where necessary. Group your publications where appropriate into "Highly Competitive Journals," "Second Tier Journals," and "Essays and Other Publications." If one of your teaching accomplishments is that you were asked eight times to guest lecture for Dr. Smith in her INT 577 course, be certain that all of your reviewers will understand what course you are referring to, that INT in this case means "International Studies" rather than "Interdisciplinary Studies," and that Dr. Smith is the president of your college who is a highly acclaimed scholar in her own right. Don't just assume that a reviewer will understand what might be a confusing entry: When in doubt, spell it out.

Format Your Résumé So That It Quickly and Easily Conveys as Much Information About You as Possible

- Always number the pages of your curriculum vitae. Whenever possible use the structure "page [NUMBER] of [TOTAL]" in your header or footer. By doing this, you'll have created a structure that can be reassembled quickly and easily if (when!) the reviewer happens to drop your résumé.

- Number the entries in each section, rather than using a bulleted list. This conveys information quickly—"Wow, 48 refereed articles!"—without forcing your reviewers to count every item in a list. (And make no mistake about it, most reviewers are going to count entries like publications and conference presentations anyway, so why not make it easier and do it for them?)

- Include dates, not just for publications and presentations, but for all activities. List the years you served on committees, held offices, or joined professional and service organizations. In a résumé that is submitted for an annual performance evaluation or merit increase, make it clear which accomplishments occurred during the period under review. For promotion evaluations, indicate your achievements since your last promotion or your date of hire. You can either separate these achievements from earlier accomplishments with a fine dotted line or note that "Accomplishments completed in the period under review are in bold-face type."

- Be consistent in listing all items the same way: in reverse chronological order. Reviewers will automatically assume that all of your publications, conference presentations, awards, and so on will be listed in reverse chronological order, with the most recent entry first. If you structure your listings in any other way (for instance, if your publications are listed in alphabetical order), a reviewer may simply look at the first listing and assume that it is your most recent achievement, even if it was written 10 or more years ago.

- Include the date on which your résumé was printed either at the end of the document or in a header or footer. This will inform your reviewers of the date on which the information they are examining was updated. And always be sure to submit the most current version you have. Never submit a résumé that was updated more than six months ago.

Plan Your Curriculum Vitae With the Assumption That It Will Be Photocopied

- Unless specifically asked to do so, never slip the pages into plastic page protectors. This will make it at best difficult to photocopy—requiring each page to be painstakingly pulled from your static-laden plastic covers before the copies can be made—and, at worst, smudged and illegible.

- Use a sturdy, plain white paper. Sturdy paper holds up better when multiple copies are made. Colored paper and paper bearing a prominent watermark or design will pose a challenge on copies and may end up making your text difficult to read.

- Avoid cramped, hard-to-read, or minute type. As a general rule of thumb, always use a font no smaller than 12 point and no larger than 14 point.

RESOURCES

Anthony, R., & Roe, G. (1998). *The curriculum vitae handbook: How to present and promote your academic career* (2nd ed.). Iowa City, IA: Rudi Publishing.

Jackson, A., & Geckeis, K. (2003). *How to prepare your curriculum vitae.* New York, NY: McGraw-Hill.

McDaniels, C., & Knobloch, M. A. (1996). *Developing a professional vita or resume* (2nd ed.). New York, NY: Ferguson Publishing.

32

Helping Faculty Members Document Excellence in Teaching

Of the three aspects of professional activity commonly evaluated at colleges and universities—teaching, scholarship, and service—assessing the quality of a faculty member's teaching frequently poses the greatest difficulty for the department chair. When individuals are going up for tenure or promotion, applying for a grant, being nominated for some type of award, or even being considered for another position, documenting their success in scholarship may seem relatively easy to do. We are all used to evaluating lists of refereed and non-refereed scholarship. We can tell from the number of successful grant awards whether that person's research has been recognized as important in the field. We can count the number of presentations each faculty member has made at national conferences, as well as the number of patents received, consultancies given, citations of their research, and similar items that regularly fall into neat categories on the résumé.

Similarly, it may seem very simple to evaluate the quality of a faculty member's service when examining a list of professional offices held, committees served, projects completed, and other contributions to the department, institution, or discipline as a whole. But how, we may often feel, can we objectively evaluate and document excellence in teaching? To be sure, many faculty members consider themselves to be excellent or even distinguished instructors within their chosen fields, even if they can present little documentation of this achievement aside from stacks of student course evaluations. Perhaps for this reason, many personnel review processes end up putting an undue emphasis on these evaluations. Since many institutions use forms for student ratings of instruction that yield quantitative scores, these scores often become the sole evidence of success or failure as a teacher. Numbers can provide a false impression of reliability. For instance, it is not uncommon in personnel evaluations to encounter such meaningless statements as "This candidate has demonstrated excellence in teaching, as indicated by an overall average of 4.89 on last semester's student ratings of instruction." The reason why this statement is meaningless is that it overlooks all of the questions we would need to ask in order to conclude anything informative from this average score.

How was the average calculated? Was it an average of the responses to every single question on the evaluation form or were questions included only if they specifically related to this instructor's teaching in this particular course? If all the questions were included, were the questions dealing with the professor's individual performance given any greater weight than those dealing with textbooks, course scheduling, and other matters over which the professor may have had relatively little control? If only some of the questions were used, were any comparative data for other faculty members calculated in the same way? Other important considerations to include are: How many students were in each class and what percentage of the enrolled students answered each question? This information can be important because very high or very low ratings with only a small percentage of students replying are highly suspect.

Moreover, in developing an overall score, were the different responses of the students truly averaged or is the overall score only an "average of the averages" for different courses? (In the latter scenario, a course that enrolls 6 and a course that enrolls 350 count as the same in the average.) When developing an average score, was the institution using means or medians, and, in either case, why was that particular statistical measure selected? Is the resulting figure statistically significant to the decimal place cited? How do the resulting scores compare to others who have been assigned the same course (either currently or in the past), the rest of the department, and all the faculty members of the institution in general? Lacking clear answers to these questions, we cannot hope to drawn any useful conclusions from that impressive-sounding "overall average of 4.89." Nevertheless, in the absence of other compelling indications of teaching excellence, presidents, deans, and committees frequently misuse or overinterpret student evaluation scores—just because they are some evidence of instructional quality. They might conclude that a faculty member receiving an overall student evaluation average of 4.56 is better than a faculty member receiving a score of 4.53, even when there is no statistically significant difference between the two numbers and even when the methodology used to generate those numbers is highly questionable.

For all of these reasons, department chairs are confronted with an opportunity and an obligation to help faculty members make an appropriate case for the quality of their instruction. To help your faculty members succeed in making their best case, there are several effective steps you can take as you review and summarize the materials that are submitted to you.

Encourage Your Faculty Members to Develop Brief "Philosophy of Teaching" Statements

A statement that reveals why an instructor has made certain choices in the classroom can go a long way toward documenting how that instructor has been effective. These short philosophy statements can be included in applications for tenure, promotion, and other types of personnel decisions. The statement might become part of the curriculum vitae itself, perhaps heading a section outlining that faculty member's contributions to instruction. For instance, you might encourage your faculty members to include a section of their résumés that is constructed as follows:

Teaching

Philosophy of Teaching

The highest form of learning occurs when students are actively engaged in applying what they encounter in their courses to their own lives, truly making a discipline "their own." College-level learning does not merely involve the transfer of information from professor to student. It also involves discovery of how to acquire information and new skills on one's own, how to work with colleagues towards the successful completion of a goal, and how to make a difference in the lives of those around one. All learning should be active, highly engaged, and inquiry based. The professor's most important purpose must be, not only to develop successful professionals in the discipline, but also to develop the best possible members of society.

Teaching Experience

[This section should contain a list of teaching appointments, in reverse chronological order.]

By constructing the résumé in this way, the instructor is indicating that he or she has carefully considered what effective teaching is and how it may be used to help students learn. Because creation of this statement calls for reflection on teaching values, there is likely to be a genuine improvement in the faculty member's instruction as a result. After formulating a statement of teaching philosophy, the faculty member should be encouraged to define what specifically is done in his or her courses—and *how* it is done—in order to achieve these goals.

When Including Data From Student Ratings of Instruction, Always Encourage Your Faculty Members to Indicate How These Data Were Calculated and to Provide an Appropriate Context for this Information

Numerical summaries of student ratings of instruction are widely used throughout academia to document success in instruction. In spite of their flaws, they do have their value. Student evaluations correlate rather closely with other measures of teaching effectiveness, including peer evaluations and appraisals by supervisors. Nevertheless, averages of student ratings of instructors are often cited rather carelessly at many institutions, presenting an ambiguous picture of a faculty member's strengths and weaknesses, or worse, leaving these schools liable to legal challenge when their decisions are questioned. If, therefore, you either wish or are required to provide summarized data from student ratings of instruction, encourage your faculty members to do the following if it is possible at your institution.

Supply Medians, Modes, and Arithmetic Means Whenever Discussing Averages

Most institutions either calculate for you or require you to calculate some sort of average score for student ratings of instruction. Generally these averages are determined by calculating simple arithmetic means; in other words, the numerical scores are tabulated for each response in the evaluation, and the resulting number is then divided by the number of responses received. Unfortunately, this type of averaging can produce very misleading results, particularly in small classes. Moreover, it is not a suitable form of averaging when students are providing *discrete* rather than *continuous* responses. (In other words, if your institution uses a scale of 1 to 5 on which students are allowed to respond "2.37," then you are receiving continuous data and arithmetic means may have some value. But if students can only fill in bubbles on a form or otherwise answer only in whole numbers, you are receiving discrete data so calculation of means does not provide you with the most reliable type of average.) Means are notoriously susceptible to outliers: one or two students who really love or hate a middling professor can distort an entire set of results. For this reason, it is a useful corrective for you to encourage your faculty members also to calculate the median and mode as an additional overall score. The *median* is the middle-most score whenever there is an odd number of responses or the average of the two middle-most scores whenever there is an even number of responses. The *mode* is the most commonly chosen response. As you will discover if you use these calculations (particularly in a course enrolling fewer than 30 students), both of these types of averages prove to be much less susceptible to the effects of outliers and really provide better portraits of the average when students are supplying discrete data.

Calculate True Per-Class and Per-Student Averages

All too frequently, the manner in which institutions or individuals calculate per-student averages results in incorrect and misleading figures. The temptation is to calculate an average score per class and then simply to average these averages, calling the result an overall average score. The problem is, as we have seen, that this does not really result in a per-student or per-response figure. It treats all classes as equivalent, regardless of the number of students enrolled in the course. The only way to derive a true per-student average is to add all the scores reported for a question in all sections of the faculty member's courses and then to divide that total by the total number of responses. This will give you an average response for that question. The real danger comes when institutions summarize results for all of the questions on the rating instrument and then generate one comprehensive score. The reason this approach is highly questionable is that student evaluation forms frequently have questions that evaluate more than just the individual professor's effectiveness in teaching, such as those that deal with the effectiveness of the course design itself, the suitability of the textbook, the structure of the lab sections, and the helpfulness of other course materials. If all of these scores are simply averaged together, you end up combining so many things that it is impossible to learn anything significant about that particular professor. So, it is far better for you as chair (even if it is not the custom at your institution) to select a few key questions—that really get to the heart of this professor's ability to engage his or her students—and focus on them in your evaluation of the faculty member.

Remember That Individual Averages Are Meaningless Unless You Provide a Context

Initially, some department chairs may feel that statements such as the following are extremely clear and detailed:

In last fall's three sections of Dr. Jones's EGYP 101 ("Introduction to Egyptology") course, students responded to the central question on 'the overall excellence of this faculty member's instruction' with a mean score of 4.33 (median: 4.0; mode 4.0) on the standard 1–5 scale, thus attesting to the high quality of instruction in Dr. Jones's introductory courses.

Nevertheless, as detailed as this statement may appear to be, it lacks at least one important element that it needs to be effective: a context for the figures cited. In other words, how does Dr. Jones' score relate to other members of the department and the college? How does this figure compare to instructors' scores in other introductory courses within the department and across the institution? Without further information, the reader simply cannot tell whether the score you are citing is good, adequate, or highly inadequate. For this reason, you should encourage your faculty member to follow the preceding statement with specific grounds for comparison such as:

Excluding Dr. Jones's own scores, the department's overall rating on this same question results in a mean of 3.21 (median 3.0; mode 3.0), while that of the whole college is 3.77 (median 3.5; mode 3.0). Similarly, comparable scores for all introductory courses across the college are . . .

Calculate Standard Deviations, If the Institution Does Not Already Provide Them
Standard deviations, which any spreadsheet program can calculate automatically, provide an indication of how much variation occurred in the students' answers to each question. If the standard deviation is low, most students tended to answer that question in the same way. If the standard deviation is high, there was widespread disagreement among students on that issue. Even more than average scores, standard deviations can be useful indicators of where faculty members need to direct their efforts at improving instruction.

Encourage the Faculty Member to Supply Other Evidence for Success in Teaching, Such as Indications That Enrollments in the Department Have Been Growing as a Result of His or Her Quality of Instruction

Student ratings of instruction—which, for all of their apparent sophistication, are essentially satisfaction surveys—are not the only measures of a faculty member's teaching ability. In many cases, the true merit of a professor is only realized by students years later. While it is possible to document some of the faculty member's strengths with alumni surveys and letters received years after a course is completed, for certain personnel decisions (such as annual contract renewal or initial tenure decisions), department chairs do not have the luxury of waiting that long. Therefore, chairs should encourage faculty members to compile indicators of their quality of instruction that go beyond standard student evaluations and alumni surveys. For example, encourage the faculty to provide data indicating that enrollments in the department have increased (or at least have stabilized after a period of decline) since his or her initial hire or some other major event in the faculty member's career. The faculty member could include a section similar to the following, either on a résumé or on an application for promotion.

Enrollment Growth	
Average number of students in Dr. Jones's courses at time of hiring:	11
Average number of students in Dr. Jones's courses at last promotion:	23
Average number of students in Dr. Jones's courses currently:	48
Development of Majors	
Number of Egyptology majors at time of hiring:	4
Number of Egyptology majors at last promotion:	7
Number of Egyptology majors currently:	12

It is certainly no guarantee that these improvements occurred only because Dr. Jones was hired and promoted, but it does appear to make the case that, with this faculty member teaching in the department, the program is growing. Certain faculty members, particularly at the junior ranks, may be reluctant to introduce this type of information on their own behalf. In these cases, you have an excellent opportunity to use your authority as chair to encourage them to do so or even to introduce the information *for* them.

Recommend That the Faculty Member Supply Information Indicating That Students Have Been Succeeding in Their Other Courses as a Result of His or Her Quality of Instruction

A brief but very compelling section of a vita or promotion application might include a simple tabulation of how students who have been prepared by this instructor faired in their upper level courses or in graduate school. One way to present this type of information follows:

Academic Preparation of Dr. Jones's Students	
Number of students advancing from Jones's EH I to Smith's EH II	89
Average grade of these students in Smith's EH II	B-
Number of students advancing from Jones's EH I to Jones's EH II	53
Average grade of these students in Jones's EH II	B
Number of students advancing from Jones's EH I to Smith's EH II since last promotion	21
Average grade of these students in Smith's EH II	B
Number of students advancing from Jones's EH I to Jones's EH II since last promotion	6
Average grade of these students in Jones's EH II	B+

Encourage Faculty Members to Provide Data That Indicate Their Students Are Succeeding After They Leave the Institution as a Result of Their High Level of Instruction

Another brief but effective way to demonstrate a faculty member's effectiveness is to provide information about advisees or students who took multiple courses from that instructor and went on successfully to graduate school in the discipline or received attractive offers of employment in the field. Statements of this sort might be phrased as follows:

Nine Egyptology graduates who were Dr. Jones's advisees advanced to graduate programs in the discipline (Jane Richardson and Mark Howard, Pennsylvania State University; Tasha Reese, Brittany Pierce, and Lloyd Maxwell, The Johns Hopkins University; Marvelle Edwards, University of Chicago; Robert Elder and Jamal Robertson, University of Michigan; Jei Li, University of Wisconsin) compared to only four such graduates in the entire five-year period before Dr. Jones's arrival.

When Quoting Comments Made By Students or Peer Evaluators, Suggest That the Faculty Member Select Only Those Comments That Indicate *Why* He or She is an Effective Instructor

A few carefully selected comments from unsolicited student letters or standardized ratings of instruction can provide a much clearer impression of what makes a faculty member successful as a teacher than can pages of numerical summaries. Nevertheless, it is far more compelling to include three to five comments that clearly state the reasons behind a faculty member's success—even if some of these comments are less than glowing—than to include numerous remarks that merely say, "Terrific professor!" or, "Best class I've ever had!" As you know if you've served on many promotion committees, any professor can locate at least a fair number of positive comments on student course evaluations. The truly informative comments are those which give the reader a sense of what precisely the professor is doing in order to engage his or her students so deeply with the material. Consider, for example, the following student comment:

> I hated Egyptology long before I registered for this class, and I wouldn't have taken this course if any other offering in the humanities had been open this semester. And now that it's over, I can't really say that I've come to enjoy the material at all. But I will admit that Dr. Jones made me *think* in a way that no other professor has. This was a hard class. We had to write something nearly every day and then turn it in. We had to critique one another's ideas and compositions. And then we wrote fresh drafts based on what we learned from one another. Okay, so I may never be an Egyptologist (thank heavens!), but maybe I'm a better writer because of Dr. Jones.

A comment such as this one is certainly not the most flattering remark any of us will ever receive on a student course evaluation but, to reviewers and selection committees, it provides far stronger evidence of what makes this particular instructor effective than could pages of "Great prof!!!!!!!!" comments.

Remind Your Faculty Members That Successful Instruction Also Occurs Outside the Classroom

Sometimes faculty members become so fixated on demonstrating their excellence as classroom teachers that they forget all of the other venues in which their instruction occurs. How successful were they as advisors and mentors to students? Have they provided guest presentations (including lectures, recitals, exhibits, online discussions, web pages, and other formats in which ideas are exchanged) that could be considered an extension of their teaching mission? Have they demonstrated excellence in teaching by updating curricula and syllabi for the department, thoroughly revising courses or recommending more pedagogically effective course rotations, proposing new courses in critical areas, or teaching students by giving them a significant role in their research? Has the faculty member been an effective "coach" in studios, lab experiences, or private lessons? Have they participated in workshops sponsored by a center for teaching and learning or undergone special pedagogical training as part of a national conference in your discipline? Have they directed theses or supervised interns in a way that significantly enhanced the students' learning?

As a Department Chair, Consider Situations That You Were in a Position to Observe That May Have Been Overlooked by Students, Peers, and Other Observers

As a chair, you may be in the best position to know all of the ways in which a faculty member has effectively incorporated new technologies into his or her teaching. You may have observed the teaching that goes on outside of class as the faculty member meets with students during office hours or discusses ideas with them in the dining hall. You may be aware that the faculty member has chosen a specific textbook, web site, or set of course materials that are significantly more effective than those in use earlier. You may be in a better position than anyone else to document that the faculty member has met or exceeded the professional standards of your discipline in terms of remaining current with advances within your field, incorporating appropriate inter- or cross-disciplinary perspectives into his or her courses, adhering to the regulations of your institution and department, and evaluating students according to the accepted standards of your field.

RESOURCES

For further suggestions on how to assist faculty members in documenting their success in teaching, the following are among the best sources currently available:

Chism, N. V. N. (1999). *Peer review of teaching: A sourcebook*. Bolton, MA: Anker.

Ryan, K. E. (Ed.). (2000). *New directions for teaching and learning: No. 83. Evaluating teaching in higher education: A vision for the future*. San Francisco, CA: Jossey-Bass.

Seldin, P., & Associates. (1999). *Changing practices in evaluating teaching: A practical guide to improved faculty performance and promotion/tenure decisions*. Bolton, MA: Anker.

Stronge, J. H. (Ed.). (1997). *Evaluating teaching: A guide to current thinking and best practice*. Thousand Oaks, CA: Corwin Press.

33

Helping Faculty Members Improve Course Syllabi

Every course taught at a college or university requires a syllabus. Many accrediting agencies mandate them. Faculty members rely on them to approve, revise, or evaluate courses. Students turn to them for essential information about an instructor's objectives and requirements. And yet only very rarely do we teach faculty members how to write an effective syllabus. While many institutions provide lists of items that must be included in course syllabi, it is relatively uncommon for faculty members to be shown how to communicate this information effectively or how to construct a syllabus that will actually improve their students' performance in the course. Department chairs who are committed to excellence in teaching may thus find it useful to mentor faculty members in the art of good syllabus construction.

A Well-Constructed Syllabus Conveys the Right Tone and Includes the Right Information

Every course syllabus includes information about the rules and expectations that will be in effect throughout the class. Too often, however, the need to establish clear policies and procedures results in course syllabi that look like little more than long lists of "don'ts" and "thou shalt nots." This negative tone can alienate students from the instructor at the very beginning of a course; students see the instructor more as a warden interested in rules than as a mentor who wants them to succeed at their educational goals. As a department chair, you can help your faculty members avoid this problem by critiquing their syllabi for tone as well as content. An undesirable tone may be conveyed through devices as simple as the sheer amount of **bold face**, <u>**bold underline**</u>, or CAPITALIZATION that appears in instructions. Similarly, too many exclamation points create a tone of suspicion or condescension that impedes rather than assists the learning process. Avoiding strict language does not mean that a professor should not set boundaries or state specific expectations. What it does mean is that it is preferable to convey one's high standards through a supportive, constructive tone than through a style that unnecessarily puts students on the defensive. Consider, for example, the following section from a hypothetical course syllabus:

Attendance Policy

Each student is expected to be in class, on time for every class period. <u>DO NOT</u> miss class more than <u>three</u> times during the semester. <u>DO NOT</u> arrive in class late or after the door is closed. *DO NOT* expect exams to be given as make-ups. <u>NO EXCEPTIONS WILL BE GIVEN!!!!!!!</u> Students who miss class more than three times may have their final grade reduced by at least a full letter grade; doing so will be completely my option. <u>THERE WILL BE NO APPEALS TO THIS POLICY!!!!!!</u>

Contrast the tone that appears in that set of instructions to the impression conveyed by the instructor in the following passage:

Attendance Policy

Since this course involves active and participatory learning, many of the activities that we'll be engaging in cannot occur outside of class. For this reason, I'll take attendance every day and base part of your grade on your rate of class participation. When you are unable to attend a particular class session for any reason, please try to find out from your fellow students what you missed that day. If you stop by my office during regular office hours, I'll be happy to give you any handouts or other materials that you may have missed. Do remember, though, that while I'm here to help, ultimately I can't do the learning for you. So please make every effort to be in class on time for each session and prepared to learn what we will cover that day.

As a student, which of these two courses would you rather take? As a faculty member, which instructor do you think is the more effective teacher?

As a department chair, which instructor do you believe is more likely to develop the sort of rapport with students that leads to better learning?

Notice that, in addition to phrasing what is essentially the same attendance policy in a manner more respectful of the students and more helpful to them than the first example, the second passage also explains *why* the instructor has required class attendance. Students, like most of us, are willing to work under many different systems, as long as they understand the rationale for the rules being enforced. Too often in course syllabi an instructor establishes a needlessly hostile tone by outlining policies that seem necessary to the instructor but that appear merely arbitrary to students in the course. A tone of inapproachability can be avoided with just a little bit of explanation and softer phrasing.

Do Not Bury Essential Information Under Dense Portions of Text

Syllabi communicate ineffectively if they consist of nothing more than page after page of fine print. Greater impact is obtained with course outlines that present material in a user-friendly manner. For instance, the presence of a few well-chosen pictures or diagrams can make an entire document seem more readable and understandable. Although a certain amount of white space can make a syllabus communicate more effectively, some carefully planned graphic design can take effective communication to an even higher level. It illustrates that the instructor has taken great care in planning the course and has considered how students are likely to best receive and understand information. In larger classes it may be necessary to reproduce syllabi in black and white, but in smaller classes it is not difficult to use the techniques of desktop publishing to create very attractive full-color course syllabi. Even if they are only printed in black and white, full-color syllabi can be posted in a variety of formats on the department's web site where they can be downloaded by current students (who invariably misplace copies of paper syllabi) and prospective students. If you do not have design skill or experience there are several easy steps that you can take to make your syllabi more graphically innovative.

Begin by Using the Templates Available in Microsoft Word™ and Other Word Processing Programs

You are unlikely to find that your word processor includes a template labeled "syllabus," but you will find plenty of attractive templates for newsletters, catalogs, and brochures. Take one of those templates, experiment with it, and modify it to include your course information.

Even Simple Graphics Can Create an Impressive Result

Most word processing programs allow you to create basic geometric shapes automatically. Several perpendicular rectangles, filled with light or pastel colors that do not interfere with reading the text, can be placed behind your course information to give your syllabus a published look.

Choose a Font for the Title of the Course That Effectively Conveys Some Aspect of the Course Material

For instance, if you are teaching medieval history, use a Gothic font in your header, find a technical font for a computer science class, record your name on an image of a marquee for a theater class, or use a cartoon font for a course in popular culture.

Add Scanned or Digital Photographs

Images of students on a field trip or working in the lab during previous semesters can instantly explain what it will be like for students to take your course. Wrap the text around the photographs for a result that can be graphically striking and simple to create. Experiment with a few photo placements to see what you like best. The students are likely to enjoy that design as well.

Include Charts or Tables

Many students understand information better when it is portrayed graphically. Clear, simple charts or tables make grade weighting and assignment due dates easier to understand.

Make Your Syllabus Look Like Something Other Than a Syllabus

In certain courses, it might be effective to design your syllabus as a menu. Where are the options among various "entrees"? Is your course prix fixé or à la carte? Or, should your syllabus be more like a concert program with a prelude, several main features, an intermission, and a coda? Choose a creative metaphor for your course and design the syllabus accordingly.

A Well-Constructed Syllabus Need Not Be a Single Document

If instructors put into their syllabi all of the information required by their institutions and all of the information that they themselves would like to include, the document can become quite unwieldy. For instance, a list of recommended or required items for a syllabus might include:

- Your full name

- How you wish to be addressed

- Your title

- The location of your office

- Your office phone number and the best times to call you

- Your office hours

- Your email address

- Instructions about calling you at home

- The course title, prefix, number, and number of credits

- The basic goals of your course

- The topics you will cover

- Essential dates and deadlines for your institution (e.g., the last date to drop a course or to take a course pass/fail)

- Your course's requirements, assignments, and deadlines

- Your attendance policy

- Information about your final examination

- How final grades will be calculated

- General criteria you will use in evaluating assignments

- Information about how best to succeed on your exams

- Your policy on retaking an exam

- Your policy on offering extra-credit assignments

If you try to include all of these items—plus any others that are important to you personally—your syllabus is likely to be so long that students will never read it in detail. If you also try to incorporate white space or the recommended illustrations, the entire document will become hopelessly bulky. One solution to this problem is to divide the syllabus into a variety of syllabus documents, including a(n):

- Course calendar

- Course goals and philosophy

- Assignment guide

- Exam guide

- Study guide

- Profile of the instructor

These syllabus documents can be distributed one at a time over the first several weeks of the course. They will receive more attention since you are introducing information to your students gradually and can take a few moments at the start of each class to explain them. Several short syllabus documents will not be as intimidating as a single mega-syllabus and will not require the entire first session of the class just for review of the syllabus. This will give you time on the first day for more interesting things, such as introducing yourself or your subject, learning about the students and their interests, or discovering what the students already know about the material. Also, if you distribute these documents on paper that has already been three-hole punched, you will be silently instructing your students to keep track of this information.

A Well-Constructed Syllabus Conveys Something of the Instructor's Personality

A brief quotation that summarizes an essential point to be covered in the course makes an excellent epigraph or conclusion to a syllabus. For example, a course on Wagner might follow Wagner's claim "I write music with an exclamation point!" with Mark Twain's observation that "Wagner's music is not as bad as it sounds." Alternatively, an instructor might personalize a syllabus with a statement of personal philosophy, a brief reminiscence about his or her own experience taking a similar course, or two parallel sections on "What I Expect From You" and "What You Can Expect From Me."

RESOURCES

Finally, in any workshop on how to improve course syllabi, you will want to point out to faculty members that many excellent resources already exist for them. These resources include two books and a superb syllabus development web site maintained by the University of Minnesota:

Grunert, J. (1997). *The course syllabus: A learning-centered approach.* Bolton, MA: Anker.

Lowther, M. A., Stark, J. S., & Marten, G. G. (1989). *Preparing course syllabi for improved communication.* Ann Arbor, MI: University of Michigan, National Center for Research to Improve Postsecondary Teaching and Learning.

University of Minnesota. (2004). *Syllabus tutrorial.* Retrieved October 6, 2005, from the University of Minnesota, Center for Teaching and Learning Services web site: http://www1.umn.edu/ohr/teachlearn/syllabus/effective.html

34

Ten Ways to Promote Creative Learning

Increasingly, department chairs are interested in exploring ways to promote more creative teaching by their faculty members and more creative learning by their students. Creativity, long regarded as the domain of the arts, is now widely understood to be an essential part of every discipline. After all, regardless of our academic specialties, we all want our students to:

- Approach problems in new ways

- Develop original questions about the material in our courses

- Discover new applications for existing knowledge

- Form interesting conclusions that can lead toward better understanding

- Question established interpretations

- Assist their fellow students in fostering their own creativity

Similarly, we—as department chairs—want the faculty members of our disciplines to be creative in designing their courses, original in their approaches to scholarship, and adaptable in their instructional methods. And yet, despite this importance, creativity is often regarded as "unteachable." We may ask, therefore, whether there are any ways in which we can help the members of our departments develop greater creativity in their courses.

A departmental workshop on creativity is an excellent way to begin addressing this issue. Such a workshop might include the study of a text followed by a discussion of how various members of the department might incorporate creative teaching or creative learning into their courses. *Creativity in Education and Learning* (Cropley, 2002), *Creativity: Flow and the Psychology of Discovery and Invention* (Csikszentmihalyi, 1996), and *Lateral Thinking: Creativity Step by Step* (De Bono, 1970) all work extremely well in workshops of this sort.

Faculty members are usually eager to learn more about what they can do to foster more creative ideas in their own work and in that of their students. Too often, however, they discover that an approach which worked well for one of their colleagues is not particularly transferable to what they do in their own courses or to their own style of teaching. As a department chair, you can assist these faculty members by exploring with them several classroom-tested approaches that promote creative learning at the college level.

Model Creativity for Your Students in Your Course Design

Students are not likely to adopt creative approaches in a course that itself seems hidebound, restrictive, or sterile. If the organization of a course is inventive—if students are frequently caught off guard by being offered new ways of seeing or doing things—they are more likely to consider even familiar concepts in unfamiliar ways. Faculty members can encourage student creativity by exercising a little instructional creativity themselves. Teachers should ask themselves: To what extent does the methodology that I use in this course fall into the typical lecture/discussion, laboratory, or studio framework? To what extent is that particular structure essential to what I'm doing? Are there ways in which I can stimulate creative thinking by having my students enter an environment that helps expand their comfort zones? For instance, how might a student view a history course differently if it were structured, described, and presented as a laboratory? How might the dynamics of a chemistry course change if instructors presented their roles as personal trainers rather than as lab instructors? What might a psychology studio be like?

Revise "From Scratch" One Course Each Year

By reorganizing a course completely—new textbook, new syllabus, new set of assignments, new structure, everything—faculty members are encouraged to look at their own teaching methods in different ways. For one course each year, each faculty member should try, not merely to improve the syllabus, but to recreate the syllabus from top to bottom. The faculty member might explore what occurs, for instance, when a course is designed, not from the top down (chronologically from the first day of the course to the end or the front of the book to the back), but from the bottom up (from the last day of class or from the final exam backward). Have the instructors ask themselves: In a perfect world, what final exam or final project would I like my students to be able to complete? Then, setting that perfect project as a goal, have the faculty member design the course backward so that this goal can actually be attained. What intermediate assignments or steps along the way would get the students to reach this goal? Plan each class period or unit, not by the material that appears in a chapter of your textbook, but by the essential steps that will lead the students to the best possible final project you can imagine.

Select an Appropriate Metaphor, Image, or Structural Principle for Each Course

Ask the members of your department to come up with an image that best describes each one of their classes. Is the course most similar to a play, a pilgrimage, a banquet or feast, an excavation, an investigation, a conversation, an experiment, a session of psychoanalysis, a saga, "Marine basic training," or something else? The more your department engages in this activity, the more creative and revealing these images will become. A faculty member may find that different metaphors are more appropriate for different courses; this is perfectly acceptable. As a department chair, you should then explore why a particular metaphor was chosen for a particular course and explore how the image selected by the faculty member could be used to shape individual assignments and requirements. Even more importantly, how might a metaphor for a course affect how the faculty member spends time in class? If, for example, the course is "an investigation," is teaching with lectures the most appropriate technique to be used?

Adopt Methods of Evaluation That Encourage Students to Take Risks

Students are less likely to be creative in their answers if they believe that their entire grade, or a significant portion of their grade, will be determined by one particular assignment. In cases where much is at stake, students tend to err on the side of conservatism; they attempt to give you what they think you want rather than what they really believe. Teachers can minimize this reluctance to be honest and to take risks by allowing revisions of assignments, by adopting portfolio or progress-based projects rather than by using one-time, discrete-task-based assignments, and by developing learning opportunities that are either not graded at all or graded in such a way that they can only help one's final grade.

Consider Assignments That Include a "Creativity Component"

Some students will only try to be imaginative or innovative if it is clear that the instructor expects, values, and rewards creativity. In these cases, it can be extremely valuable for an instructor to explain how he or she intends to acknowledge a particular assignment that has been innovative, elegant, or effective in its approach to some problem. The professor might then address these issues: What are some examples of solutions that would be deemed suitably creative? What are some examples of approaches that might seem lacking in creativity? What are the qualities that the creative approaches tend to have that are missing from their non-creative counterparts? If the creativity component of the assignment is to be graded, the instructor has options in assigning an appropriate and minimally subjective score. The instructor can develop a rubric that clearly outlines the qualities and expectations for this creativity component and how these qualities and expectations will be graded. Alternatively, the instructor could assign the creativity component enough value to make it worth taking seriously, but not enough to threaten or intimidate those students who are particularly challenged by having to think in new ways. A weight of 5% or less of the project's total grade is probably appropriate. The instructor can also have these creativity scores set by a group or even by the class as a whole—an approach that will be both fairer and will expose students to other examples of creativity. When using group grading, the instructor may wish to calculate the median score of the group so as to minimize the effect of "outliers."

Reflect Seriously on Which Aspects of a Course Must Be in an Instructor's Control and Which Can Be Left Flexible

Students get excellent experience in creative problem solving when they are given an opportunity to design or organize certain parts of the course themselves. Students may be permitted, within certain limits, to choose the relative weighting of various course components, the specific focus of individual units or subunits, or the method of evaluation to be used at the end of one or more units. By giving students this opportunity, faculty members encourage them to become active participants in the course rather than passive recipients of instruction. They also provide a practical lesson in how creativity can often involve imagination, negotiation, and the inventive use of scarce resources such as time.

Consider Structuring Each Course Around a Specific "Problem" or "Inquiry"

With the inquiry method of instruction, students are asked, not simply to learn a set of disparate facts, but to solve a mystery. The mystery they set out to solve might be a puzzle (a problem having only one solution) or a conundrum (a problem that has several possible answers but no single solution). For example, in a course on Roman Civilization, the instructor might begin with the following conundrum.

During the reign of the emperor Trajan (who ruled A.D. 98–117), the Roman Empire was at its greatest size and strength. In fact, the opening line of Gibbon's *Decline and Fall of the Roman Empire* states that "In the second century of the Christian era, the Empire of Rome comprehended the fairest part of the earth, and the most civilized portion of mankind." Almost immediately after the reign of Trajan, however, the Roman Empire began to shrink in size and, before the medieval period was over, cattle were grazing on the site of what once had been the Roman Forum. Your goal in this course will be to figure out what went wrong.

Adopt Collaborative Learning Techniques Such as "Jigsaw Groups"

Jigsaw groups were developed by Elliot Aronson as a means of promoting collaborative learning and helping students break issues down into manageable parts, master those parts, and then synthesize small pieces of information into a larger picture. Like a classic jigsaw puzzle, jigsaw groups involve a number of interlocking units. For example, in a history course, each student might be assigned: 1) a specific city, region, or nation; 2) a specific era; 3) a specific topic: art, literature, warfare, politics, or architecture; and 4) a specific resource: a book, web site, collection of essays, or CD-ROM. When subgroups are needed for discussions or to critique each others' assignments, they are then organized according to one of these pre-established categories. (The instructor can say, for instance, "All right. Let's have all the Paris people over here, Rome over there, London in that corner, and Madrid across from them. The issue that I want you to talk about today is …") After 20 minutes or so of this discussion, the students might be asked to leave their "city groups" and reorganize according to their "era groups;" they would then address the same issue, but from a different perspective and with a different group of peers. The advantage of this approach is that students tend to be more creative when given frequent opportunities to work with other students, modifying and improving their ideas based on the suggestions of their classmates. The usual disadvantages to these team-based approaches are that groups all too often move no faster than the level of the least productive member, share work assignments inequitably, and receive grades that are not reflective of individual effort or learning. Instructors can minimize the effect of these disadvantages by constant reconfiguration of groups according to the jigsaw method and then by encouraging group critique and improvement of assignments that are ultimately the responsibility of each individual student.

Develop "What If" Assignments

In "what if" assignments, students are asked to consider what the world would be like if we could "waive" a certain historical event, natural law, or social constraint. They may be asked, for instance: What would have been the consequences if the French rather than the English had made extensive use of the longbow at the Battle of Agincourt or if there were no Second Law of Thermodynamics or if the verification principle of the logical positivists were to be regarded as invalid? Such exercises not only encourage students to engage in creative speculation but also reinforce for them what the actual consequences of the given event, law, or constraint proved to be. For excellent historical examples of this approach, see Cowley's (2000, 2001) *What If?: The World's Foremost Military Historians Imagine What Might Have Been* and its sequel *What If? 2: Eminent Historians Imagine What Might Have Been.*

Encourage Students to Remain Physically Active

As early as the mid-1980s, Gondola (1985, 1986, 1987) conducted several studies that indicated the creativity of students is enhanced—at least as measured by several standard measures—when they engage in physical exercise. Although this effect tended to be most pronounced among students who adhered to a regular program of physical exercise, certain differences could be measured after even a single session of strenuous physical exercise. Such findings indicate that instructors would be well served to encourage activity by their students or, at least, to get them out of their seats and moving around the classroom on a regular basis. By so doing, students are likely to be more creative in their solutions to problems and in their approaches to unfamiliar ideas.

REFERENCES

Cowley, R. (Ed.). (2000). *What if?: The world's foremost military historians imagine what might have been.* New York, NY: Penguin Putnam.

Cowley, R. (Ed.). (2001). *What if? 2: Eminent historians imagine what might have been.* New York, NY: G. P. Putnam's Sons.

Cropley, A. J. (2002). *Creativity in education and learning: A guide for teachers and educators.* London, England: Kogan Page.

Csikszentmihalyi, M. (1996). *Creativity: Flow and the psychology of discovery and invention.* New York, NY: HarperCollins.

De Bono, E. (1970). *Lateral thinking: Creativity step by step.* New York, NY: Harper & Row.

Gondola, J. C. & Tuckman, B. W. (1985). Effects of a systemic program of exercise on selected measures of creativity. *Perceptual and Motor Skills, 60,* 53–54.

Gondola, J. C. (1986). The enhancement of creativity through long and short term exercise programs. *Journal of Social Behavior and Personality 1.1,* 77–82.

Gondola, J. C. (1987). The effects of a single bout of aerobic dancing on selected tests of creativity. *Journal of Social Behavior and Personality 2.2.1,* 275–278.